Youth Mediations and Affective Relations

Susan Driver · Natalie Coulter
Editors

Youth Mediations and Affective Relations

palgrave
macmillan

Editors
Susan Driver
York University
Toronto, ON, Canada

Natalie Coulter
York University
Toronto, ON, Canada

ISBN 978-3-030-07551-4 ISBN 978-3-319-98971-6 (eBook)
https://doi.org/10.1007/978-3-319-98971-6

Cover credit: MirageC

This Palgrave Macmillan imprint is published by the registered company Springer Nature Switzerland AG
The registered company address is: Gewerbestrasse 11, 6330 Cham, Switzerland

This book is dedicated to
passions and possibilities of young people everywhere.

Contents

Notes on Contributors

Morgan Bimm is a Ph.D. student in the department of Gender, Feminist, and Women's Studies at York University in Toronto, Ontario. Her research interests include integrating fandom studies and feminist affect theory, especially as they relate to performances of girlhood and queerness in relation to popular culture objects and texts, the affect infused in girls' cultural spaces, and instances of community built around traditionally 'girly' objects and aesthetics. Morgan's work also appears in the forthcoming collection *The Spaces and Places of Canadian Popular Culture*, which includes her co-authored chapter on the affect and implicit nationalism of Canadian pop singer Carly Rae Jepsen.

Sophie Bishop is an Associate Lecturer in the Department of Arts, Technology and Innovation at the University of East London. Her Ph.D. research looks at the political economy of YouTube vlogging, algorithmic materialities and self-optimisation practices on the platform. Her work has been published in peer-reviewed journals including *Feminist Media Studies* and *Convergence*.

Natalie Coulter is currently an Assistant Professor at York University in the department of Communication Studies. She is currently completing a SSHRC-funded research project entitled, The Embodied Tween: Living Girlhood in Global and Digital Spaces. She co-edited the special issue, Locating the Tween Girl, of *Girlhood Studies* in 2018. Her book *Tweening the Girl: The Crystallization of the Tween Market* was published in 2014. She has published in the *Canadian Journal of Communication*,

Journal of Children and Media, *Popular Communication* and *Jeunesse*. She is a founding member of the Association for Research on the Cultures of Young People (ARCYP).

Susan Driver is an Associate Professor at York University in Communication Studies. Her books include *Queer Girls and Popular Culture* (Peter Lang). She has also edited books including *Queer Youth Cultures* (SUNY) *and Engaging Affects, Thinking Feelings: Social, Political and Artistic practices* (Cambridge). Her current work focuses on using affect theories and new materialist feminist and queer scholarship to rethink youth and media through relational ontologies and epistemologies. She is writing a book that rethinks young people's engagements with social media in terms of complex dynamics of attention, connecting, caring and sharing.

Christine Feraday obtained her Master's in Communication and Culture at Ryerson University, where she researched queer identity language used on Tumblr. She currently lives in Washington with her wife and their dog.

Johanna Luanne Fraser is a Ph.D. student in Communication and Culture at York University. Her research interests tend to relate to media, gender identity, and youth studies, with particular emphasis on youth masculinity and boyhood. She holds an M.A. in Political Science with a focus on Political Theory from McMaster University, where her research theorized the public washroom as Third Space and investigated the policies on gender-accessible washrooms (and their lack) at Canadian Universities. Her current research refocuses her attention on the problem of gender itself in the context of youth's experience with contemporary media. Grounding her work in Feminist and Queer theory, she is passionate about crossing the boundaries of disciplinarity in her research and writing.

Eileen Mary Holowka is a writer, editor, and Ph.D. student who also makes games and music. Her current research focuses on feminist social media practices, "sick women," and vulnerable acts of resistance. She has published on self-imaging, Instagram, online affective labour, and the intersections of media and trauma. For her master's thesis, she created a digital narrative called *circuits* about the act of narrating sexual trauma within institutional spaces. *circuits* can be played for free online. In 2017, she worked in a team to create a playable art project (*Place des ALTs*) for Montreal's largest ever public art event, *KM3*.

Alejandro MayoralBaños is an Indigenous activist and Ph.D. Candidate, who is currently working with organizations in Canada and Mexico deploying participatory and community-driven ICT projects by/with/for Indigenous peoples. He is the creator and founder of the Indigenous Friends Initiative (Canada) and Magtayaní (Mexico). His participatory action research explores the cultural, economic, social and political implications of ICTs within Indigenous contexts. His examination includes inquiries about Indigenous Software Protocols, STEM Pedagogies for Indigenous peoples, Indigenous Social Media, Intellectual Property and Traditional Knowledge, Indigenous identities and embodiment in digital spaces and ICT4D by Indigenous peoples. Alejandro has plenty of experience volunteering, leading, collaborating and participating in different projects around Indigeneity and social action in Canada, Mexico, Peru, Chile, and Bolivia.

Whitney Monaghan is an Assistant Lecturer in Film and Screen Studies at Monash University, Australia. Her background is in screen, media and cultural studies and her research examines the representation of LGBTIQ youth on screen. She is the author of *Queer Girls, Temporality and Screen Media: Not 'Just a Phase'* (Palgrave Macmillan, 2016).

Shazlin Rahman is an established engagement specialist and nonprofit marketing and communications professional; credited with developing, marketing and implementing stakeholder engagement initiatives, online community engagement, and fostering deeper online and in-person conversations on identity-based discrimination and marginalization. She earned her M.A. in Communication and Culture from York University. Her thesis looked at how Muslim women vloggers used social media platforms and personal networks to bypass mainstream media and speak in their own voices. Shazlin has contributed to a number of community engagement projects including: building solidarity with Muslim communities; the 4Rs. Youth Movement; and Toronto's first Open Iftar, where she brought over 400 community members to break fast at Dufferin Grove Park. In her own practice, Shazlin marries her passion for city-building and journalism by marketing and hosting neighbourhood walks that build solidarity between Muslim and non-Muslim communities. Shazlin utilizes social media to share microstories aimed at broadening the narrative around resilience and labour among women of colour through her project, hersarong. In her free time, Shazlin sits on the Toronto Ward Museum's programming committee, the 4Rs Youth steering committee, and on the board of directors of The Tessellate Institute, Canada's first Muslim-led research organization.

Claudia Sicondolfo is a Vanier Scholar and Doctoral candidate at York University, in the department of Cinema and Media Arts. Her research projects address topics including film festivals, screen publics, youth and digital media cultures, decolonizing research methodologies and the creative industries' relationships with theories of affect. Her doctoral research project examines educational and community outreach strategies of Canadian digital screen institutions, collectives, and film festivals. Claudia has worked extensively with educational communities across Canada and she has published educational companion curriculum for interactive and traditional documentaries, including *Highrise* and *Offshore*. In addition to publications within various anthologies, her writing has also been published in *Public Journal* and *Senses of Cinema*.

Anastasia Todd is an Assistant Professor of Gender and Women's Studies at the University of Kentucky. Her research broadly looks at the intersections of disability and affect from a feminist disability studies perspective. Her book project, Affective Citizen: Disabled Girlhood and U.S. Disability Exceptionalism, traces how contemporary representations of disabled girlhood are affectively mobilized to shore up the logics of ablenationalism. She is currently collecting narratives for a project about invisible disability and young womanhood.

List of Figures

CHAPTER 1

Introduction: Open-Ended and Curious Explorations of Youth Mediations and Affective Relations

Susan Driver and Natalie Coulter

In recent years, there has been a proliferation of academic and popular interest in the ways young people engage with digital media as a pervasive, integral and immersive part of their everyday lives. On the one hand, celebratory approaches position youth as generational leaders with unique knowledge and skills to operate devices and applications, navigate complex networked environments, design and code digital texts and collaborate creatively. Valorized as "digital natives," the experiences of youth become totalized in ways that naturalize competence as a given and overlook broader social conditions that produce inequities and differences within and between young people. On the other hand, young people are positioned in passive ways as compliant users of adult-driven media systems, or even more disturbingly as victims of corporate

S. Driver (✉) · N. Coulter
Department of Communication Studies, York University,
Toronto, ON, Canada
e-mail: sdriver@yorku.ca

N. Coulter
e-mail: ncoulter@yorku.ca

S. Driver and N. Coulter (eds.), *Youth Mediations and Affective Relations*,
https://doi.org/10.1007/978-3-319-98971-6_1

technologies that shape their identities and delimit their social relations within narrow and normative boundaries. Big data and overarching structures become primary sites of fascination, losing touch with the voices, embodiments, feelings and practices of youth within their local contexts of learning, creativity and socialization. In both these framings, young people are homogenized according to dominant cultural notions and institutions of the digital capitalist economy. Neo-liberal ideologies of individualism, along with sweeping critiques of them, leave out the provisional, messy and ambiguous relations through which young people learn over time and through diverse modes of engagement across a range of digital media.

Alternatively, the desire to hone in closely on young people's media practices has often proven to be invasive, bound up with moral evaluations that rigidly interpret the subjective and interpersonal lives of young people, judging how they connect, play games, make profiles, text each other, upload images and gather information. And within this process, it is striking how much interest and surveillance get placed on the emotional and affective dimensions of young peoples' experiences. It is precisely the feelings, passions and bodily encounters of young people that grip moral panics about the excess and dangers of online interactions: sharing too much information, immersing too fast, going too far within virtual realities, fictionalizing the self, taking sexual risks, becoming violent or addicted, and losing control. What seems to trouble adult onlookers are precisely those facets of youth digital culture that appear to be too intense, to evoke unruly sensations, suggesting bodies and emotions gone awry. The affective lives of young people online are sites of intensified adult concern and action as they appeal to rationality and often conceal their own affective investments. In this way, young people come to bear the burden of affective excess to be tamed by the implementation of knowledge and power that tries to make sense of it all. This approach reduces youth to dramatic examples that highlight visible transgressions, spectacularizing youth at the level of their passions, bodies, desires, abstracting them from the relational dynamics through which youth respond to each other in specific and changing ways. What is often lacking are materially and relationally honed, along with empirically detailed and ethically nuanced, ways of understanding connections between youth, affect and digital mediations.

Multiple Approaches, Directions and Visions

Responding to the historical and contemporary predicaments that have limited conceptualizations and representations of young people, scholars have taken up affect theories as speculative and practical tools through which to approach youth with an openness to the unpredictable and marginalized dimensions of their mediated embodiments and relationships. Innovative scholarship has begun to grapple with the affective contours of youth mediations using supple and complex interdisciplinary tools that recognize the urgent need to think beyond conventional binary paradigms and imagine alternatives. Nancy Lesko's deconstructive approach (Lesko 2012) to modern normalizing conceptions of youth offers a brilliant starting point to reconsider how youth affect gets erased, reified and misrepresented. Feminist approaches to the study of girls media engagements have been especially responsive to the creative emotional and symbolic negotiations of young people across a range of media formats (McRobbie 2007; Fine 1988; Harris 2003; Coleman 2009; Coulter 2014; Ringrose 2012; Keller 2015; Hickey-Moody and Page 2015; Renold and Ringrose 2011). Critical attention to youth sexualities has also turned toward the ways desire and power play out in a multitude of ways, against restrictive heteronormative expectations (Halberstam 2005; Talburt 2008; Monaghan 2016; Stockton 2009; Driver 2007; Rasmussen et al. 2004). Focusing on how racial and national identities and embodiments become articulated and resisted, scholars have designed research to consider how and why race matters across media (Rose 2008; Pough 2004; Dimitriadis 2009; Maira 2016; Gopinath 2005). These lists are in no way exhaustive but what is striking are the ways in which thinking through affects of joy, fear, desire, anxiety, hope, longing, anger, pleasure and grief (among many others) become central to the process of understanding young people's mediated lives across a range of youth scholarship. Recognizing the interconnected embodied, affective, psychic, social, cultural, political worlds of young people becomes vital within research grappling with experiences of marginalization and oppression. These diverse and overlapping bodies of work are at the forefront of attending to the historically mediated and situated dynamics of young people's affective lives and the conceptual mappings and discursive formations that make them thinkable and politically relevant.

Our book aims to expand upon this emerging research, insisting upon theoretical applications that are partial, specific and historically grounded. Attending to the emerging networked publics and social media landscapes that elicit young people's intense interest, we want to address changing intersections of technology, practice, representation and affect. We are excited to explore how youth activism and networking have been propelled through the affectively charged and nuanced participations that mobilize a range of political, social and cultural practices by, for and about young people. We also want to attend to the detailed ways youth use and transform media technologies and platforms, for multiple purposes, faced with unequal opportunities and drawing upon a range of resources. As the title of a recent book linking youth online cultural and political participation asserts, young people seek to connect and communicate with others "By Any Media Necessary" (Jenkins et al. 2016), working out of the constrained material conditions and local vernacular styles that shape and propel them. With the popularity of sharing user-generated content on mobile devices through platforms such as YouTube, Instagram, Snapchat and Tumblr, youth are telling stories, imaging themselves and forging connections in prolific ways that articulate relations between selves and others, intimacy and community, creativity and politics that go beyond adult expectations. We value research that engages with the small data realms of young people through which ephemeral and fluid online interrelations become noticeable and meaningful, giving rise to new interpretive styles and methodologies that refuse totalization and closure.

Passionate Research: Questioning, Participating, Researching, Writing

This collection acknowledges and builds upon the exciting work by youth scholars interested in the productive possibilities of considering affect as a mobile term, with multiple genealogies and potential directions. Affects move and traverse human and nonhuman bodies, acting as connective and/or disruptive forces, propelling new social configurations and shifting symbolic meanings. Affect is an intrinsically relational concept that defies rigid borders and either-or formulations, shifting toward in-between dimensions that are impossible to reduce to binary and individualizing ways of thinking. Along these lines affect defies stable boundaries, compelling us to think outside the lines through which youth have been positioned, defined and controlled. There are very different theoretical approaches to the articulation of affect ranging from a focus on realms of psychology, phenomenology, political economy, material assemblages, posthumanism and immaterial labor to name a few. And contributors draw upon these expansive interdisciplinary fields of thinking, using ideas as tools that help to reconfigure how selves, bodies, technologies, belongings, and institutions are affectively imbricated. Tracing various workings of affect to understand how hierarchies of power are reproduced within ordinary micro spaces of everyday life, the essays simultaneously consider openings through which youth exceed expectations, creating relations and paths unforeseeable within dominant frameworks of knowledge.

Philosophical speculations about affect have elaborated those dimensions of affects that precede and exceed language, emotion and cognition, attending to intricate bodily relations of force and intensity (Spinoza, Deleuze, Massumi). These ideas have been a basis for a wide range of applications by youth researchers, who make use of concepts in ways that help provide insights into the fractious experiences of youth within concrete spaces of media participation. In this way, notions such as affect unfold through the ethical and methodological considerations of youth doing things with media in specific ways. What matters is not the purity of the ideas but their effectiveness in spurring questions and new ways of approaching youth with curiosity, care and imagination. The pragmatic research projects on youth and media within this book take up affects in ways that grapple with their entanglements with material and discursive processes such that it is impossible to consider them in isolation or opposition. Analysis of discursive and mediated power is vital to understanding affective dynamics but at the same time they resist reduction to dichotomous ways of approaching bodily and textual worlds. Grappling with ephemeral intersections of affect helps to overcome dualistic ways of thinking that have tended to simplify and delimit how we understand young peoples' engagements with media. Rather than isolating the effects of representation, approaches attuned to affect think through representation within broader ecologies linking language to social, corporeal, technical and material practices. Attending to these interwoven dimensions of youth experience helps us to consider areas overlooked within social scientific accounts centered narrowly on the effects of media representation or too broadly on institutional structures; at the same time, it also decenters fixed categories and identities bound to rational individualism.

The essays here offer glimpses into the relational processes through which affect circulates within the everyday lives of young people as they engage with social media to socialize with friends, explore queer desires, protest injustice, share stories and express their suffering and joys. The turn to affect and youth does not focus on isolated texts, bodies or subjects, but rather stays close to young peoples' relations with others and the worlds around them, attending to how they respond, feel and think in the flux of their daily networked lives. As the contributors explore, there are many ways of practicing and experiencing digital mediations, and by turning attention onto the active and diverse doings and becomings of youth in relational formations, it becomes possible to resist universalizing conceptions of youth. Vital to this work is a questioning of static ideals of what it is to be a child, to develop as an adolescent or to struggle as a teen, since the terrain of research becomes the living contingencies that shape multiple becomings rather than unified subjects. At stake is a process of challenging the ways youth are stabilized for the sake of epistemological and moral evaluations. In this way, an ontological richness and variability of becoming afford a way to shift how research on youth is framed and carried out.

What connects the essays is an acknowledgment that the process of becoming a "youth" is amazingly complicated not only because of accelerated technological transformations but equally contingent on the changing contours of young peoples' specific passions, embodiments, histories, and locations. The research explored in this book is attentive to the changing mediated social conditions of the affective relations of young people across gender, sexual, racial, national and class differences. Through an affective lens, differences are not abstract categories, but dynamic embodied relations that are in a continual process of articulation. And while dominant media systems seek to capture these differences and commodify their value, youth are amazingly nuanced and unpredictable in what they do in response. This is vividly demonstrated throughout the chapters as authors pay close attention to creative endeavors by youth in the process of making apps, playing games, sharing selfies, vlogging experiences, protesting through memes or networking events. Many of the authors in this collection are or were participants in the communities and networks they study, and perhaps this allows for a sharper attunement to the ways affects shape not only what happens online but also in the layering of offline experiences as they complicate and give rise to knowledge by adult researchers.

Participatory involvement does not erase the ethical dilemmas of researching youth, but it does enable a degree of intimate experiential entanglement through which the hierarchies of researched/researcher and the distancing of academic protocols become recognized and reconsidered. Personal connection does not guarantee clarity or authenticity, but it does allow little things to get noticed, unforeseen problems to be addressed in specific ways and difficult questions to be posed using the language of youth themselves. These chapters provide engaging and accessible examples of emerging scholarship precisely because they unfold from the relational flux of feeling and thinking in close proximities to the worlds they seek to understand, offering partial yet passionate perspectives that push readers to stay open and learn in new ways rather than to figure things out once and for all.

The book starts with Anastasia Todd's piece on disabled vloggers Charisse and Rikki Poynter. Their vlogs, Todd argues, offer spaces of mediated intimacies that affectively reorient able-bodied publics into tolerant, neoliberal citizens. By using the comments sections of the vlogs as a means to unearth the affective readings of the vlogs, Todd extrapolates that the vlogs reorient the able-bodied viewer into being accepting of the diversity of the disabled body. As intimate publics, they are co-opted as signs of neoliberal inclusionism. Building on the work of Sara Ahmed, Todd states that the promise of diversity is future oriented and in being included, erases the signs of exclusion. The affective reorientations that image futures of tolerance thus function to depoliticize disability. This connects with many other chapters in the book that simultaneously analyze the limitations of normalizing powers while also imagining affective formations online that disrupt dominant structures of feeling, discourses and institutions.

Also writing within a vein of research that complicates the process of self-representation and community building on Youtube by, for, and about youth who have been historically excluded from mainstream media representations, Shazlin Rahman's piece on three young female hjabi vloggers begins with the premise that hijabi is a social practice. The vloggers each have different approaches to hijabi, and were diverse in their articulations of being a Muslim woman. Rahman reflects upon her own early hopes that the hijabi vlogs would offer digital platforms for women's self expression and become sites free from more oppressive narratives on Muslim women in mainstream media narratives. While the opportunity to vlog has given these young women opportunities to challenge common misconceptions about themselves, in the end, Rahman expresses her disappointment at how the hijabi vloggers are circumscribed by the impulses and logics of consumer culture. Also grappling with the tensions between hegemonic consumer and fashion discourses and localized affectively embodied engagements, Sophie Helen Bishop's online ethnography of British beauty vloggers Zoellla and Gabriella Rose pays attention to complexities that go beneath the surface of visual representations. Bishop explores the anxiety video, in which vloggers reveal their struggles with anxiety. Anxiety videos, Bishop argues, provide insight into the affective labor undertaken by vloggers as they build their profiles in the digital visibility economy. The videos are designed to strip away professional artifice of beauty vlogs and to construct narratives of authenticity. The anxiety videos by these high-level vloggers are affectively charged strategic performances designed to reset the vlogger's authenticity. Bishop's chapter opens up the possibility of reading such affective and authentic performances as merely postfeminist masquerades.

What links the essays is an acknowledgment that the process of becoming selves and political subjects in the life phase of youth is connected to the struggles over self-representation by vloggers. Along these lines, Eileen Mary Holowka explores the ambivalent ways women of color participate within mainstream photo sharing digital platforms. She considers the critical and playful potential of popular digital memes on Instagram, using the work of @GothShakira as examples of a reflexive feminist artist who intervenes within social media spaces with creative mobilizations of meme images. Against the hegemonic styles and messages within male-centered meme culture, Holowka discusses the social and political dimensions of activist art and affective labor enacted by racial and gender marginalized subjects. This chapter is attentive to exploitative and empowering conditions of image reproduction and circulation within social media platforms and considers the ways in which researchers need to thoughtfully engage with the digitally mediated subjects so as to foster care and responsibility. Memes are interesting in terms of how they reclaim, re-present and juxtapose popular images and words in ways that provoke strong feelings and political messages. Also working with the process of digital image remixing, Whitney Monaghan's interest in the ephemeral affective dimensions of mashup video by queer girls also thinks through the creative possibilities of editing and recombining video clips within subcultural practices of invention and resistance. Thinking about the value of queer girl mashups within a broader context of visual exclusion becomes important in helping Monaghan to make sense of the cultural and emotional value of these participatory fan texts. Exploring the tensions between the desire to archive cherished popular culture elements that are part of creative projects that are fleeting and provisional within online digital environments, she demonstrates the unique ways in which queer screen cultures are situated and altered in relation to shifting affects and temporalities.

Whereas digital remixing provides interesting examples of youth intervening using mainstream images, it is also vital to consider alternatives excluded by dominant forms of popular culture. Nuanced ways of thinking that engage affect and youth need to expand beyond the Western philosophical traditions in order to encompass rich histories, knowledges and cultural practices that have interwoven thinking about the body, affect and relationality beyond the hierarchies that mark out dominant institutional discourses. Alejandro MayoralBaños's chapter explores the layers of a process through which he has developed the *Indigenous Friends App.* at York University in Toronto. He draws upon a rich field of indigenous thought and practice at every stage of his work designing the app. by for and about indigenous youth. His chapter traces the ethical, social and technical dimensions of his project, situating it amongst scholarship reorienting digital social media in ways that account for the unique needs and approaches of diverse indigenous identities and communities. Focusing on possibilities for decolonizing virtual environments, Banos attends to the importance of designing digital spaces capable of attending to emotional bodily and spiritual realms of experience. His project draws upon and integrates a wealth of traditional knowledges through dialogue with elders at every stage so that technical considerations are guided by community interests and approaches. His app. situates the importance of networking within a broader context of cultural recognition and possibilities for support and healing. MayoralBaños' approach works hard to connect emotional, embodied, social and cultural realms of indigenous youth experience through design and implementation. In this way digital technology becomes framed in new ways that help us to envision possibilities for attending to indigenous youth as dynamically involved in reorienting social media as tools for embodied belonging, community building, and empowerment.

Theorizing the limits of liberal individualist models of the self, Susan Driver's chapter works to reconceptualize social media as a dynamic realm of affective practices by marginalized youth. Her chapter addresses how youth selfies are framed in ways that fixate on normalizing conceptions of self and representation. Deleuzian theories of affect and becoming are introduced as productive in displacing individualistic modes of thinking and reorienting our perceptions and conceptualizations of selves and selfies within dynamic material, social, embodied and technological assemblages. Following creative and relational contours of queer youth selfie circulation on Tumblr, Driver is interested in methods that stay close to the flux of affective relational experiences in terms of a process of becoming. She refuses epistemological certainties, leaving room for doubts and uncertainty, her essay turns toward a multiplicity of ways youth make selfies and do things with them that exceed our expectations and prescribed judgments leaving room for imaginative alternatives. Christine Feraday is also interested in creative experimentations by marginal subjects to name themselves beyond fixed normative categories through collective dialogue and supportive communities on Tumblr. Focusing on the elaboration of diverse languages that comprise neo-identities, Feraday explores processes through which youth experiment with naming and communicating themselves outside the parameters of binary gender, sexual and romantic identities. She attends to the specific ways in which Tumblr as a social media platform provides fluid and anonymous spaces for connecting and learning between youth who identify in heterogeneous ways. While experimenting creatively with words is vital for youth seeking alternative forms of self-identification, Feraday highlights the affective power of language to help youth overcome alienation and isolation.

Affect becomes a useful conceptual tool for analyzing realms of youth digital experimentation and play. Johanna Fraser's chapter explores the affective contours of desire in the performance of gender within the online role playing game World of Warcraft. She argues against a hermeneutics of suspicion and paranoia that would focus on the dominant visible structures of design and representation at the expense of the subtle ways young people engage in gaming through complex modes of fantasy and imagination. Listening to how youth talk and feel about gender swapping and ambiguous gender identifications within the context of the game, Fraser notices a striking shift in the embodiment of shame as an affective orientation among participant accounts. Theorizing the ways shame is a predominant affective force through which gender is policed within young peoples social worlds often tied to fear of social rejection and devaluation, this chapter calls attention to an alternative affective economy of gender relations. Fraser turns attention toward the affirmative ways in which desires for gender differences spur game play outside the binary lines of identity regulation, opening up possibilities for queer modes of role playing. Also considering affect within digital game play, Natalie Coulter uses the children's online game *Moshi Monsters* to explore the affective modalities of children's digital cultures within the context of neoliberal capitalism. The goal of the game, which mimics many of the mundane practices of capitalism, is too maintain one's avatar (in the form of pet monster) level of happiness at a high rating. Coulter uses Sara Ahmed's work to argue that the promise of happiness is political in that it maintains and justifies social oppressions. Coulter concludes her piece by suggesting that Moshi Monsters is an example of Lauren Berlant's cruel optimism, in that we attach ourselves to promises of future happiness through institutions that diminish us.

Taking a different approach, Claudia Sicondolfo's piece documents the labor practices of four young feminist film critics who each started a feminist film collective. Based on interviews with the women, Sicondolfo argues that they fill, or rather '*fille*'—as she playfully suggests—the lack of spaces for female film criticism. Towards filling/*fille*ing these gaps, the four young women in response to precarious nature of the neoliberal economy are moved to create their own meaningful work through their feminist subjectivities and creative exchanges. She shows how these four are part of a new youth led, creative labor force who forge their own employment opportunities. For Sicondolfo this research calls for a wider understanding of the affective labor practices of young people in the face of current policies and socioeconomic realities.

Whereas most of the chapters in this book focus on realms of youth cultural practice that are relatively autonomous from direct adult involvement, Morgan Bimm's chapter questions the complex ways that girls take up space online and navigate the nuances of digital politics and expression within online communities in terms of the continuing power and authority of adults. Her questions build upon an exploration of a digital moment on Tumblr in which Tumbler user *virjin* critiqued YA novelist John Green. Green and his fellow adult YA authors swiftly responded with vitriol. The critique and the subsequent response reflect the messy and ambiguous tensions between the digital practices of teenaged readers/consumers and adult media creators, and in doing so reveals the unequal value of girls' voices, that are valued as fans but not as critical thinkers and political actors. Building on the theoretical traditions of girlhood studies and feminist studies, Bimm's work expands the definitions of feminist resistance, and suggests that digital moments such as this one offer small points of rupture that jar mainstream formations.

The chapters throughout this book actively work within the dynamic, local sites of youth social engagement, imaginative play, creativity and labor, offering readers a breadth of texts, experiences and contexts that defy the tendency to generalize and unify knowledge about youth and social media. This book is interested in the multiplicity of stories, images, actions and concrete details that emerge out of the expansive empirical work being undertaken by scholars working with a diverse range of theoretical and methodological tools. There are many possibilities for thinking about affect and youth mediations. The goal here is to provide conceptual and material openings in which to consider the complexities of youth in their everyday activities that interweave on and offline relations. These chapters are necessarily provisional and open-ended in terms of their desire to grapple with the difficult and changing worlds of youth without providing closed interpretations or pat evaluations. They aim to acknowledge and portray those realms of youth desire, embodiment and belonging that have been devalued as trivial or ignored as irrational. Integral to all this work is an awareness of the limitations, and at times the impossibility, of making fixed coherent claims about the messy, fleeting and mobile affective lives of young people. Our hope is that this collection makes this unique contribution within youth scholarship, to admit that adults do not know it all in the here and now, and should not always have the final say in matters affecting youth. It is not for us to decide what is possible for the future of youth mediations and affective relations, but at least we can remain open, curious and engaged in a caring ethical way.

References

Coleman, Rebecca. 2009. *The becoming of bodies: Girls, images, experiences.* Manchester: Manchester University Press.

Coulter, Natalie. 2014. *Tweening the girl: The crystallization of the tween market.* New York: Peter Lang.

Dimitriadis, Greg. 2009. *Performing identity performing culture.* New York: Peter Lang.

Driver, Susan. 2007. *Queer girls and popular culture: Reading, resisting and creating media.* New York: Peter Lang.

Fine, Michelle. 1988. Sexuality, schooling, and adolescent females: The missing discourse of desire. *Harvard Educational Review* 58 (1): 29–54.

Gopinath, Gayatri. 2005. *Impossible desires: Queer Diasporas and South Asian public cultures*. New York: Duke University Press.
Halberstam, Judith. 2005. *In a queer time and place*. New York: NYU Press.
Harris, Anita. 2003. *Future girl: Young women in the twenty-first century*. New York: Routledge.
Hickey-Moody, A., and T. Page. 2015. *Arts, pedagogy and cultural resistance: New materialisms*. London: Rowman & Littlefield International.
Jenkins, Henry, et al. 2016. *By any media necessary*. New York: NYU Press.
Keller, Jessalynn. 2015. *Girls' feminist blogging in a postfeminist age*. New York: Routledge.
Lesko, Nancy. 2012. *Act your age: A cultural construction of adolescence*. New York: Routledge.
Maira, Sunaina Marr. 2016. *The 9/11 generation*. New York: NYU Press.
McRobbie, Angela. 2007. Top girls? Young women and the post-feminist sexual contract. *Cultural Studies* 21 (4): 718–737.
Monaghan, Whitney. 2016. *Queer girls, temporality and screen media* (Not 'Just a Phase'). London: Palgrave.
Pough, Gwendolyn. 2004. *Check it while I wreck it: Black womanhood, hip-hop culture, and the public sphere*. Boston: Northeastern University Press.
Rasmussen, Mary Louise, et al. 2004. *Youth and sexualities: Pleasure, subversion, and insubordination in and out of schools*. London: Palgrave.
Renold, E., and J. Ringrose. 2011. Schizoid subjectivities? Re-theorizing teen girls' sexual cultures in an era of 'sexualization'. *Journal of Sociology* 47 (4): 389–409.
Ringrose, Jessica. 2012. *Postfeminist education*? New York: Routledge and Littlefield Publishers Inc.
Rose, Tricia. 2008. *The hip hop wars*. New York: Civitas Books.
Stockton, Kathryn Bond. 2009. *The queer child or growing sideways in the twentieth century*. New York: NYU Press.
Talburt, Susan. 2008. Queer imaginings. *Journal of LGBT Youth* 5 (3): 99–103.

CHAPTER 2

"I Am Crying…This Really Touched My Heart": Disabled Intimacy and the Thick Materiality of the Virtual

Anastasia Todd

"Charisse's Story—My Life Journey with Cerebral Palsy" is Charisse Living with Cerebral Palsy's most watched YouTube video. This seventeen-minute video, with over 228,945 views and 800 comments, alternates between video footage of present-day Charisse and still photographs of her as a baby. As the title suggests, within the space of video, Charisse sits on the floor, an Americana quilt draped behind her, and narrates her disability story, or "life journey." As baby photographs linger in the frame, Charisse takes us through her birth. The viewers learn that her umbilical cord was wrapped around her neck, cutting off oxygen for seven minutes. She explains that she was not diagnosed with low tone Cerebral Palsy and Ataxia[1] until she was two years old. We first see photos of toddler Charisse, using a walker in a pink tutu, and we follow along through school photographs, as present-day Charisse narrates her journey from walker, to forearm crutches, to walking unassisted with a bit of a limp. The video alternates between discussions of

A. Todd (✉)
Gender and Women's Studies, University of Kentucky,
Lexington, KY, USA
e-mail: anastasia.todd@uky.edu

S. Driver and N. Coulter (eds.), *Youth Mediations and Affective Relations*,
https://doi.org/10.1007/978-3-319-98971-6_2

the materiality of her disabled embodiment, for example, her experiences with seizures, and how her embodiment structures her being-in-the-world, for example, how she did not realize she was disabled until someone at school started bullying her in the second grade.

Similar to Charisse's other videos on her channel, which range from informative, "Talking About Driving with Cerebral Palsy," to mundane, "A Day in the Life of Charisse Living with Cerebral Palsy," "Charisse's Story" invites viewers into some of her most intimate moments. As McGlotten (2013) notes, intimacy can describe a sense of belonging or a feeling of connection. It refers to things that we feel and do. Intimacy is a force. McGlotten writes, "In contemporary American culture, intimacy names the affective encounters with others that often matter most, while also functioning as a juridical form, an aspirational narrative, and therapeutic culture's raison d'etre" (2013, p. 11).

The YouTube video blog, or vlog, is a phenomenon that has often been theorized in media studies within the framework of a turn toward confession or therapeutic culture, and has been connected to new post-feminist, neoliberal, and, as this chapter forwards, post-Americans with Disability Act (ADA)[2] economies of visibility (Raun 2012; Banet-Weiser 2014). Intimacy is the force that constitutes these contemporary cultures and economies. Historically, people with disabilities have had a paradoxical relationship with intimacy and visibility, and this chapter interrogates what happens when *certain* people with disabilities are welcomed into, and work to create, a specific "intimate public." An intimate public can "legitimate qualities, ways of being, and entire lives that have otherwise been deemed puny or discarded" (Berlant 2008, p. 2). Most remarkably, an intimate public "creates *situations* where those qualities can appear as luminous" (Berlant 2008, p. 2).

This chapter explores how the vlogs of differently abled girls function as intimate publics, or spaces of technologically mediated intimacy, where I understand intimacy in terms of "affects own immanence," or a "necessary precondition for certain affective states to bloom, especially those that have to do with other people" (McGlotten 2013, p. 9). Through a critical analysis of the virtual intimate publics that are produced by 'Charisse Living with Cerebral Palsy,' and a fellow disabled vlogger, Rikki Poynter, I explore the mechanisms that "cause us to be moved," or generate the specific individual and collective affective states that circulate in and through Charisse and Poynter's vlogs. I explore the comment sections and argue that these YouTube videos function, in phenomenological terms, as devices of able-bodied reorientation. I argue that this able-bodied reorientation is undergirded by ablenationalist logic, which functions to reorient, or rehabilitate, the able-bodied viewer into a tolerant post-ADA neoliberal citizen. Ultimately, these intimate publics are co-opted as a sign of neoliberal inclusionism. This capture is contingent on the very production and circulation of an atmosphere of post-ADA tolerant futurity, which is, in part, generated through the 'disabled girl' subject.

Disabled Girlhood 2.0

> Hello, my name is Rikki Poynter and welcome to my channel. On my channel, you will see videos about these topics: closed-captioning awareness, Deaf awareness, me learning ASL. But being deaf isn't all that I am. I also like to talk about my favorite things: Pokémon, Sailor Moon, coffee, YouTube. I upload videos every Monday and Thursday. So make sure you subscribe and look out for those. And I will see you later. Bye! ("RIKKI POYNTER—Channel Trailer" 2016)

I came across and became interested in disabled girl YouTubers somewhat accidentally. I subscribe to and watch a variety of makeup YouTubers and daily vloggers, and I stumbled upon Rikki Poynter's channel organically, as I was searching to expand my repertoire of channels to subscribe to. As her channel trailer cited above articulates, the current videos on her channel range from informative, "3 Ways to Caption Your Videos!," to more personal, "Storytime: My Teacher Made Fun of Me in Class." However, a few years ago when I first came across her channel, she was exclusively producing makeup videos. Her channel was like many of the others that I watched at the time, a profusion of "Chit Chat Get Ready With Me," "Monthly Favorites," and "Empties" videos. Her Deaf identity was not the focus of her channel, when I clicked the subscribe button it was acknowledged, it was just not the focus of the content of her videos. I was already writing about representations of disabled girlhood in other spaces, so it was a bit serendipitous when I looked in my subscription box, in early October 2014, to find her video "Q&A: Deaf Awareness Week." Poynter's departure from her typical makeup upload was so well received that she decided to change the direction of her channel shortly after, and she is now what I would term, a "disability vlogger." Poynter's transition piqued my interest in this genre of YouTube videos, and from there I stumbled across many more emergent channels that addressed the embodied reality of disability. This chapter takes Poynter and one of the channels I stumbled across, Charisse Living with Cerebral Palsy, first introduced in the opening, together as its point of departure.

Although these two YouTubers are both disability vloggers, their channels are aesthetically quite different. Poynter has been making videos since 2010, but as I previously mentioned, she rebranded as a disability vlogger in 2014, evidenced by the hashtag she promotes: #deaftalent. She has over 30,000 subscribers and 1.5 million views. Charisse has been making videos since 2009, but her channel is a much smaller channel with just under 7000 subscribers. Interestingly, her 1.2 million views are comparable to Poynter's channel views. The aesthetic of Poynter's channel has become increasingly more polished and produced (e.g., professional lighting, corporate sponsorship videos, etc.), as her brand gains traction and circulates online. Her "About Me," attests to her productive virality as an effect of building and marketing her new brand:

> Rikki Poynter is a twenty-four year old Deaf vlogger on YouTube. After four years of being a beauty blogger and vlogger, she took a hiatus in October 2014 to focus on more lifestyle vlogs and vlogs about deafness and Deaf culture. Since making her first deaf related video on October 1, 2014, Rikki has been on the Huffington Post, Mic News, Upworthy, ABC News, BBC Newsbeat, BBC Ouch, BBC See Her, and other news outlets in various countries. Also, she has been working on her new closed captioning campaign, #LIGHTSCAMERACAPTION, to try to get more YouTubers to closed [sic] caption their videos. After hopefully one day taking over YouTube, she wants to work on the rest of the internet.

In contrast, Charisse's aesthetic is less produced, and one could consider the style of her videos derivative of early vlogging culture, characterized by dim lighting, clunkier editing, and informal filming spaces (e.g., her actual bedroom, as opposed to a dedicated filming space that imitates the look of a bedroom). One could read her "About Me" as a metonym for her channel's aesthetic:

> Hi everyone! My name is Charisse! I was born with low tone Cerebral Palsy and Ataxia. In my videos I share my disability with the world to spread awareness and understanding of disabilities. My main goal is to show others that people with disabilities can do things other people can do, we just sometimes do things differently in our own unique way.

> I also want to inspire others to always keep hope and never give up during struggles. I film, edit, and upload all my videos by myself. Thank you for checking out my channel!

Although the current aesthetic of their channels differ, Poynter and Charisse both produce videos that explicitly reflect on their embodied reality as disabled girls, and their stated goal for their respective channels is similar in that they want to, as Charisse eloquently articulates, "spread awareness and understanding of disabilities." For both of the girls, creating YouTube content is their full-time job. In several videos, Poynter and Charisse recall the painful ways ableism has essentially excluded them from the traditional job market. Through YouTube, Poynter and Charisse have successfully leveraged this exclusionism, and have become re-capacitated by way of a new brand of disability entrepreneurialism.

Poynter and Charisse become valuable through this brand of disability entrepreneurialism, because of the ways in which it functions to position the girls as disabled "future girls." Many scholars of girlhood studies argue that girls are the privileged subjects of neoliberalism. For example, Anita Harris argues that "future girls," endowed with an imagined capacity for weathering the attendant crises of neoliberalism, are envisioned as flexible, resilient, adaptive, and ultimately successful in managing their own "choice biography" (2004, p. 8). The rhetoric of autonomy, choice, flexibility, and responsibility "facilitates the coalescence of global economic motives with girls' individual life decisions" (Harris 2004, p. 183). As I have argued elsewhere, it is easy to mistakenly imagine this ideal girl proto-citizen subject as always, already able-bodied (Todd 2016). However, disabled girls, like Poynter and Charisse, who successfully manage their life and their future, become intelligible to the nation because of their ability to productively rehabilitate their own lives, or appear to overcome and paradoxically rebrand their disability, in order to insert themselves into the market. As disability entrepreneurs, Poynter and Charisse effectively and *affectively* rehabilitate their disabled identity, and construct a self-enterprising choice biography that emphasizes self-determination, individual hard work, and flexibility.

The disabled future girl emerges under a particularly insidious spotlight, cast by the contemporary post-ADA production of disability, which can be characterized through the tension of the material failure of the ADA, the attendant fraying of the welfare state and the framework of ablenationalism, or exceptional neoliberal inclusion efforts. Mitchell and Snyder (2015) argue that ablenationalism manifests through "open rhetorical claims of a new era of inclusion for people with disabilities issued by the state [...] Disabled people now perform their representational work as a symbol of expansive neoliberal inclusion efforts" (p. 116). In this chapter, I deploy post-ADA as a sensibility that can be conceptualized by an entanglement of discourses and affective states that work to enfold disability and neutralize it in the process of enfolding. In a post-ADA America, disability politics and activism are rendered irrelevant on the assumption that disability rights have been achieved. In this space, the hypervisible figuration of the disabled girl serves as a testament to this final frontier of American benevolence. In a post-ADA America, Charisse and Poynter are welcomed into the diversity economy through their capacity to successfully re-orient the able-bodied who participate in their intimate publics.

Virtual Disability Intimate Publics

Intimate Publics

The disabled girl emerges as an index of the problem of the present, or to manage the contradictions inherent in a post-ADA neoliberal moment. Within the spaces of Poynter's and Charisse's intimate publics, they offer up a roadmap to ideal neoliberal citizenship, which has been reshaped and modified over the past 30 years. In *The Queen of America Goes to Washington City*, Berlant (1997) maps the reshaping of citizenship during the ascendancy of the Reaganite right. Central to this reshaping was a privatization of citizenship, which occurred through many different forces: rhetorical shifts to a "culture-based concept of the nation as a site of integrated social memberships"; antifederal, patriotic nationalism of Reagan Republicanism; the marketing of a nostalgic American aspirationalism; and, "the expansion of a mass-mediated space of opinion formation" (Berlant 1997, p. 3). This reformulation of citizenship was, in part, configured through the "rerouting of energies" into the "sentimental spaces of an amorphous opinion culture," which became possible through a narrative of a traumatized national identity, premised on an entanglement of suffering and citizenship (Berlant 1997, p. 3). Overcoming this trauma, the personal became the (a) political; the nation's survival depended on rehabilitation through "personal acts and identities performed in the intimate domains of the quotidian"

(Berlant 1997, p. 4). As such, national politics is no longer exercised through a political public sphere, but rather, the political public sphere has become an intimate public sphere. This new intimate public sphere figures citizenship through belonging, which is produced by "personal acts and values" (Berlant 1997, p. 5).

What is striking about this vexed evocation of intimacy is the ways in which it works to intertwine affective orientations and economies. Berlant notes that the Reaganite cultural revolution foregrounded "normal intimacy" as the key to a citizen's happiness, while at the same time operated rhetorically to cover over the precarity inherent in neoliberal capitalism, espousing that the causes of job instability and income inequality were "rephrased in terms of individuals' capacity to respond flexibly to the new 'opportunities' presented to them within an increasingly volatile global economy" (Berlant 1997, p. 8). This configuration of the intimate public sphere works to individuate citizenship and misdirect energies from the structural into the personal.

An intimate public names a space of belonging, wherein the participants consume common texts and objects, they "***already*** share a worldview and emotional knowledge that they have derived from a broadly common historical experience" (Berlant 2008, p. viii). Participants in these spaces structure the conventions of belonging, while experiencing and expressing an embodied sensation of living as a certain kind of being in the world. An intimate public is a space of recognition and reflection, or, in other words, it is an achievement. Berlant (2008) explains:

> Whether linked to women or other nondominant people [it] flourishes as a porous, affective scene of identification among strangers that promises a certain experience of belonging and provides a complex of consolation, confirmation, discipline and discussion about how to live as an *x*. (p. viii)

The participants in an intimate public may have freely chosen to identify as an *x*, or participants may have been marked as an *x* by outside taxonomies, but regardless, an intimate public provides its participants with an "anchor" and material for "enduring, resisting, overcoming, and enjoying being an *x*" (Berlant 2008, p. ix). Intimate publics provide an affective frame for being in the world.

As a mass-mediated, nondominant community, an intimate public operates "juxtapolitically," thriving in proximity to the political, sometimes crossing over to the political, but largely "acting as a critical chorus that sees the expression of emotional response and conceptual recalibration as achievement enough" (Berlant 2008, p. x). An intimate public necessitates a turn inward, and it requires perpetual self-management and self-reflection as conditions of belonging.

Disabled Girl Intimate Publics

With over 71,000 views and 1000 likes in September 2017, "Q&A: Deaf Awareness Week" is Poynter's most-watched and "liked" video on her channel. As I have previously stated, this video was the catalyst for a rebranding of her channel. In the video, filmed in what we would presume to be her bedroom, she sits in front of her bed on the floor. A wooden armoire sits behind her bed, and a NASCAR quilt sits on top of her bed. The video has a distinctly amateur aesthetic—characterized by dim lighting and the mundane bedroom space. During the video, Poynter toggles between educational facts and figures about deafness, personal narratives, and, what I can only describe as, pleading with her viewers to: consider captioning their videos; consider how they are potentially complicit in dehumanizing deaf persons in their everyday lives; consider how they would feel if they were deaf, living in a hearing world. Throughout the video, and despite the different terrain that Poynter covers, she maintains a distinctly humorous and even sarcastic tone. For example, she begins the video by discussing an offensive meme that she recently came across, a picture of a green dinosaur looking inquisitive, its claw to its chin, with this text overlain, "When people yawn, do deaf people think they are screaming?" She points to the meme that she inserted into the corner of the video frame and, with an incredulous face, she says, "I don't know who the hell made this shit up, but um, it's shit."

Poynter invites her viewers into the space of her bedroom—to joke with, to tell personal stories with, to plead with. This is an intimate encounter. Intimacy can describe a sense of belonging or a feeling of connection; it refers to things that we feel and do; intimacy is a force (McGlotten 2013). This video is strikingly similar in aesthetic and content to Charisse's most watched video, "Charisse's Story—My Life Journey with Cerebral Palsy."

In "Charisse's Story—My Life Journey with Cerebral Palsy," Charisse sits stoically in the center of the frame, staring intensely at the camera, as she delivers this monologue:

> In 10th grade I started making Youtube videos and I didn't really know how many people would actually watch them. So I just continued making more and more. And later on kids from my school found my videos some told me that they understood me more now and understood more about Cerebral Palsy and that inside I'm not as different as them and I can do what they do just in my own unique way. It helped a lot, just seeing my videos they started understanding me. More and more people began talking to me at school, and it was just really great. So I continued my videos and hoping they can help others understand that people with disabilities can do what other people do, just in their unique way, and spread the awareness of the disabled and show what we can do and that on the outside we may be different, but on the inside we're like everyone else.

Her tone is unwaveringly calm, and although her ataxia affects the smooth cadence of the monologue in unpredictable ways, words crescendo into being, and her mouth slowly mimics the uptick in her narrative. She starts to smile as she articulates:

> My 12th grade year was so much better than the two past years. A lot more people started talking to me and I started helping with the mentally challenge [sic] students and I love helping them they would make me smile and amazed me with everything they do. And when I get older I would love to have a job helping with special needs children because I love being around them.

Charisse goes on to talk about how she joined the varsity basketball cheerleading squad her senior year, "overcame" her fear stage fright through her drama class, started dating the boy she went to prom with, and walked across the stage at graduation. She notes that it "felt so amazing to walk across the stage because [she] struggled so much in high school." Charisse ends the video by firmly, yet optimistically, stating that she "knows life is going to give her more challenges along the way, but [she] thinks she is ready to face them, and [she] can't wait to see what [she has] in her future."

Both videos invite viewers into the space of the disabled girl vloggers' bedrooms, and both vloggers directly address their imagined audience, they narrate their inner worlds—reminiscent of engaging with a teenage girl's diary. Media scholar Susanna Paasonen (2005) argues that the creators of amateur video productions are assumed to have a lack of skill, and the overly non-manufactured aesthetic of their videos reads as "real," or, authentic. This authenticity resonates with the audience, exemplified both by the atypically high number of views on these two videos relative to other lesser known vloggers' average video views, as well as the similarly impassioned comments that are left on both videos. For example, in response to Poynter's video, Sassy G writes: "THANK YOU SO MUCH.<333333333." The palpable ecstatic affective state, illustrated by the less than 3 heart emoticon, is similar to It's Your Girl Miah's response to Charisse's video: "You are amazing I cried watching this video love. Just stay cool xxx." The affectivity of these videos is intense.

The internet has "become an ersatz space" that facilitates "reaching out, fetishizing, and touching other individuals" (Hillis 2009, pp. 15–16). Vlogs hinge upon touch—the viewers are touched by the vlogger and the vlogger is touched by the viewers—and this establishes virtual intimacies. These virtual intimacies manifest in various ways: through vloggers' direct address to their viewers, the vlogs' confessional and therapeutic aesthetic, and through the mundane and ordinary content. Kuntsman's (2012) concept of cybertouch is useful here, and although this approach mobilizes the term to talk about the affective entanglements of war and violence online and off, cybertouch can help us think through how Poynter and Charisse, through their videos, "create an immediate emotional response (sadness, rage, pain, compassion, joy)—an affective charge of investment, of being 'touched'" (Cvetkovich qtd. in Kuntsman 2012, p. 3). The intimate publics of the disabled girl are structured by way of the palpable touch, charge, or energy force that draws the viewers in. However, this thick materiality of the virtual is not value neutral. It is embedded within, and constitutive of, a post-ADA affective cartography, wherein the disabled girl emerges as luminous, moving viewers in specific ways within the confines of ablenationalism.

Ahmed (2006) argues in *Queer Phenomenology* that, "it involves painstaking labor for bodies to inhabit spaces that do not extend their shape" (p. 62). When bodies "take up spaces that do not extend their shape," they effectively and affectively labor to "reorientate bodies and space" (Ahmed 2006, p. 61). When Charisse and Poynter upload videos, and, thus, when their disabled bodies extend into the virtual, "something other than the reproduction of the facts of the matter happens" (Ahmed 2006, p. 62). Through the affective labor that they perform, to create and sustain a virtual intimate public, they become intelligible to their able-bodied peers by way of the extension of their disabled bodies into the space of YouTube. This extension is premised upon the pedagogical promise offered by way of their disabled embodiment.

"I am crying this really touched my heart," reads a comment Rafael Beck left in response to Charisse's "Charisse's Story—My Life Journey with Cerebral Palsy." Ach1088 concurs, "This video made me cry it's so beautiful and inspiring. Thanks for sharing." These utterances of being driven to tears, are found sprinkled throughout the comments section of Charisse's videos. Not only are commenters being driven to tears after watching Charisse recount her experience with bullying, isolation, and loneliness, they are similarly affected as they watch Charisse perform the mundane. In response to a video where Charisse explains how she ties her shoes, AgentJayZ comments that Charisse "tugs at my heart strings... whatever they are." In response to "Baking Cupcakes with a Disability," a video where Charisse shows us her mini cupcake maker, JayGirl711 writes, "You made me cry. Those cupcakes were great<3☺ Now I'm craving for cupcakes! I haven't seen a person with Cerebral Palsy. When you cracked the egg, I felt something in my heart and cried."

The feeling of Charisse's touch, "or the sensation of the skin surface," is not "in the object of the body, but instead takes shape as an effect of the encounter" (Ahmed 2006, p. 119). The touch of a disabled body, or an encounter with a disabled body is a moment of disorientation. Moments of disorientation, according to Parrey (2016), "occur when one realizes that an encounter has led to a different sense of being in the world or, more accurately, the realization that they are already in the world differently" (n.p.). Theoretically, disorientation is about 'being turned' by an encounter, and in the process of 'turning,' one is reoriented. Through the viewer's 'turning,' they are affectively rehabilitated. We can see the process of this reorientation, and how this undergirds a post-ADA rehabilitative logic, more clearly in the following discussion of Charisse's "What I Want the World to Know" video.

Viral Intimacies: Disabled Girlhood and Affective Reorientations

In "What I Want the World to Know," Charisse departs from her typical upload. She is sitting square in the frame, the lighting is dim, and, with a somber face, she lifts up a white notecard. In her shaky handwriting it reads, "My Name is Charisse." The video continues with Charisse holding up a series of notecards: "This is what I want the world to know/ people with disabilities are like/ everyone else." She urges her viewers to "Please be careful with what you say," and reminds able-bodied folks that they should not "say what [disabled folks] can't do," because they "can do what others can do." She asks us to consider that people with disabilities "just do things/ in their own unique way." The video ends with Charisse explicitly directing able-bodied individuals away from judgment and toward a shared humanity: "Before you judge us/ Just like everyone, we want to be/ accepted the way we are/ Look past the disability/ and accept the person." She ends the video by pulling the last notecard to the side of her face and smiling directly at the camera. Like most of Charisse's videos, "What I Want the World to Know" addresses a presumably able-bodied audience; however, unlike Charisse's other "doing being ordinary" videos, such as tying her shoes, this video attempts to explicitly reorient able-bodied viewers.

New modes of capitalist production require different energizing narratives; a successfully flexible subject must cultivate emotions the *right* way, or what Elman (2012) characterizes as a properly "managed heart." The intimate publics that Charisse engenders, offer up a roadmap to a successful cultivation of a post-ADA managed heart. For example, in response to "What I Want the World to Know," Autoteck1951 writes, "I see a very beautiful courageous and strong young woman with a very unselfish heart making a big difference in the world." Batmanbeyond1939 adds, "Your [sic] super brave, and stronger than most people in the world. Your [sic] awesome and no one should ever change that." Similarly, William Collier writes, "Awh, I accept you and everyone like you, or with any disability, people are amazing! And it's amazing what we can do if we put are minds to it, regardless of conditions!" These comments are striking because of the ways in which they illuminate how affect, as it traverses through this intimate public, works to uphold certain contemporary truths about disability. Fritsch (2013) argues that the contemporary production of disability is tangled up with positive affects, whether the disabled body is overcoming obstacles and inspiring hope, or suffering and inspiring a future-oriented optimism. Charisse's intimate public is at once a producer of, and produced, by this tangle of "positive affects." However, these positive affects are always produced as an effect of Charisse's capacity to reorient viewers. We can see this most clearly in Sam Curnow's comment, "One of my classmates said that people that have disabilities are stupid when I heard it I went over and hit him and said u [sic] wach [sic] dis [sic] video and then he relised [sic] what he did." Sam was affectively reoriented after watching Charisse, and as a dutiful member of Charisse's intimate public, he felt the call to rectify his classmate's act of ignorance. Under the regime of ablenationalism, "disabled people now perform the nation's representational work as a symbol of expansive neoliberal inclusion efforts" (Mitchell and Snyder 2015, p. 49). Thus, as a disabled "future girl," Charisse not only successfully manages her own future, but she manages the future of the nation: one that is tolerant of disability, the last frontier of American benevolence.

"Good News" in Post-ADA Times

Shortly after Poynter uploaded her Deaf Awareness week video, an article was posted on the Huffington Post: "This Beauty Vlogger is Hard of Hearing, and She's Stepping Up Her Game on YouTube." The article ends with a similar sentiment: "If one of her goals is to raise awareness for what she calls a 'hidden disability,' her online presence, mixed with the vibrant colors showcased on her Instagram page, makes it pretty hard to look away" (Matthews 2014). The Huffington Post article illustrates how this video instigated a stir of public feelings—intense flows of affect spilled over from Poynter's intimate public to other online outlets. Poynter articulates in the video she uploaded following the Huffington Post article, "Deaf Awareness: I'm on the Huffington Post!":

> I can't believe I'm actually getting to say this in real life, I'm on the Huffington Post! I'm on the Good News portion of the Huffington Post world. To be completely honest with you, I thought the entire thing was fake all weekend until the very second that the article actually went live. I mean it's not every day that somebody from the Huffington Post emails you and says, 'Hey! I wanna write about you.' After the Deaf Awareness video went viral after 3000 views—FYI: to the little YouTuber people like us, 3 K is viral—Cate Matthews from the Huffington Post emailed me [...] and said, 'I'd like to do an interview.'

Poynter discusses her video in terms of virality, or, "the ability to cross time and space and reach a large audience" (Ash 2015, p. 120). If we understand affect as "what allows our content to resonate beyond ourselves," then we can consider affect as both what enables Poynter's virality, as well as what sustains it (Pybus 2015, p. 242). Both Poynter and Charisse are welcomed home, into the national imaginary, through their intimate publics, because of the ways in which they work, perhaps unwittingly, to establish a rehabilitative promise of tolerance. As Wendy Brown argues, "although tolerance has been constructed as a transcendent virtue, it is instead a 'historically protean [...] vehicle for producing and organizing subjects'" (qtd. in Elman 2014, p. 91). Tolerance, as a dominant mode of U.S. governmentality, functions affectively, working insidiously through disabled intimate publics, such as those nurtured by Charisse and Poynter's.

For example, Deadeye87 writes in response to Poynter's Q&A:

> You are an amazing person. Thank you for informing hearing people, like me, about what it is like to be deaf. You helped me understand some of the hurdles deaf people have to jump through in life. I am not a YouTuber, but if I ever start uploading videos I will be sure to Closed Caption them. Keep doing what you're doing - you are helping make the world, and the Internet, a better place.

This comment specifically calls attention to the ways in which Poynter has "helped" Deadeye87 to "understand some of the hurdles deaf people have to jump through in life." Not only has Poynter helped Deadeye87 to perform an internal epistemological and ontological shift, but now Deadeye87 will remember to always caption their videos, if they decide to become a YouTuber. As Berlant would say, Deadeye87 is learning to become *x*, or we could say that they are being rehabilitated into *x*. For many, to belong to Poynter's virtual intimate public is to be rehabilitated, or *affectively reoriented* into a tolerant neoliberal (virtual) citizen.

This act of affective reorientation relies on imagining a "future-oriented" version of tolerance, wherein we all imagine "a good society yet to come," which effectively depoliticizes disability (Elman 2012, p. 91). An affective atmosphere of tolerant futurity undergirds many of the comments that are found on Charisse and Poynter's videos. For example, Bleed peroxide comments about how Poynter's Q&A video *will* make them "pause before getting irritated" at their hard of hearing roommate for playing the television "really loud." Similarly, Robert Croft comments on Poynter's "Is the Internet Real Life?" video:

> Coming across your videos has informed me about something I did not know. You are a very smart person and give your heart to what you believe and do. The things you bring up has given me what I can take into the real

> world and live it out in real life. In closing ...Talking about issues on the internet can move us into action.

Both of these comments are future-oriented, as well as exemplify that this future orientation is one that is premised on a turn inward—on becoming more tolerant, more understanding, more knowledgeable—and, through this turn inward, we can take it "into the real world and live it out in real life." Thus, Poynter effectively and affectively reorients able-bodied people through her affective capacity to cybertouch her viewer's hearts and minds, as well as through her symbolic embodiment of a new American tolerance, illustrated through the positioning of her Huffington Post article in the "Good News" column.

What enables Poynter's and Charisse's virality, are their affective capacities, and ultimately, their self-brand as YouTube "disability educators." They are recapacitated through this symbolic and literal work of tolerance, and welcomed into neoliberal capitalism by virtue of their pedagogical labor, helping to rehabilitate able-bodied people into properly affective citizens of a new post-ADA America. These intimate publics unwittingly function to shore up ablenationalism, which is premised on a surface-level inclusionism. Inclusionism has come to be defined as a superficial "embrace of diversity-based practices by which we include those who look, act, function, and feel different" (Mitchell and Snyder 2015, p. 4). Or, in Ahmed's (2012) words:

> Perhaps the promise of diversity is that it can be both attached to those bodies that 'look different' and detached from those bodies as a sign of inclusion (if they are included by diversity, then we are all included). The promise of diversity could then be described as a problem: the sign of inclusion makes the sign of exclusion disappear. (65)

Poynter and Charisse are both producers of and produced by inclusionism; their intimate publics offer affective roadmaps for the able-bodied to follow and attain certain virtues that scaffold the "promise of diversity." In the specific terms of post-ADA America, Charisse and Poynter are made luminous as disabled "future girls," however, this luminosity works in concert with insidious and slippery modes of compulsory able-bodiedness. Rehabilitation and reorientation are premised upon disability as a sign of tolerance—an exceptional and inspiring way of being-in-the-world; a hollow promise that tomorrow is a better day—not on disability as desirable, lived, and real.

Notes

1. Charisse explains that low tone cerebral palsy affects her movement—her muscle tone is low, which makes it difficult to control her movements. Her body also is subject to uncontrollable jerks because of her ataxia.
2. The Americans with Disabilities Act (ADA) is one of the United States' most comprehensive pieces of civil rights legislation regarding disability. Signed into law by President George Bush in 1990, the ADA prohibits discrimination on the basis of disability. The ADA aims to provide disabled people with the "same opportunities" as able-bodied people to "participate in the mainstream of American life," e.g. through the ability to attain employment opportunities, purchase goods and services, and participate in state and local government (ada.gov). It is imagined as an "'equal opportunity' law for people with disabilities" (ada.gov).

References

Ahmed, Sara. 2006. *Queer phenomenology*. Durham: Duke University Press.

Ahmed, Sara. 2012. *On being included: Racism and diversity in institutional life*. Durham: Duke University Press.

Ash, James. 2015. Sensation, networks, and the GIF: Toward an allotropic account of affect. In *Networked affect*, ed. Ken Hillis, Susanna Paasonen, and Michael Petit, 119–134. Cambridge: The MIT Press.

Banet-Weiser, Sarah. 2014. Am I pretty or ugly? Girls and the market for self-esteem. *Girlhood Studies: An Interdisciplinary Journal* 7 (1): 83–101. https://doi.org/10.3167/ghs.2014.070107.

Berlant, Lauren. 1997. *The queen of America goes to Washington city: Essays on sex and citizenship*. Durham: Duke University Press.

Berlant, Lauren. 2008. *The female complaint: The unfinished business of sentimentality in U.S. culture*. Durham: Duke University Press.

"Charisse's Story—My Life Journey with Cerebral Palsy." YouTube Video, 17:35, posted by Charisse Living with Cerebral Palsy, June 13. https://www.youtube.com/watch?v=0nnuHj5M5FE.

Elman, Julie Passanante. 2012. 'Nothing feels as real': Teen sick-lit, sadness, and the condition of adolescence. *Journal of Literary & Cultural Disability Studies* 6 (2): 175–191. https://doi.org/10.1353/jlc.2012.011.

Elman, Julie Passanante. 2014. *Chronic youth: Disability, sexuality, and U.S. cultures of rehabilitation*. New York: New York University Press.

Fritsch, Kelly. 2013. The neoliberal circulation of affects: Happiness, accessibility and the capacitation of disability as wheelchair. *Health, Culture and Society* 5 (1): 135–149. https://doi.org/10.5195/hcs.2013.136.

Harris, Anita. 2004. *Future girl: Young women in the twenty-first century*. New York: Routledge.
Hillis, Ken. 2009. *Online a lot of the time: Ritual, fetish, sign*. Durham: Duke University Press.
Information and technical assistance on the Americans with Disability act. *ADA.gov*, September 17. https://www.ada.gov/index.html.
Kuntsman, Adi. 2012. Introduction: Affective fabrics of digital cultures. In *Digital cultures and the politics of emotion: Feelings, affect, and technological change*, ed. Athina Karatzogianni and Adi Kuntsman, 1–18. New York: Palgrave Macmillan.
Matthews, Cate. 2014. This beauty vlogger is hard of hearing, and she's stepping up her game. *Huffington Post*, October 6. http://www.huffingtonpost.com/2014/10/06/rikki-poynter-deaf-hoh-beauty-vlogger_n_5941160.html.
McGlotten, Shaka. 2013. *Virtual intimacies: Media, affect, and queer sociality*. New York: SUNY Press.
Mitchell, David T., and Sharon L. Snyder. 2015. *The biopolitics of disability: Neoliberalism, ablenationalism, and peripheral embodiment*. Ann Arbor: University of Michigan Press.
Paasonen, Susanna. 2005. *Figures of fantasy: Internet, women, and cyberdiscourse*. New York: Peter Lang.
Parrey, Ryan C. 2016. Being disoriented: Uncertain encounters with disability. *Disability Studies Quarterly* 36 (2). http://dsq-sds.org/article/view/4555.
Pybus, Jennifer. 2015. Accumulating affect: Social networks and their archives of feelings. In *Networked affect*, ed. Ken Hillis, Susanna Paasonen, and Michael Petit, 235–250. Cambridge: The MIT Press.
Poytner, R. 2014. Q&A: Deaf awareness week|close captioned. YouTube video, 22:22, posted October 1. https://www.youtube.com/watch?v=5PApS9aKH58.
Poytner, R. 2016. RIKKI POYNTER—Chanel trailer. YouTube video, 1:05, posted May 10. https://www.youtube.com/watch?v=KMIxKwCXpBM.
Raun, Tobias. 2012. DIY therapy: Exploring affective self-representations in trans video blogs on YouTube. In *Digital cultures and the politics of emotion: Feelings, affect, and technological change*, ed. Athina Karatzogianni and Adi Kuntsman, 165–180. New York: Palgrave Macmillan.
Todd, Anastasia. 2016. Disabled girlhood and flexible exceptionalism in HBO's *Miss You Can Do It. Girlhood studies* 9 (1): 21–35. http://dx.doi.org/10.3167/ghs.2016.090103.
What I Want the World to Know. YouTube video, 4:09, posted by Charisse Living with Cerebral Palsy, September 11. https://www.youtube.com/watch?v=n_VADDvHxCY.

CHAPTER 3

Decolonizing Technology: Presence, Caring, Sharing, and Orality Within the Indigenous Friends Mobile App

Alejandro MayoralBaños

Indigenous[1] research can only interpret the world from the place of our personal and communal experiences in order to be congruent with a system based on relationships (Wilson 2008, p. 123; Kovach 2009, pp. 110–111). Therefore, the autobiographical narrative along with the introduction of the mobile application is a fundamental element of the presentation of this research, as it is used to understand how the knowledge around this project was constructed.

My name is Alejandro MayoralBaños. I am an Indigenous *Mestizo* scholar and activist and am originally from Mexico. My journey around this work began when I was doing my undergraduate studies in computer science in 2006. During that time, I started visiting several Indigenous communities in the countryside of Mexico, primarily the Totonac and Huastec peoples. I realized the differing realities that Native peoples, and especially Indigenous youth, were facing, in comparison with their non-Indigenous counterparts. In the context of Canada, I have worked within Mi'kmaq

A. MayoralBaños (✉)
Indigenous Friends Association, Toronto, Canada
e-mail: alejandro@indigenousfriends.org

S. Driver and N. Coulter (eds.), *Youth Mediations and Affective Relations*,
https://doi.org/10.1007/978-3-319-98971-6_3

communities in Nova Scotia in 2011, where I realized the significant and common challenges and threats that Indigenous peoples face across North America, such as isolation, misunderstanding of traditional worldviews, and discrimination. In January 2015, during the first year of my master's degree, I had a conversation with the Métis Cree Elder Laureen Waters Gaudios (who is better known as 'Blu Waters'), and the Mohawk Traditional Knowledge Keeper Ruth Koleszar-Green, about Aboriginal youth in the context of York University (Toronto). This conversation became the birthing ceremony of the *Indigenous Friends App*. In this ceremony, we talked about the opportunities to possibly impact Aboriginal youth through innovative solutions that are familiar to them, such as mobile technologies and social media (MayoralBaños 2016, pp. 78–79).

During the first development phase of the mobile application, I had the role of Fire-keeper in the Tipi that is located at York University, in the traditional territories of different Indigenous peoples.[2] In this role, I discovered the similarities of the methodology to create a mobile application in comparison with the procedure that is needed to raise and maintain a traditional Tipi, as a safe space for Indigenous bodies. I decided to disrupt standard software design methodologies, and modify the design process, in order to follow the protocols and knowledge of the Tipis. Although the complex specifications of this development process are beyond the scope of this particular research, several implications and considerations will be mentioned within the analysis of certain features of the mobile application. The result was a mobile software application that could support some of the needs of Indigenous peoples, as well as a space which might connect Indigenous youth to virtual and physical traditional experiences. In other words, the *Indigenous Friends App* became a mobile virtual Tipi for Indigenous youth (MayoralBaños 2016).

This mobile application aims to generate a supportive space for Native youth within educational institutions, by providing access to Indigenous counselling, creating Indigenous social networks, and offering information about resources and events. The app is in continuous flux, based on the feedback of Indigenous community members and allies. Currently, there are several opportunities for this virtual Tipi, as the community members try to reach more educational post-secondary institutions in order to create larger support networks. Furthermore, this software creates virtual spaces that offer new opportunities to explore Indigenous bodies and identities. The creation, maintenance, improvement, and research of this space have incorporated several aspects of Indigenous *ways of knowing*, as well as web epistemologies that are exploring innovative forms of interaction, expression, and methodology. The construction of this application (app), as an Indigenous virtual space with significant cultural, emotional, and spiritual elements, supports processes of embodiment and healing in cyberspace.[3] It is within this framework that my paper will provide some insights about practices and concepts that are new in cyberspace, in relation to Indigenous peoples, such as presence, sharing, caring, and orality. My analysis of these insights is through the exploration of different features within the *Indigenous Friends App* that have a direct relation with Indigenous embodiment and healing.

To unpack this examination, first I briefly explain the use of Indigenous methodologies and epistemologies. Next, I explore the possibility of Indigenous embodiment in virtual spaces and its decolonizing character around Indigenous principles. Finally, I explore how presence, caring, sharing, and orality are incorporated into the *Indigenous Friends App*.

Indigenous Ways of Knowing

This mobile app was designed and created through a process of sharing circles and conversations with Elders, students, faculty, and staff members during 2015, at York University. Several considerations and features were created, to address some of the challenges that Indigenous community members face in the context of post-secondary educational institutions. The usage of Indigenous *ways of knowing*, or Indigenous paradigms, throughout the full process of research is essential in order to acknowledge the history of colonization and to show respect for the communities. Therefore, before the analysis is elaborated, it is necessary to frame this work around Indigenous knowledges and paradigms.[4] Typically, Indigenous scholars are compelled to justify their research and knowledge systems within the dominant perspective in order to gain credibility and to support their results for academic purposes (Wilson 2008, p. 12). In this brief section, I will clarify and justify why Indigenous research paradigms are essential to this research. I will examine how these paradigms are indispensable in creating new, effective decolonizing technologies and spaces.

The first aspect to take into consideration is the guarantee that non-Indigenous epistemic content would not override Indigenous knowledge (Wilson 2008, pp. 35–37). In other words, the voices, experiences, and teachings of Indigenous Knowledge Keepers and Elders are acknowledged to have the same value as academic sources. The failure of this fundamental aspect would undermine essential cultural aspects of Indigenous ways of knowing, and therefore, significant understandings and perspectives might not be heard (Kovach 2009, p. 81). Secondly, Indigenous epistemology influences the way in which methods are practised. In a *good way* is a traditional Elder's expression, which literally means to speak truthfully, as well as to offer validity, relational accountability (i.e. the recognition of relationships), and credibility (Kovach 2009, p. 52). Otherwise, Euro-centric methods would impose conditions of validation that would not consider all dimensions of Native communities. Furthermore, this *good way* describes relationships within Indigenous knowledges and practices that are more significant than abstract discussions of 'evidence' or mathematical accuracy. This is because Indigenous methodologies emerge as a result of the experience of these relationships (Wilson 2008, p. 77). In other words, all beings and their actions are 'related and interconnected, so knowing about the world involves actively seeking out newly emerging connections between experiences' (Norton-Smith 2010, p. 58). Thirdly, an essential principle of relational accountability is that I should be accountable, not merely to the reader, but also to the Indigenous communities, and to myself in my role as a researcher (Wilson 2008, p. 123). This personal accountability means that I will state my positionality with humility and honour, as well acknowledge the lessons that I have received in my journey. This humility means that I am no more important or knowledgeable, than anyone else, and that I will share the relationships and connections that make up this research in a *good way* (Wilson 2008, p. 134).

Finally, this research aims to continue giving back to the Indigenous communities in a way that is useful for them—not merely for the world of academia. In order to do so, this research aims to continue exploring the possibilities of the mobile application to assist Aboriginal members in creating support networks within post-secondary institutions. In other words, this research aims primarily to benefit the 'researched' community (Kovach 2009, p. 29).

Decolonizing Virtual Environments: Healing Through Indigenous Embodiment in Digital Spaces

According to Elder, Blu Waters, the body represents the physical dimension that should be in balance with the other three dimensions of human beings: mind, heart, and spirit.[5] Our connections to (our) Indigenous bodies shape the ways in which we tell our stories and our history. Indigenous bodies are also shaped and defined by the stories and the history. In this regard, Diana Taylor (2003) states that the Indigenous body is an essential element of the translation of memory, social knowledge, and identity (p. 16). Moreover, she asserts that Indigenous bodies are sites of convergence, where the individual is merged with the collective, the private blurs into the social, and memory and knowledge are joined (p. 80). This aspect helps us to understand the importance and relevance of 'community' for Indigenous bodies. The body cannot be isolated from other bodies. Taylor claims that problems started when Indigenous bodies were marginalized and turned into a site of shame through the discourse of European colonization, which was just based on texts and narratives that rejected and devalued notions of embodied practices (Taylor 2003, p. 16). In the same way, Indigenous scholar Qwo-Li Driskill (2008) writes about the historical process of Indigenous bodies and colonization:

> Colonization is a kinesthetic reality: it is an act done by bodies and felt by other bodies. Violence is not an intellectual knowledge, but rather one that is know because of damage done to our skin, flesh, muscles, bones and spirits. It is both our homelands and our bodies that are violated through colonization. If colonization is a kinesthetic wounding, then decolonization is a kinesthetic healing. (p. 155)

As Waters, Taylor, and Driskill claim, damage to Indigenous bodies through colonization has an effect upon identity, collective memory, and social knowledge. Therefore, any type of decolonization must include the healing of Indigenous bodies. As already noted, this type of healing is not simply the healthy condition of the biological organs, but the balance between the body, mind, heart, and spirit. This balance is extremely difficult to reach and maintain within the context of global neoliberalism. According to Statistics Canada (STATCAN) over 50% of Indigenous peoples are not in their community of origin (quoted in MayoralBaños 2016, p. 54). This percentage translates to the disconnection of the majority of Indigenous youth from their families, social circles, and communities. Alongside the violence of colonization, this aspect has been shown to result in Indigenous youth continuing to experience higher rates of marginalization, crisis, substance use, and suicide in comparison with their non-Indigenous counterparts (Snowshoe et al. 2016, p. 2).

How can Indigenous bodies be healed, if they are far from their communities and scattered all over Canada? If the embodiment of

Indigenous peoples within digital spaces is possible, then a new significant opportunity emerges for healing. Mainstream, non-Indigenous embodiment in virtual spaces has been discussed largely in academia, while only a small number of Indigenous authors have studied the relation between Indigenous corporality and virtual spaces. Before the era of mobile devices, most Indigenous scholars and activists argued that Indigenous embodiment in virtual spaces was not possible because Indigenous paradigms are based on the body, and the virtual embodiment of Indigenous bodies entails a loss of corporality. Craig Howe (1998) asserted that virtual spaces are not a place for Indigenous bodies because people anonymize their presence (which means, further, that their relationships are not acknowledged), and he claimed that virtual spaces do not include spatial, social, spiritual, and experiential dimensions (pp. 21–22, 27). Moreover, Diana Taylor (2003) states that the Indigenous bodies are at risk of disappearing in virtual spaces that elude embodiment, because cyberspace is based on a Western writing culture (p. 16). In this regard, Salazar (2002) asserts that virtual spaces are mainly written about and developed for use in English, and they are not adapted to the language needs of Indigenous communities (p. 75). Non-Indigenous scholar Garcia Canclini (2005) asserted that Indigenous bodies had been used frequently as a sign of opposition to the emerging digital technology and globalization. He claims that Indigenous cultures and bodies are seen as forms of historical preservation of the past, whereas digital technology is used as the iconic symbol of the future (xxviii). Garcia Canclini implies that Indigenous cultures are a form of historical folklore that oppose the consequences of technology and capitalism. In other words, Indigenous bodies are reduced to a form of static and ahistorical preservation.

Since the proliferation of mobile technologies and social media in 2010, there has been a significant shift in the debates surrounding Indigenous cultures, embodiment, and virtual spaces in ways that no longer focus on the threat of losing Indigenous corporality and presence, because digital technology is primarily serving as an extension of the body. In what might seem to be a disembodying process, 'technology' is not interacting with technology; rather, people are interacting with people. Laurel Evelyn Dyson (2016) claims that mobile technologies are improving communication among individuals and communities, as well as extending Indigenous educational and health systems through the embodiment of Indigenous peoples in virtual spaces (pp. 18–45). In this regard, social media is being used within remote First Nations' communities to facilitate communication between family members and friends because this type of technology enables oral communication across different locations (Molyneaux et al. 2014). Moreover, Kevin Kemper (2016) claims that mobile technology is creating shared spaces where people can easily access language and culture. These spaces are not just written mediums, but they are designed with several modes of expression and representation of bodies and spaces, such as pictures, sounds, and videos (pp. 299–310).

In 2016, the Indigenous social movement against the Dakota Access Pipeline at Standing Rock Sioux Reservation showed how thousands of peoples around the world virtually embodied themselves at the Reservation, through checking-in at that location on Facebook, in order to confuse government prosecutors (Miller 2016).[6] This embodiment of the people is an expression of *giving back*, because the users of these social media channels protested against the negative effects of the pipeline on the environment, as well as the exploitation of natural resources in North Dakota. Although this type of activism was not enough to stop the pipeline project, it tried to provide actions in favour of the environment. The people who posted did so on devices that relied on natural resources for their production; however, in the spirit of 'giving back', these devices were, in turn, used to draw attention to the political and environmental implications of Standing Rock.

There is evidence that suggests that, nowadays, digital spaces can begin to ethically embody Indigenous peoples in cyberspace, because mobile technologies and social media are enabling the inclusion of important principles of Indigenous Knowledges. This includes the capability to be virtually present with other members (presence), the opportunity to look after others (caring), the possibility of providing for others (sharing), and the character of these spaces being spoken or verbally communicated (orality).

Presence: Indigenous Bodies Within the Indigenous Friends App

If Indigenous peoples can embody themselves in digital spaces, then a possibility emerges for virtual environments to be healing spaces. The embodiment of Indigenous youth implies the possibility of interacting with other people who are part of their community, without the necessity of being located in the same geographic space. In this way, virtual and mobiles devices become an extension of Indigenous bodies, representing physical, emotional, intellectual, and spiritual dimensions. The possibility of the extension and convergence of all these elements within virtual spaces might enable healing processes. The *Indigenous Friends App* relies on the possibilities opened up by this virtual Tipi, created to support healing processes of Indigenous bodies, and therefore to be a potential decolonizing tool. Enabling embodiment and presence are the most difficult challenges I faced, when creating the *Indigenous Friends App*. The inclusion of virtual Indigenous bodies in a safe cyberspace is a recent topic that is opening up new areas of exploration and creation. In this regard, I relied completely on the voices of the community to guide our project. The initial requirement of the community was to create a registration form (signing up) that captured some initial parameters, or fields, for identification purposes, such as specific community, gender, and year of birth (Fig. 3.1a). For each identifier, there is also an option for those who wish to self-identify outside the traditional parameters. These parameters have the purpose of organizing some of the internal spaces depending on gender, group, and age specifications. All of them aim to follow the principle of self-determination (i.e. a personal decision grounded in embodiment).[7]

In the case of group identification, the initial options for potential *partners*[8] are: 636 First Nations, 5 provincial Métis Federations, 51 Inuit communities divided into 4 Arctic regions, Non-Indigenous identification for adopted allies, Indigenous groups outside Canada, and also, the Unknown option. In the gender field, there are 8 different choices. All the previous information, along with name, educational institution, username, and password, can be changed on the *Profile Screen*, when the partners log into the app. When the first signing-up screen was tested, several community members were concerned about the safety of their identities within the space of this virtual Tipi (i.e. a first sign that they were beginning to embody themselves in the space). They did not want a completely open space where any person can register and enter inside this virtual Tipi because they were concerned with the potential of being bullied, threatened, or harassed by non-Indigenous peers.

In the Anishinaabe tradition, the conical shape of a physical tipi is compared to the skirts of women and how they can provide shelter for young children when they feel scared or threatened. For that reason, Tipis have protocols, and certain people may not be granted entrance to specific types of Tipis.[9] Therefore, in order to guarantee the safety of

Fig. 3.1 The *Membership Screen* (**a**) and the *Signing up Screen* (**b**) (*Source* Indigenous Friends App 2016)

the space, throughout a long process of negotiation and deliberation,[10] we made the decision, together with the community, to create a *Membership Screen*, to restrict the access to the signing up process of the app. In other words, we created a restrictive mechanism that allows only Indigenous peoples and non-Indigenous allies entrance to this space (Fig. 3.1b). This membership tag is completely free of charge for all peoples, and is expected to be shared by the native centres of post-secondary educational institutions through their emailing list and social media platforms. In the case of non-members of educational institutions, a contact email address is provided.[11]

Despite this first layer of safety, community members stated that some Indigenous individuals might also be potentially harmful (i.e. sexist) towards other members. Therefore, we designed another layer of safety that was based on the virtual bodies of the partners. Each of the partners, through their virtual bodies, belongs to a 'cyber' animal clan (in the case of First Nations and Métis peoples) or colour group (in the case of Inuit peoples). Each of these seven clans or colour groups has a responsibility inside this virtual community.[12] The seven clans or groups are: Eagle-Yellow, Owl-Red, Wolf-Black, Bear-Blue, Marten-White, Turtle-Green, and Beaver-Orange.[13] The Wolf-Black and Bear-Blue clans/groups are the members who take care of this virtual space, watching that all the public spaces are free of harassment and discrimination. Any member, who feels threatened in any private or public environment, can send a report to these clans.

Finally, when the safety of the people is addressed and they begin the process of embodiment, the possibility for healing begins. The potential healing process is guided by wise, prepared, and responsible people who have the knowledge and experience to heal the body, but also the mind, heart, and spirit (i.e. guiding people towards the balance of the Healing Circle). The Eagle-Yellow and the Owl-Red clans/groups are Elders and Traditional Knowledge Keepers who take care of the Indigenous bodies inside the virtual Tipi.

Caring: Anishinaabe Healing Circle and the *Indigenous Friends App*

One of the most important teachings that this virtual Tipi inherited from traditional Knowledge was the Medicine Wheel or Healing Circle. Paula Gunn Allen defines the Medicine Wheel as 'a tangible object seen as possessing non-rational powers to unite or bind diverse elements into a community, a psychic and spiritual whole' (in Graveline 1998, p. 14). This circle is divided into four sections which have different meanings depending on the Nation or Indigenous group.[14] However, all of the interpretations of this Sacred Circle have the common goal of 'mutual balance and harmony among animals, people, elements of nature, and the Spirit World' (Archibald 2008, p. 11).

The *Indigenous Friends App* inherited the Anishinaabe Knowledge of the Medicine Wheel because York University is geographically located on the traditional territory of the Anishinaabe peoples (i.e. the Mississaugas of New Credit First Nation and Huron-Wendat Nation). The incorporation and recognition of this teaching and its origin are important in order to develop the app in a *good way*. Indeed, Snowshoe et al. (2016) have recently shown that Indigenous Knowledge and cultural elements have a significant positive impact on the health of Aboriginal youth. Elder, Blu Waters, asserts that the Anishinaabe Medicine Wheel[15] represents the four dimensions of human beings: North-Mind-White (Intellectual), West-Body-Black (Physical), South-Heart-Red (Emotional), and East-Spirit-Yellow (Spiritual).[16]

The Anishinaabe Medicine Wheel is acknowledged in a physical Tipi through four coloured cloths that are tied at the extreme top of four poles, which face the four cardinal points on the top part of the Tipi. In the case of the virtual Tipi, the Medicine Wheel is recognized through the graphical logo of the app, which is also displayed through the colours of the menus and interfaces. Indeed, the significance of the Anishinaabe Medicine Wheel became the central consideration in creating a safe space within the *Indigenous Friends App*. It enables the caring for Indigenous youth and their bodies in a traditional manner, within a digital environment, through intergenerational communication. The logo is the first element that partners see when they access the app (Fig. 3.2a).

In the Anishinaabe Medicine Wheel, human beings are depicted in a spiritual phase at the beginning of their lives, because children are connected with the Creator, since they do not have complete autonomy over their actions (spiritual dimension). As people then begin to grow, they are aware of their emotions and belong to the youth stage (emotional dimension). Next, when a person reaches twenty-one years old, they are said to belong to the adult stage, because the physical body reaches its full capacity (physical dimension). Later, when people are older and wiser, they become more intellectual and belong to the Elder stage (intellectual dimension). Finally, at the end of their days, there is a return to the spiritual phase, when, typically, humans become like 'babies' again, because they require help and support from their families, in order to survive. This is the cycle of life, and the connection among these stages can usually be seen when people gather inside a Tipi.[17]

Following the previous principles within the *Indigenous Friends App*, the community and I decided to create the *'I need help' Screen*, recently renamed as *Peer Support* (Fig. 3.2b).

This healing space is where partners have seven different buttons that they can use to communicate with different resources, such as their mentor and guide, as well as a Native centre and a Native crisis line. These communications follow through the embedded technologies of the mobile device (e.g. phone calls and SMS text messages). When a partner taps one of these buttons, the dial screen of the phone will pop up with

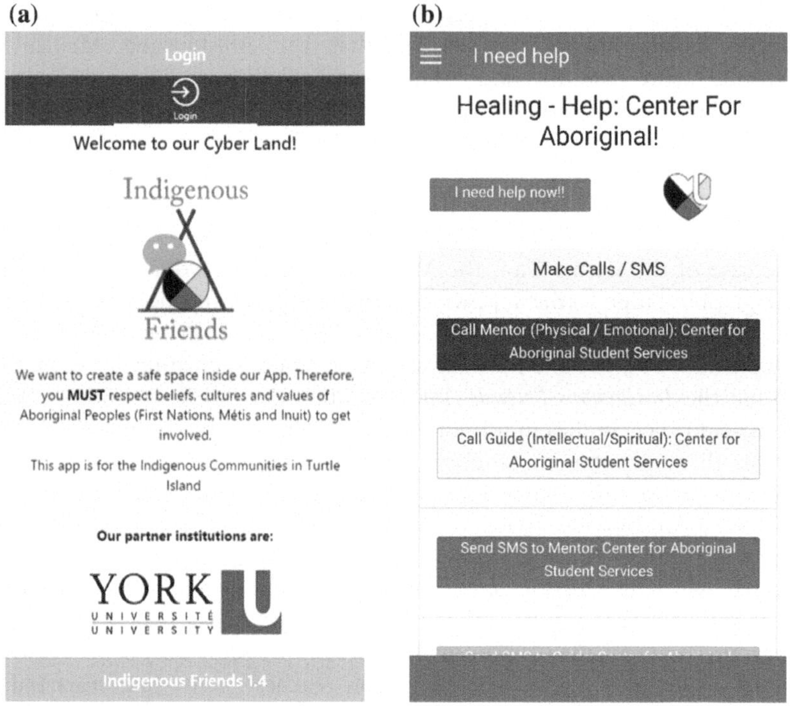

Fig. 3.2 The *Login Screen* (**a**) and *Healing Screen* (**b**) (*Source* Indigenous Friends App 2016)

the cell phone number of the resource that was tapped. In the case of SMS, a message is automatically written with an example of content and the phone number of the sender.

The mentors are Elders who belong to the Eagles-Yellow clan/group and are in charge of the West-Body-Black-Physical and South-Heart-Red-Emotional dimensions. The guides are Traditional Knowledge Keepers, who belong to the Owl-Red clan/group and are in charge of the North-Mind-White-Intellectual and East-Spirit-Yellow-Spiritual dimensions. In other words, the Elders should primarily take care of the body and heart, while the Traditional Knowledge Keepers should care for the mind and spirit. In the *Profile Screen*, the partners can select their mentors and guides (they must belong to the Eagle-Yellow and Owl-Red clan/group).

These mentors and guides have the responsibility of caring for Indigenous peers within this space. The healing process, which is possible through Indigenous embodiment in this virtual space, is based on the mutual balance of the human dimensions of the Healing Circle. This balance is promoted through a traditional, intergenerational communication. In this way, the process of healing follows traditional knowledge and protocols. The *Indigenous Friends App* is merely the space where this healing process might begin. As already argued, this is a space that promotes the healing of the body; it is a form of decolonization.

Through the feedback of various community members, the community and I are designing training for Elders and Knowledge Keepers, who want to learn more about the capacities (and limitations) of this type of technology, so that they can better support other members or partners. Along with this educational preparation, we are designing a new feature of caring based on Push Notifications.[18] This form of caring consists of interacting with the partners, to inquire about their emotional status, and offer any needed support. In other words, when someone is not feeling well, then an Eagle-Yellow or Owl-Red can contact the member or partner to start, or continue, a healing process. Also, this push notification system will enable Elders and Knowledge Keepers to send information, or teachings, to the partners at certain moments, or through regularly scheduled contact (expected release date: June 2017).

When the Métis historian, David McNab, learned about the caring character of this project, he acknowledged that the *Indigenous Friends App* has a spirit.[19] In other words, the app has a purpose and should be embraced by the entire community. Moreover, he asserted the potential character of the app as an *Electronic Buffalo*,[20] that has the purpose to connect different generations of Indigenous peoples who are located in different geographical spaces, and therefore, this virtual space can be the medium through which healing, sharing, and reconciliation can begin.

Sharing: Providing Others Within the *Indigenous Friends App*

According to the Elder, Blu Waters,[21] the *Indigenous Friends App* is a space to share and support Indigenous identity, cultural connection, and intergenerational communication. When people gather inside a Tipi, regardless of its form (virtual or physical), they share experiences, knowledge, and food. It is a common space for these types of sharing.

The sharing between members and partners is promoted through several features in order to foster healing processes in this virtual space.

First, on the *Directory Screen*, partners can search for peers from the same community of belonging, gender, year of birth, or educational institution (Fig. 3.3a). The objective of this feature is to promote the sharing of information between members, so that they may find people with whom they feel comfortable, and who can support them and build relationships. They may not necessarily find people from the same location, but they can discover peers from contiguous communities or reserves.

Also, community members can share and express ideas through public spaces, such as the forums, or private spaces, such as group or individual conversations. The sharing of traditional knowledge and meaningful information between members is promoted in these spaces. These virtual places are regulated by the Wolf-Black clan/group.

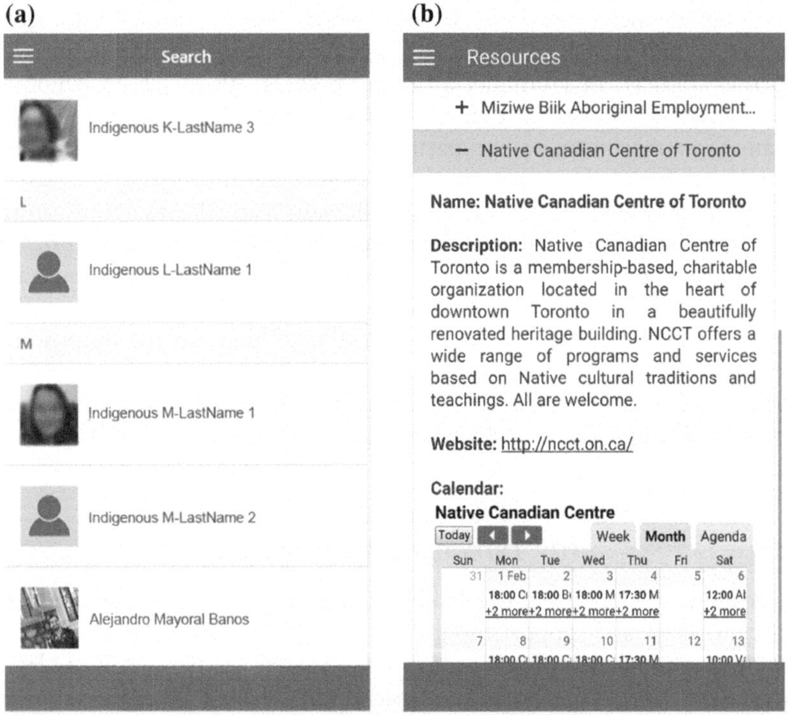

Fig. 3.3 The *Directory Screen* (**a**) and *Resources Screen* (**b**) (*Source* Indigenous Friends App 2016)

Third, partners can share information about the community through the features: *Frequently Asked Questions*, *Events*, and *Community Resources*. In *Frequently Asked Questions*, Wolf-Black and Bear-Blue clans/groups can share common inquiries that Indigenous members have about the area where they are living, or the educational institution where partners are studying. In *Events*, Wolf-Black and Bear-Blue clans/groups can invite other partners to physical events that are performed within the surrounding community. These events can also be initiatives of political action or resistance. Finally, under *Community Resources*, a list of Indigenous organizations, collectives and institutions, which are located in the geographical area around the educational institution, is provided (Fig. 3.3b).

As already noted, one of the main objectives of these spaces is to create Indigenous social networks that can support the needs of Aboriginal students in post-secondary educational institutions.

Orality: The Role of Media Within *Indigenous Friends App*

As Molyneaux, O'Donnell, Kakeskaspan, Walmark, Budka, Gibson, and Kemper have mentioned, the new mobile technologies and social media offer Indigenous peoples a forum to embrace and preserve the traditional culture, based on nature, through images, sounds and videos (Molyneaux et al. 2014; Kemper 2016). Even though the *Indigenous Friends App* does not currently have the capability to store all of these types of media, this virtual Tipi provides an initial receptacle storage for all the links and addresses of this media within the *Community Resources* section and in public forums.

Relying on the humility principle of Indigenous paradigms, *Indigenous Friends App* is just the starting point to store and preserve the references to all these types of media. We recognize that Indigenous and non-Indigenous organizations, communities, governments, educational institutions, and even individuals are investing a significant number of resources to create and design better ways to store this type of information. Therefore, this virtual Tipi follows the principle articulated by Beaton et al. (2016) in the First Mile approach, which is based on the research OCAP principles—Ownership, Control, Access, and Possession—developed by Schnarch. These principles recognize the right of Indigenous peoples to own, control, access, and possess their data.

Therefore, the community members who have signed up for the app have the full rights to their information. In other words, their information is not going to be provided to any third party under any circumstances (e.g. advertising agencies, governments).

Conclusion

Digital spaces can support the healing of, and connections between, Indigenous peoples because the design and implementation of mobile technologies and social media can be based on the fundamental principles of Indigenous paradigms. As I have argued throughout this analysis, the *Indigenous Friends App* enables processes of healing in the digital space of a virtual Tipi. This environment adopts cultural and spiritual aspects of Anishinaabe Knowledge, to create a supportive, respectful, and safe dynamic as much as possible, which relies on the principles of presence, caring, sharing, and orality. However, it is important to emphasize that, with the previous analysis, I am not implying or arguing that this mobile application is the only solution or form of healing for Indigenous youth, but that this mobile app is an instrument to support these processes.

Nonetheless, there are still some internal inconsistencies in the designing of the mobile application which must be addressed. The development journey of this potentially decolonizing tool is a work in progress that implies the deconstruction and reuse of several types of neoliberal technologies and colonial structures. In other words, it is not possible to conceptualize and construct the elements of the app outside of these boundaries. However, complex and ethically nuanced considerations could potentially guide the design and implementation processes according to principles of reconciliation and decolonization.

New and diverse virtual spaces, which social media and mobile technologies are opening up for Indigenous peoples, provide new areas of exploration and creation. These areas include the possibility to listen to more Indigenous voices, which might previously have been difficult to hear due to location and accessibility factors. The reconciliation between technology and Indigenous bodies provides alternatives to recover and embrace traditional Knowledge in the context of a neoliberal global economy. Community-based mobile technologies are already enabling Indigenous peoples to give back to other people and Mother Earth through community building, active participation, and healing, and the new *Indigenous Friends App* would allow this process to continue.

Notes

1. The terms Native, Aboriginal or Indigenous refer to peoples who identify their ancestry with the original inhabitants of Canada and other countries worldwide, who are unique in their cultures, but who share common experiences of colonialism and understandings of the world. The epistemological, political, and historical differences and intrinsic implications embedded in the terms Native, Indigenous, and Aboriginal are beyond the scope of this research. However, these terms are used interchangeably throughout this research. In the Canadian context, this term refers to First Nations, Métis, and Inuit peoples.
2. The area known as Tkaronto has been taken care by the Anishinabek Nation, the Haudenosaunee Confederacy, the Wendat, and the Métis. It is now home to many Indigenous Peoples. The current treaty holders are the Mississaugas of the New Credit First Nation. This territory is subject of the Dish with One Spoon Wampum Belt Covenant, an agreement to peaceably share and care for the Great Lakes region.
3. Cyberspace is sometimes also called digital or virtual spaces. Cyberspace is 'an infinite artificial world where humans navigate in information-based space' (as stated by Gibson in Benedickt 1991).
4. The plural form of the word knowledge and paradigm are used to recognize the diversity of traditions or ways of knowing among different Indigenous groups and communities.
5. Elder Laureen Waters Gaudios, personal communication, 26 October 2014.
6. Checking-in at a specific location in Facebook is the capability to create a post.
7. There is an ongoing tension between the uses of parameters alongside with self-determination because they forced the categorization of the individual.
8. The concept 'partners' alludes to the notion of software 'users', however, as part of the decolonization process, the concept usage around people was avoided.
9. Elder Laureen Waters Gaudios, personal communication, 28 October 2014.
10. There was a negotiation period with Apple Inc. to publish the *Indigenous Friends App* in their apps market (Apple Store), which ended after 47 days, due to their restricted and closed guidelines.
11. In the case of York University, the membership tags are managed by the Center for Aboriginal Student Services.
12. In the real world, most Indigenous peoples belong to a clan or group, which are instrumental in traditional occupations, intertribal relations, and marriages.

13. To see the full description of the responsibilities and duties of the seven clans or groups, consult MayoralBaños (2016, pp. 128–130).
14. The full description and significance of the Healing Circle for Indigenous peoples are beyond the scope of this research; however, certain aspects related to the mobile application will be explored later on the analysis.
15. It is important to emphasize that there are several interpretations of the Anishinaabe Medicine Wheel that imply a change of the order of the colours. However, all of them follow the same principles of balance and cyclical meanings.
16. Elder Laureen Waters Gaudios, personal communication, 26 October 2014.
17. Elder Laureen Waters Gaudios, personal communications, 26 October 2014, 26 November 2014.
18. Push Notification is 'the delivery of information from a software application to a computing device without a specific request from the client. Push notifications let applications notify users of new messages, updates or events, even when the users are not actively using such applications' (quoted in MayoralBaños 2016, p. 98).
19. David McNab, sharing circle, 30 June 2016.
20. The Sacred Buffalo has always held great meaning for First Nations and Métis people. For Métis people, the Buffalo represents their spirit and remind them of how their lives were once lived in harmony with nature (Laureen Waters Gaudio, pers. comm.).
21. Elder Laureen Waters Gaudios, personal communication, 5 October 2016.

References

Archibald, Jo-ann "Q'um Q'um Xiiem." 2008. *Indigenous storywork: Educating the heart, mind, body, and spirit*, First Printing ed. Vancouver: UBC Press.

Beaton, Brian, Terence Burnard, Adi Linden, and Susan O'Donnell. 2016. Keewaytinook mobile: An indigenous community-owned mobile phone service in Northern Canada. In *Indigenous people and mobile technologies*, ed. Laurel Evelyn Dyson, Stephen Grant, and Max Hendriks, 149–171. New York and London: Routledge.

Benedickt, Michael. 1991. *Cyberspace: First steps*. Cambridge: The MIT Press.

Canclini, Nestor Garcia. 2005. *Hybrid cultures: Strategies for entering and leaving modernity*, trans. Christopher L. Chiappari and Silvia L. Lopez. Foreword by Renato Rosaldo. Expanded edition. Minneapolis: University of Minnesota Press.

Driskill, Qwo-Li. 2008. Theatre as suture: Grassroots performance, decolonization and healing. In *Aboriginal oral traditions. Theory, practice, ethics*, ed. Renée Hulan and Renate Eigenbrod, 155–168. Black Point, NS: Fernwood Publishing.

Dyson, Laurel Evelyn. 2016. Framing the indigenous mobile revolution. In *Indigenous people and mobile technologies*, ed. Laurel Evelyn Dyson, Stephen Grant, and Max Hendriks, 149–171. New York and London: Routledge.

Graveline, Fyre Jean. 1998. *Circle works: Transforming Eurocentric consciousness.* Halifax, NS: Fernwood Publishing.

Howe, Craig. 1998. Cyberspace is no place for tribalism. *Wicazo Sa Review* 13 (2): 19–28. https://doi.org/10.2307/1409143.

Indigenous Friends App. 2016. What is Indigenous friends? *Indigenous Friends mobile application.* http://www.indigenousfriends.org. Accessed 1 Dec 2016.

Kemper, Kevin. 2016. Cultural hybridity, resilience and the communication of contemporary Cherokee culture through mobile technologies. In *Indigenous people and mobile technologies*, ed. Laurel Evelyn Dyson, Stephen Grant, and Max Hendriks, 299–317. New York and London: Routledge.

Kovach, Margaret. 2009. *Indigenous methodologies: Characteristics, conversations, and contexts*, 1st ed. Toronto, Buffalo and London: University of Toronto Press, Scholarly Publishing Division.

MayoralBaños, Alejandro. 2016. *Decolonizing technology through a Tipi: Creation of an Indigenous mobile application.* MA thesis, New York University, June. http://yorkspace.library.yorku.ca/xmlui/handle/10315/32700. Accessed 28 Nov 2016.

Miller, Ryan W. 2016. How the Dakota access pipeline battle unfolded. *USA Today.* http://www.usatoday.com/story/news/nation/2016/12/02/timeline-dakota-access-pipeline-and-protests/94800796/. Accessed 4 Dec 2016.

Molyneaux, Heather, Susan O'Donnell, Crystal Kakekaspan, Brian Walmark, Philipp Budka, and Kerri Gibson. 2014. Social media in remote First Nation communities. *Canadian Journal of Communication* 39 (2). http://www.cjconline.ca/index.php/journal/article/view/2619.

Norton-Smith, Thomas M. 2010. *The dance of person and place: One interpretation of American Indian philosophy.* New York: State University of New York Press.

Salazar, Juan Francisco. 2002. Activismo Indígena En América Latina: Estrategias Para Una Construcción Cultural de Las Tecnologías de Información y comunicación. *Journal of Iberian and Latin American Research* 8 (2): 61–80. https://doi.org/10.1080/13260219.2002.10431783.

Snowshoe, Angela, Claire V. Crooks, Paul F. Tremblay, and Riley E. Hinson. 2016. Cultural connectedness and its relation to mental wellness for First Nations youth. *The Journal of Primary Prevention*, November 1–20. https://doi.org/10.1007/s10935-016-0454-3.

Taylor, Diana. 2003. *The archive and the repertoire: Performing cultural memory in the Americas.* Durham: Duke University Press.

Wilson, Shawn. 2008. *Research is ceremony: Indigenous research methods.* Black Point, NS: Fernwood Publishing.

CHAPTER 4

Becoming More Than a Self: Affective Relations and Queer Selfie Lines of Flight

Susan Driver

On the surface, selfies appear to valorize the appearance of individuals as they turn mobile cameras onto themselves, being reduced to images, constructing static self-representations of how they want to look. In this way, selfies have been understood to mark sharp boundaries between self and other, reducing subjects to perfectly framed and filtered faces, promoting pictures and pleasures of autonomous subjects. Henry Giroux writes that

> Selfie culture pushes against the constructive cultivation of fantasy, imagination and memory, allowing such capacities to deteriorate in a constant pursuit of commodified pleasure and the need to heighten the visibility and performance of the self. The culture of atomisation and loneliness in neoliberal societies is intensified by offering the self as the only source of enjoyment, exchange and wonder. (Giroux 2015, p. 159)

S. Driver (✉)
Department of Communication Studies, York University,
Toronto, ON, Canada
e-mail: sdriver@yorku.ca

S. Driver and N. Coulter (eds.), *Youth Mediations and Affective Relations*,
https://doi.org/10.1007/978-3-319-98971-6_4

Such accounts emphasize how the isolation of the self epitomized by selfies becomes the apex of neoliberal societies. The tendency to center on surface images of selves as symptomatic of broader social problems has exacerbated the already atomistic and visually centered ideologies of youth and digital culture. Debates have pivoted on either the anti-social tendencies of selfies as diminishing our capacities to connect in deep and meaningful ways or else on the invigorating social possibilities for representing and networking marginalized subjects (Goldberg 2017, p. 1). On both sides, what remains foundational is the status of the individual subject. Abstracted through mediated repetition and generic templates, selfies seem the last place to consider the relationally entangled worlds of young people. And yet, some of the most inspiring scholarship focusing on young peoples' selfie cultures has mobilized new ways of conceptualizing visual images within social media that complicate how we think about youth embodiments and mediated relations through Deleuzian theories of affect and becoming (Gill-Peterson 2013; Renold and Ringrose 2016; Warfield 2017). Against the reification of selfies as static images, new materialist research unfolds the specificities of everyday life in-between surface and depth, proximity and distance, intimacies and publics, touch and vision, feeling and thinking, restraint and freedom, exploring contingent, ephemeral and indeterminate worlds that defy individualizing depictions of the subject.[1] Going beyond the content of an image as reflective of a unified subject, research turns outwards in distributive fashion to follow embodied sensibilities, signifying connections, networked publics and politicized hashtags. Unique within this work are explorations of the entanglements of technologies, bodies, subjectivities and social relations. Along these lines, some of the most critical insights have emerged that refuse the gendered and racialized normalizations of selfie stereotypes, interrogating the ways girls become rigidly aligned with selfies in simplified duck face poses and moral panics around sexting. Refusing such characterizations, projects work to map affective forces, desires and communicative possibilities that displace binary logics while also recognizing the continuations of power that limit selfie practices and meanings.

In this paper, I want to draw out some possibilities within materialist-affective ways of thinking about selfies in terms of complex and relational embodiments, drawing upon Deleuze and Guattari's conceptualizations of affect and becoming that exceed individualistic frameworks of self and selfies. In their words, "becoming is a verb with a consistency all on its own; it does not reduce to, or lead back to, 'appearing,' 'being,' 'equaling' or 'producing'" (Deleuze and Guattari 1987, p. 263). Starting with an analysis of the power of individualizing discourses framing what, how and why youth are culturally visible and valuable becomes an important basis for affirming theoretical and empirical interest in affectively intensified becomings. The containment of youth within humanist individualist formulations has profoundly circumscribed ways of thinking about selfies. As a ubiquitous locus of visual identity construction within networked spaces, selfies mark an expansive mode of self-representation that is often evaluated through rational and homogeneous norms of individualized consciousness. Yet, this is a very partial and reductive mode of understanding what self and selfies can do and become. It is remarkable what happens when our perspectives shift toward affective and socially articulated expressions by, for and about youth that are not reducible to normative individualized foundations privileging visual hierarchies of race, class and gender. Shifting an onto-epistemological orientation toward material, situated, sensuous and symbolic relational enactments, it becomes possible to map selfies within the social and media ecologies of daily life—at school or at home, in malls or parks, in work or play, immersed in nature or on the streets. Selfies are mobile, they move across spaces, they shift locations and perspectives, they refuse the stasis that often circumscribes how youth are categorized and represented, and yet, they continue to be understood as prefixed and inert. And this is precisely what I want to think about here: how do our limited ways of seeing and thinking about selfies remain bound to humanistic epistemologies and ontologies that obscure other more historically embedded, socially entangled, affective desiring modes of understanding youth? Might we look beyond the discreet contours of individual subjects and texts, and the institutional regulations rigidly encoding them, in order to grapple with the relations that compose, engage and transform them? To take selfies seriously in this regard is to address the diverse social and corporeal becomings of youth, it is to see the changing flows and formations of selves and selfies, without predetermining them in advance.

Decentering Individualism: Rethinking the Self of Selfies

> "The ultimate cultural manifestation of the internet is the "selfie." The "selfie: as the quintessential, almost inevitable conclusion, where all we are left with is ourselves. We are not able to see anything in the world

> except ourselves. What the internet has done is placed us at the center of the universe". (Keen as quoted in Maddux 2015)

While the focus of this chapter is oriented toward reading for complex material-discursive- affective relations, it is important to acknowledge that the dominant frameworks for approaching selfies reduces what we come to perceive and think about their possibilities. Andrew Keen's words are indicative of journalistic, academic and popular accounts describing selfies as detrimental to psychic and social life. Making simplified clear cut claims about youth and selfies has become a common practice and this reinforces what Julian Gill-Peterson refers to as the arrogant reproduction of "adultomorphism" (2013) that defines youth experiences through universalizing concepts valorizing adult rationality. We can trace this across news articles, parenting guides, academic reports, film and TV portrayals as well as everyday gossip that generates pat assumptions about youth and selfies such that understanding stops at the level of surface appearances. Often dismissed as trivial pursuits suggestive of immaturity (Saltz 2014) or slammed as inappropriate, risky and dangerous (Bratskeir 2016), youth and selfies are caught up within contradictory judgments that equate youth with narcissism or a susceptibility to peer pressure and crowd mentalities. Alternatively, selfies are valorized as giving youth control over self-representations, as markers of empowerment and sovereignty within new media terrains. While this suggests a plurality of perspectives, they converge in ways that naturalize and fixate upon what Nancy Lesko calls "confident characterizations" (1996, p. 147) about adolescents, hinged to hegemonic discourses and social relations. Lesko reveals how gendered, racialized and heteronormalized ideals become deeply inscribed within taken-for-granted thinking about what youth are, do and become.

With the proliferation of contradictory yet "confident" common-sense ideas about youth taking, sharing and enjoying selfies, the very notion of a unified self linked with the selfie as transparent mediation of that self is often left unquestioned. In this way, selfies provide a productive entry point for grappling with assumptions about youth as subjects, and specifically the reproduction of individualistic ideologies that restrict our ways of perceiving and thinking about what selfies do and mean within their everyday worlds. On one level, selfies appear as the perfect visual symbol of the individualizing logics of neo-liberal capitalist culture. They represent difference as sameness, multiplicity as uniformity, choice as control, democratization as self-commodification. The abstract individualism surrounding selfies works to universalize the desires and identities of youth, erasing exclusions bound to racial, gender, class and sexual differences along with a disregard for specific ways marginalized youth engage in networked self-mediations. The homogenization of selfies within the popular imagination has reified particular kinds of images and ways of seeing youth that detracts from the experiential differences comprising their enactments, materializations and circulations. Kate Miltner and Nancy Baym argue that selfies are "more frequently described as juvenile, frivolous, and narcissistic, reflecting a greater interest in the self than the world" (2015, p. 1706). They go on to situate selfies within a history of "previous moral panics around technology in which youth have been depicted as both dangerous and at risk" (p. 1706). Cast in negative psychologizing terms, selfies become evidence of self-absorption and narcissism, to the point where youth are regarded as oblivious to the world around them, evidence of their solipsistic desires that disconnect them and inhibit ethical ties of belonging.

Within popularized psychological discourses, young people's selfies are understood within a logic of lack, diminishment and isolation that underpin binary ways of thinking about me and you, self vs. other, us and them.

> It's about, 'How should I edit myself, cut myself up... so you'll consume me in a way that's pleasurable to you?' Rather than me liking who I am. (Dr. Linda Papadopoulos quoted in Foster 2017)

> Selfies, when used to excess, show a lack of depth and a shallow personality. If someone is obsessed with taking selfies it is most likely because the individual is self-absorbed and narcissistic. (Dr. Bart Rossi quoted in Schirripa 2015)

These quotes are examples of how psychologists emphasize separation and psychic impoverishment. This can be seen in how selfies are defined as instrumental technologies that edit and cut in the service of egotistical aspirations to visually project idealizations of beauty and personality. They emphasize not only the autonomous white heterosexual girl's face at the center of the image, but also linear accounts of developmental identities and the motivations and longings that come to define them. Within the terms of expert knowledge, selfies restrict an always already enclosed self, offering circular accounts as to who youth are and what they should become. Assumed to be physically and linguistically coherent, caught within a unified photographic frame, the self is secured as a locus of possessive individualism. And while the selves and identities of young people are pervasively cast as lacking or in need of further development, the goal of bounded mature selfhood is implied and valorized. As Fleur Gabriel argues, developmental discourse entrenches "certain natural stages of physical, emotional and cognitive development" (Gabriel 2014, p. 107) regulating pathways into adult selfhood that guide scientific and moral judgments about the proper and improper effects of social media on youth. And while youth are positioned as ambiguous, incomplete or in-between, as they learn to become a self, the horizon of their completion and success as adults is the attainment a recognizable autonomous selfhood. Interest in youth selfies, and the ways they are problematized, has revealed deeply entrenched ideologies of individualism, and the developmental models they rest on.

Individualistic and developmental frames emerge forcefully through the use of psychological discourses shaping popular notions about youth and selfies. Emphasizing how selfies interfere with proper development and socialization, experts call attention to pathological forms of narcissism and self-esteem disorders associated with selfies. Quoted extensively in the press and blogs, psychological accounts center on unhealthy patterns of self- absorption and one-sided preoccupations of how the self looks and is seen by others. This characterization of youth who invest too much in appearances and popularity suggests a loss control and are often linked to a string of problems including addiction and depression. What is significant is that the problem of selfies becomes reduced to mental disorders attached to individual youth. Another vein of commentary highlights the risks of peer immersion within social media, suggesting a pathological loss of self when measured against a normative standards of individuation. Quoted in the popular press, Dr. Jessamy Hibberd warns against the ways selfies make youth vulnerable to abuse, dependent on others and at risk of low self-confidence, offering prescriptive advice "Young people should not have to seek approval from their peers but celebrate who they are inside which is far more important" (quoted in Woollaston 2013). Well-being hinges upon an independent bounded self that displays just the right amount of self-regulation and containment. Problems emerge when youth exceed these boundaries, becoming too self centered and/or too social.

As Nancy Lesko argues, adolescents have been negatively targeted as engaging excessively with peer groups throughout modernity across the psychological and social sciences, as well as, more wide-spread moral panics (1996). Threatening civilized subjecthood, the unruly social desires and engagements of young people propel intensive forms of categorization and management. It is interesting to trace the intensification of these ideas and policies in relation to discourses about youth and social media where youth appear as "over-sexed and over-exposed, subject to excessive pressure from peers and the wider consumer culture" (Gabriel 2014, p. 106). Targeting selfies as a source of youth unhappiness, illness, sexual promiscuity and danger such perspectives draw upon a range of prescriptive assumptions that police how youth should look and act. Connecting psychologized and moral panic discourses is a threat of boundary transgression against norms of individual rational control in which the boundaries of self and other, bodies and intimacies, publics and privates are normatively regulated. Yet, attention returns repeatedly to what normalizes the subject in predictable forms, instituting protectionist or prohibitory methods of control.

As decades of feminist and postcolonial critiques have shown so powerfully, universalizing norms that underpin conceptions of individual rationality and agency reproduce exclusionary powers. When it comes to youth, the very status of a recognizable individual self is deeply burdened with class, gendered, racialized and sexualized norms that constitute talk about selfies. Proliferating images of white heterosexual middle-class teens to exemplify and glamourize selfie genres have once again privileged those faces whose visibility signifies a whole range of characteristics, investments and protectionist responses denied to marginalized youth. Commercialized media representations of selfies almost exclusively depict conventional feminine white girls as highly desirable and active users. This is the crux of selfie commodification that gets reiterated within commentary centered on the pressures selfies put on girls toward enacting conventional beauty and body ideals. Such accounts reproduce narrow gendered and heteronormative frames of recognition. Discussion of sexy and beautiful feminine bodies becomes narrowly circumscribed in terms of a limited range of physical characteristics and assumptions about how girls uniformly desire to portray their bodies in sexual, fashionable and likable ways. But it is not only the ways girls look that matters, as Heather Warren-Crow demonstrates, the digital itself has become configured as girlish in its plasticity and malleability (2014). Within this broader picture, "girls" are cast as quintessential selfie selves valorizing their fluidity and adaptability, and belittling them as superficial and silly. This drives attempts to educate and protect the "innocence" of girls from dangers posed by inappropriate sexting. Young feminine bodies and personalities are cast in simplified and homogeneous terms, as either highly vulnerable or agents of innovation and hyper-participation, making it difficult to grapple with the ambiguities and nuances of bodies, selves and images. This way of seeing and talking about youth and selfies not only inscribes individualizing ideals but also centers upon a determinate range of normative subjects and texts as representative and worthy of concern and intervention.

Julian Gill-Peterson analyzes the limits of discourses that render girls as vulnerable and passive victims of selfie technologies and, also, how feminist reparative work on sexting that recasts girls as knowing digital agents often remains tied to liberal notions of sovereignty that reinforces exclusionary powers. Gill-Peterson examines how reverse discourses that promote girls as creative producers of media often fail to address the ways technological sovereignty presumes norms of whiteness and continues to embed notions of girlhood within capitalistic notions of youthful feminine plasticity at the heart of neo-liberal individualism (2015). He argues for "a different scenography of gender and the digital" one that no longer "relies on a mode of agency that relies on whiteness to overcome passivity" (2013, p. 146). Such ideas compel us to think radically about the conceptual tools we use and the need to question the gender and racial assumptions that shape our understandings about youth and their self mediations. Gill-Peterson concludes that "perhaps curious adults must suspend their will to know and focus instead on the underlying assumption about sovereignty that frame girls as trapped between vulnerability and agency in the first place" (2013, p. 153). While he suggests the need to resist our desire to know, to let go of the impulse to seek truth beneath the surfaces of youth selves, he has also written on his blog (Gill-Peterson 2013) about the need to experiment with alternative material-affective theories and methodologies that refuse Western humanistic logics through which young people are defined as immature, incomplete not-yet-subjects measured in terms of their capacities to become sovereign rational subjects. He turns to Deleuze and Guittari's *A Thousand Plateaus* to consider "the generation of children as a question of affect," (Gill-Peterson 2013) so as to engage with multiple becomings and creative involutions, to hone our attention to the open-ended process of their embodiments and mediations. No longer measured or judged according to external prescriptive ideals and transcendent moral theories that assert rules about what youth should be and become, possibilities emerge for considering what happens in the flux of living, in the here and now of their bodily, material and technological engagements with the world around them.

Becoming, Affects and Lines of Flight

> A becoming is not a correspondence between relations. But neither is it a resemblance, an imitation, or, at the limit, an identification. (Deleuze and Guittari 1987, p. 262)

Deleuze and Guattari's theories[2] of affect and becoming guide my research enabling new ways of thinking about bodies and selves that depart from liberal representational models and methodologies. Becomings are transformations that call for new ways of imagining individuation, they attend to what happens between entities rather than fixating on one or the other. As I have shown, selfies have been difficult to think about outside of formulaic notions of imitation, identification and individuality. The turn to Deleuzian theory helps to focus on how youth and selfies might become thinkable without becoming predictable, experimenting with what is contingent and unexpected, mapping relational experiences without necessarily having ready made explanations, exact words or familiar narratives. Integral to engaging with affect theory and research is an acceptance that what we see, hear and know might elude our common sense and transparent paradigms and compel us to consider forces beyond the individualized conscious subject, to attend to "neither unities nor totalities, but multiplicities" (Deleuze and Parnet 1987, p. vii). Thinking across a multiplicity of lines through which social, subjective and technological assemblages are composed takes us far beyond a narrow humanistic notion of a self and a selfie.

According to Deleuze, affect is not a psychic orientation, an individual feeling, a physical characteristic or a discursive construction. Affect is not a thing to be characterized and defined, but rather comprises an assemblage of relations in a continual process of reconfiguration and duration. Drawing upon Spinoza's philosophy, affect becomes "an ability to affect and be affected," that implicates human and nonhuman materialities within a monistic ontology that defies humanistic hierarchies centered on rational consciousness and language. Affect "is not confined to the image or idea; it is of another nature, being purely transitive, and not indicative or representative, since it is experienced in a lived duration that involves the difference between two states" (1988, p. 49). The body and its representations are not definable according to form or function but rather are understood as dynamic affective intensities that connect to and change others in contingent ways. Affects are prepersonal, nonlinguistic, mapped in terms of forces and intensities, imbricated within relations of power that alter what bodies can do in the world, how their capacities are generated and changed, augmented or diminished, transformed relationally over time and across spaces. They involve an "effectuation of a power" (1987, p. 265) that is constituted through situated actions and interactions. Deleuze and Guattari write:

> We know nothing about a body until we know what it can do, in other words, what its affect are, how they can or cannot enter into composition with other affects, with the affects of another body, either to destroy that body or be destroyed by it, either to exchange actions and passions with it or to join with it in composing a more powerful body. (1987, p. 284)

These ideas focus on "what bodies can do" with and against others, attentive to tendencies of power that congeal characteristics of subjects within molar assemblages that are "stable forms, unifying, structuring and proceeding by means of heavy aggregates…organizing the crowds" (1984, pp. 286–288). Along these lines, selfies have been largely confined to their molar status that capture affect and contain identities. Yet, Deleuze's project affirms what escapes majoritarian molar organizations, against the territorialization of desire and affect within them, turning toward relational entities whose specific affective relations propel alternatives with potentials to displace them. In this way, molecular assemblages propel desires beyond representational stabilizations with potentials for deterritorializations and "lines of flight" that enable openings and desires elsewhere, propelling new modes of becoming. Todd May writes:

> A line of flight is not a flight from reality but a flight within it. It does not create from nothing but rather experiments with the difference that is immanent to our world. There is always something more than we can perceive. The question before us, and it is a question of living, is whether we are willing to explore it, or instead are content to rest upon its surface. (2005, p. 171)

In my understanding of youth and selfies, following a "line of flight" urges us to think beyond static surfaces or fixed meanings, experimenting in ways that refuse a predictive quest for truth remaining open to surprises and differences. I am inspired by Jessica Ringrose's extensive work on young peoples' social media practices, as she grapples with the simultaneity of molar and molecular tendencies surrounding gender and sexuality within networked and institutional spaces such as schools. Her work is compelling as she maps ambivalent and complex relations with an eye for disruptive lines of flight alongside persistent constraints of structural inequalities online and offline (2011). This method of attending to molar tendencies within young people's everyday practices as they congeal differences and powers, while also following affective flows that trouble and exceed them, offers a productive way forward.

Deleuzian theories of affect and assemblage disrupt the narrow lines of heteronormative developmental teleologies, dualistic languages and methodological individualism that have limited ways of studying youth and media. Against linear models of growth and maturation tied to arborous metaphors grounded in fixed origins and unidirectional branches, it becomes possible to envision "rhizomatic" modes of becoming that helps to shift away from persistent attempts to root youth in the expectations to grow up following straight lines of normative development and sovereign agency. This jibes with Kathryn Stockton's notion of "growing sideways," enabling unruly queer routes of emergence and becoming (2009). Because affects produce multiple capacities and are splayed outwards in relation with others, a rhizomatic conception emerges to help reorient youth becoming, looping back, branching out, converging and breaking apart without set beginnings or endpoints. Forging new rhizomatic pathways, through which to envision a multidirectionality of young bodies and subjectivities, becomes especially crucial in efforts to think about the problems of queer youth digital mediations. When it comes to researching queer youth on social media, the constricting force of hetero and homonormativity necessitates new modes of conceptualization receptive to varied embodiments of desire and affect. Approaching queer youth selfies on Tumblr, I am struck at how normative selfie discourses seems all the more limiting and exclusionary. The pictures and words that flow within and across platforms evoke the very multiplicity and transitivity that Deleuzian notions of affect and becoming open up.

Queering Selfies: Mapping Affective Relations

In this section, I gesture toward an array of networked images and words to get a sense of the heterogeneous ways young people articulate and orient selfies within the social media platform Tumblr. Against clear typologies that pinpoint their visual and verbal content or explanations that delve into to what selfies are and why youth make them, I suggest a more oblique experimental approach that guides us along affective lines of flight. What emerges are fleeting and unsteady networked assemblages of objects, affects and ideas. While selfie images are often wordless, they are sometimes juxtaposed with words that enable loose mappings of the desires and thoughts of the senders. A teen addresses his selfie public with the words: "daring you to hear, see and feel my queer self;" a queer activist writes: "I'm sending out some selfie love to challenge so much fear and hatred;" a defiant girl asserts that she is "facing the world with fierce femme beauty;" and as a tender gesture of longing, a selfie becomes a vulnerable declaration: "I am dreaming of seeing you." "Daring," "sending," "facing," "dreaming," these words echo out of ephemeral bodily and signifying enactments, orienting selves and selfies as a process of doing and becoming. They do not capture identity or seek closure, they gather loosely in hashtags or fracture as they are reblogged across communities. Images and words are poised as communicative gestures, provocative appeals to be seen and heard by friends and strangers. Against the assumed conformism of self-referential narcissism these selfies call out to others, turning images outwards, reaching for multiple, difficult at times impossible receptions and connections. In images and words traced across marginalized youth communities and profiles, selfies can be understood to act as invitations, eliciting feelings, evoking complex responses, enacting a process of becoming through affective "reverberations" (Kuntsman 2012, p. 1) within the "affective fabrics of digital cultures: the lived and deeply felt everyday sociality of connections, ruptures, emotions, words, politics and sensory energies, some of which can be pinned down to words or structures, others are intense yet ephemeral" (Kuntsman 2012, p. 3). Perhaps if we read selfies as productive of these "affective fabrics," indicative of a process of becoming within everyday social media, we will be able to stay close to what youth do and feel, catching glimpses of their mediated lives that challenge what we know and expect of them.

Toward an approach receptive to the shifting subjectivities, modes of address, stylizations and contexts of queer youth, I attune myself to the multivalences of selfies shared and conjoined by queer hashtags on Tumblr. I am drawn to those that actively engage in conversations and even provocations. An eighteen-year old posts a playful fashion selfie with the direct question "queer enough?" performing ironic and ambivalent feelings in asking a question that is unanswerable yet addresses so much more than an individual image, reverberating with pride, frustrations and pleasures of many followers who relate to that question on multiple levels in conflicting ways. This spurs affects and thoughts that connect to the specific experiences of other bloggers who come across the image and are moved by the question to comment and reblog it through their own personal stream. The active questioning of this selfie pushes those who come across it to pause and reflect and perhaps feel uncomfortable. This selfie has a queerly flippant attitude that winks at knowing lookers but also challenges them to consider what they assume a queer self should look like.

In another instance, a sixteen-year-old self-described Japanese transyouth captions a shy yet determined looking image with the words "I will come out to my transphobic parents next year" sharing a vulnerable moment of emotional and physical reflection. This selfie taken in the present marks an affective force of defiance that projects onto future imaginings. Affective becoming is precisely the passage between real bodies and virtual futures, imagining a horizon of possibilities. This durational quality of change over time gets transferred through this selfie, a promise of something else to come, a strong desire to be "out" and yet unknowable in how this will turn out. Here, a selfie comes to articulate the possibility of transformative desires and events that are impossible to represent in completion but can spur hope and touch others, witnessed by those who follow and respond in return. This selfie launches a story that departs from the immediate moment captured in the image and travels outwards. The complex temporalities and intimacies that selfies can generate in this way go far beyond what is visible without disregarding the ways young queer subjectivities express how they appear to others as part of a more expansive process.

For queer youth, the public sharing of a selfie is a gesture that embodies personal and political significance. And while much as been written about the political deployment of selfies across various movements to show evidence of participation and resistance (Kuntsman 2017), it is striking how queer youth selfies also embody politics at a more intimate level of engagement. In a spirit of solicitous outrage, a black gay youth writes "Can you see me?" under a close up picture of a face soliciting attention, recognition and awareness. His eyes offer an open tender call to look, feel and think in complex ways. Here, queer and racial differences are assembled within a question that compels more than a simple response. As bell hooks has argued, for racially marginalized subjects, looking is always fraught with power and potential erasure (1994). The decision to direct the gaze of ones selfie toward strangers on Tumblr is not a neutral act but is burdened by historical relations inseparable from personal desires. In this example, a simple question is directed to the viewer, one with forceful affective reverberations tied to a subtle ethical plea. What is striking is the relational work of coaxing others into an exchange, soliciting affective proximity and complicity. Far from being evidence of youth narcissism, the boundaries of the self are in flux and porous in their connections with others.

While some selfies evoke serious attention in their affective pleas for attention and reflexivity, many stay close to the fleeting surface of ordinary events and the joys of daily life. In a selfie that seems to burst with anticipation, the desiring gaze of a teen tells others of her excitement about seeing her girlfriend that night, an image lived in the transient sharing of how thrilled she feels in the present. Offering a glimpse of the desire to physically connect with her girlfriend, the image is shared as a spontaneous impulse to convey the intensities she feels. The image has a whimsical style showing a smiling face that is caught up in the moment of affirming her queer date that is on the verge of happening. It is so interesting to focus on the affective ephemeral stirring conveyed in an image composed to share experiences that exceed the self. Not bound to representing a static identity, these selfies open up networked connections, mobilize prolific ways of feeling, doing and understanding around the queer subjectivities they convey and address.

What matters in these scattered examples and partial readings is not what unifies queer youth selfies but awareness of how singular and nuanced they are in practice, as they open outwards to emotionally affect and touch someone else, burst out in ways that evoke passion and surprise, create attachments and resentments, foster care and support, generate belonging and exclusion, spur ideas and passions. This is about refusing to reduce selfies to simple data, to resubjectivize and enliven them beyond existing axioms and hegemonic structures of identity and feeling. What matters is challenging what appears to fit into a generalizable pattern, what seems fixed within a static frame or revealing of the truth behind the image, turning instead to relational actions located within a time and place yet on the go to somewhere else. The goal is not about categorizing or clearly pin pointing the actual bodies of youth nor their virtual elaborations, but rather an effort to become receptive to what happens in-between, both inside the realms of representation and visibility and beyond their reach, as uneasy signs of present experience and glimpses of an unknowable future.

Words counterpoised with images, images grouped with other images, blurry, off-center and playful images, all these variations complicate and interrupt our ways of seeing and feeling what selfies might become, propelling encounters between subjectivities, generating responsive calls and responses through which singular desiring subjectivities unfold over time and across spaces. I am hesitant to go further documenting queer youth selfies, listing their qualities, analyzing them in detail, categorizing their elements. The power of surveillance and data mining is all too pervasive, invasive and fragmenting for this generation. Less important than a study of discrete subjects and texts is ethical attention to what they do as affectively dynamic capacities to reach out, elicit, accumulate connections, create intimacies, reverberating and gaining momentum through daily acts of sharing as youth post and reblog over and over again. Staying close to the sensuous, mobile and contingent process of selfies opens room for queer seeing and thinking, for displacing stable subjects, objects and categories, to consider how facial expressions, bodily gestures, material stylizations and movements, might be perceived in queer ways. It is remarkable how heteronormalized discourses surrounding selfies have territorialized their meanings so pervasively, marginalizing or erasing queer youth. At the same time, gender and sexually marginalized subjects have embraced selfies with creative and political gusto, compelling research and writing that looks at selfies from different angles, with alternative questions and conceptual frameworks.

Queer youth engage with selfies as part of their expansive material social media worlds. Research receptive to the flow of sensibilities, desires and affects, values and makes sense of the becoming of young queer bodies without rendering their visibility transparent and bounded. This displaces the binary structures that often exclude queer youth as impossible or else incorporate them as productive and resilient. Thinking beyond individualistic and heteronormative selfie frames, the point is not to center on the visibility of marginalized youth, but to forge new ways of understanding selfies as dynamic mediations, not to exhaust what there is to know but to open up room through which to imagine alternatives. Rather than securing new forms of knowledge, the turn to affect allows for uncertainty and the impossibility of naming and codifying selfies once and for all.

Staying with Uncertainty

Theorizing youth and selfies in terms of affective becoming helps us to reorient our attention toward thinking about what they do within diverse forms of relationships, how they invite intimacies, eroticism and caring, how they spur thoughts, actions and desires in the lives of young peoples in multiple directions. In this way, selfies are hard to pin down, they defy our will to truth. Mapped in terms of nonlinear potentials for affecting and being affected, selfies enter into and shape the networked events and relationships of young peoples lives. I am still figuring out how to study affective doings and becomings, connecting elements, following intensities that move me, undertaking intertextual and transversal modes of reading digital traces as they flow, gather and change through hashtags and sharing, are replaced and erased, and archived as collective and personal memories. The challenge is to leave room to consider the idiosyncratic ways selves and selfies emerge as a process of becoming through and against others, accounting for the small ordinary subtle movements, words and gestures that complicate what is seen and valued in the moment and over time. In other words, the research process itself emerges as an activity both interested in and productive of the composition of assemblages through and beyond selfie images. In practice, this involves moving in different directions and following several lines, ones that territorialize youth and also lines of flight that disrupt oppressive identity categories and hierarchies. Selfies are complicated, they flow and get stuck, are mobilized or forgotten within and across platforms, they are received in activist contexts and savored in more private intersubjective exchanges, emerging within diverse relationships and social scenes, propelled onwards or left without comment, unnoticed and forgotten. Ultimately, they might be impossible to define as we stay "immersed in the changing state of things" as Brian Massumi writes (1987, p. xiii). We might need to back off and refuse to pry too closely into their intimate lives, to leave them alone, to afford them an affective-material-technological space of their own. These are ethical issues that are urgent in a time of commodified hyper-surveillance. The ethical dilemma of selfie research may require us to step back and accept how little we know even as we open ourselves to the abundance and complexities this work unfolds.

Working against a will to truth in relation to young subjects and their desires and creative expressions online, Deleuzian theory becomes useful in helping us to learn to accept epistemological limits; it helps us to avow how little we actually know about the virtual and material worlds of youth we study. In this way, knowledge turns toward an ethical engagement, and a perpetual questioning of our assumptions that shape what and how and why we speak of youth so anxiously and authoritatively. Rather than seeking more truth, research along these lines needs to generate curiosity and attunement that help us pay attention to the ontological contours of young people's affective relational experiences, including the sometimes awkward relations between adults and youth. The hope is to generate thinking in multiple directions along lines of flight such that selfies might be understood for how they mobilize desires and differences between selves in a process of becoming that always exceeds our grasp.

Notes

1. The special issue in the International Journal of Communication Studies opened up diverse theoretical and methodological explorations that ranged from the intimate bodily gestures and haptic contours of selfie production, the situated uses of selfie making within marginalized communities, alongside the macro dimensions of big data projects.
2. I am primarily referencing the work of Deleuze and Guatarri, *A Thousand Plateaus* (1987).

References

Bratskeir, Kate. 2016. Selfies are more dangerous than you think. https://www.huffingtonpost.ca/entry/selfies-are-dangerous-distracting_us_56d841c5e4b0000de40373b9.

Deleuze, Gilles. 1988. *Spinoza: Practical philosophy*. San Francisco: City Lights Books.

Deleuze, Gilles, and Claire Parnet. 1987. *Dialogues*, trans. Hugh Tomlinson and Barbara Habberjam. New York: Columbia University Press.

Deleuze, Gilles, and Felix Guattari. 1984. *Anti-oedipus: Capitalism and schizophrenia*. London: Athlone.

Deleuze, Gilles, and Felix Guattari. 1987. *A thousand plateaus*, trans. Brian Massumi. Minneapolis: University of Minnesota Press.

Foster, Alistair. 2017. Selfies can damage your mental health, expert warns the young. https://www.standard.co.uk/lifestyle/health/selfies-can-damage-your-mental-health-expert-warns-the-young-a3461446.html.

Gabriel, Fleur. 2014. Sexting, selfies and self-harm: Young people, social media and the performance of self-development. *Media International Australia* 151: 104–112.

Gill-Peterson, Julian. 2013. Childhood blocks: Deleuze and Guattari's infant affects. https://juliangillpeterson.wordpress.com/2013/04/29/childhood-blocks-deleuze-and-guattaris-infant-affects/.

Gill-Peterson, Julian. 2015. Sexting girls: Technological sovereignty and the digital. *Women and Performance: A Journal of Feminist Theory* 25 (2): 143–156.

Giroux, Henry. 2015. Selfie culture in the age of corporate and state surveillance. *Third Text* 29 (3): 155–164.

Goldberg, Greg. 2017. Through the looking glass: The queer narcissism of selfies. *Social Media and Society* 3 (1): 1–11.

hooks, bell. 1994. *Black looks: Race and representation.* Boston: South End Press.

Kuntsman, Adi. 2012. Introduction: Affective fabrics of digital cultures. In *Digital cultures and the politics of emotion*, ed. Athina Karatzogianni, Adi Kuntsman, 1–17, London: Palgrave Macmillian.

Kuntsman, Adi. 2017. *Selfie citizenship.* London: Palgrave Macmillian.

Lesko, Nancy. 1996. Denaturalizing adolescence: The politics of contemporary representations. *Youth and Society* 28 (2): 139–161.

Maddux, Catherine. 2015. *Author Andrew Keen warns of internet's disastrous impact.* https://www.voanews.com/a/digital-revolution-disastrous-for-culture-says-internet-skeptic-andrew-keen/2649154.html.

Massumi, Brian. 1987. Translator's forward. *A thousand plateaus*, trans. Brian Massumi. Minneapolis: University of Minnesota and Continuum Press.

May, Todd. 2005. *Gilles Deleuze: An introduction.* Cambridge: Cambridge University Press.

Miltner, Kate, and Nancy Baym. 2015. The selfie of the year of the selfie: Reflections on a media scandal. *International Journal of Communication* 9: 1701–1715.

Renold, Emma, and Jessica Ringrose. 2016. Selfies, relfies and phallic tagging: Posthuman participations in teen digital sexuality assemblages. *Educational Philosophy and Theory* 47 (11): 1–14.

Ringrose, Jessica. 2011. "Beyond discourse? Using Deleuze and Guattari's schizoanalysis to explore affective assemblages, heterosexually striated space, and lines of flight online and in school. *Educational Philosophy and Theory* 43 (6): 598–615.

Saltz, Jerry. 2014. Art at arm's length: A history of the selfie. *Vulture.* http://www.vulture.com/2014/01/history-of-the-selfie.html.

Schirripa, Jessica. 2015. How this generation's obsession with selfies correlates with mental disorders. https://www.elitedaily.com/life/selfies-self-love-surgeries/902152.

Stockton, Kathryn. 2009. *The queer child, or growing sideways in the twentieth century*. Durham: Duke University Press.

Warfield, Katie. 2017. 'I set the camera on the handle of My Dresser': Re-materializing social media visual methods through a case study of selfies. *Media and Communication* 5 (4): 65–74.

Warren-Crow, Heather. 2014. *Girlhood and the plastic image*. Hanover, NH: Dartmouth College Press.

Woollaston, Victoria. 2013. Selfies are 'damaging' and leave young people vulnerable to abuse, claims psychologist. http://www.dailymail.co.uk/sciencetech/article-2401017/Selfies-damaging-leave-young-people-vulnerable-abuse-claims-psychologist.html.

CHAPTER 5

Vlogging the Hijab: Subjectivity, Affect and Materiality

Shazlin Rahman

Muslim women—particularly those who are visibly Muslim—are largely absent from the mainstream media. In response to this lack of representation, young Muslim women have become vloggers on YouTube. As a journalism student, these vloggers were appealing to me because they were just like me: young, visibly Muslim, and living in non-Muslim majority countries. They were creative in their practice of the hijab and spoke confidently to a global audience. Most importantly, they seem perfectly comfortable in their identities as both Muslims and as Canadians, Britons, Swedes or Americans. However, the vlogs had affective impacts on my body and the way I "fashioned" my identity as a Muslim woman. I began to emulate the vloggers style and practices which entailed significant material consumption, such as, wearing make-up or purchasing particular clothes, despite the fact that there were mixed signals pertaining to modes of covering and what they implied about my religiosity and piety as a Muslim woman.

This chapter looks at three young Muslim vloggers for whom the hijab is an affective "practice", not just a material item. The hijab as a practice includes the act of wearing the hijab, the motivation to cover,

S. Rahman (✉)
Communications and Engagement Professional, Toronto, Canada

S. Driver and N. Coulter (eds.), *Youth Mediations and Affective Relations*,
https://doi.org/10.1007/978-3-319-98971-6_5

the embodied experience of wearing the hijab, as well as how different—often less conventional modes of covering—signal the practice of the hijab. I elucidate how vlogs[1] communicate the hijab wearer's individuality, and how cultural and ethno-religious influences shape the practice of the hijab. The three vlogs demonstrate how the hijab as a practice is strongly circumscribed by consumer culture and the logics of digital capitalism, which has significant implications upon the vloggers' gender subjectivities and Muslim identities. The young Muslim women's vlogging practices are dynamic, multifaceted and intuitive to how social media algorithms function.

The Practice of Hijab

The term "*hijab*" is Arabic for "cover" or "barrier". Today, it refers to various forms of religious head coverings worn by Muslim women, including the head scarf; the burka, commonly worn by women in Afghanistan, Iraq, Iran, and Pakistan, which covers their bodies from head to toe; and the niqab, a face covering sometimes worn in addition to head scarves. The practice of covering varies from one ethno-religious group to another. Some women only wear it on particular cultural or religious occasions such as weddings or Eid, the Muslim holy day, while others wear it all the time. The degrees to which they cover and the styles in which they cover also vary widely. Some wear it loosely draped around their heads with parts of their hair visible while others wear it tight to their head with no hair showing. A small number of women in Canada cover all parts of the body except for the eyes. Just as the practice is different for Muslim women, it is different for the Muslim women vloggers. Some vloggers began practising the hijab at a young age, eventually wearing it on a regular basis as part of a progression into womanhood; others began wearing it as adults out of a personal religious conviction, and some stop the practice of hijab briefly when the pressure to conform became too overwhelming. Most vloggers are motivated to wear the hijab out of religious observance. This diversity among the young women's practice of religious covering is rarely reflected in Western mainstream media, be it in news, advertisements, films and television shows. Rather, they are commonly misrepresented as a monolithic group of voiceless, oppressed, and subjugated women; their practice of religious covering is seen as the manifestation of the patriarchy inherent in Islam.

Pushing against these narratives of oppressed victimhood, Hijabi vloggers articulate a strong level of personal agency. They produced videos on a range of topics, including their choices of consumer products, how they dress for different occasions and their struggles with issues of faith and motherhood. Although many vlog entries focus on *hijabi*[2] fashion, make-up and consumer items, vloggers inhabit multiple cultural frames that overlap and nest within one another, illustrating that there is not one single narrative of 'the Muslim woman'. There is also a social dimension to the women's vlogging practice as each vlogger has her own fan base. Their YouTube channels have thousands of followers who actively comment, like and share the vloggers' videos across platforms, and these numbers are steadily growing.

The broad geographical distribution of these vloggers indicates that this trend is part of a larger transnational, transcultural discourse within the Muslim diaspora. While the mainstream media and discourses are failing to capture the full spectrum of Muslim lives in non-Muslim majority countries, these women are engaged in their own networks of transnational discourse.

Research Methodology

To complete this research, I conducted interviews with three popular Hijabi vloggers who I am calling here, *Amina, Fatima* and *Sarah* to protect their anonymity. All three were born and raised in Canada by first generation immigrant parents. Amina comes from a Caribbean background, Fatima from a South Asian background and Sarah from an Arab background. To explore their vlogging praxis, I used a method that privileges individual lived experiences and accompanying minutiae of everyday life. The nexus where Western Muslim women, questions of identity, online communications and self-expression converge is still a new research terrain. This is further complicated by the changing political and religio-cultural contexts within which the vloggers operate and which spurred their move to online self-expression. I conducted individual interviews with each of the three vloggers, for an intimate look into individual narrative accounts which allowed for an inductive analysis of the social processes that shape their narrative accounts. The interview questions mainly focused on the ways in which Muslim women vloggers in Canada utilize YouTube as a disruption of mainstream discourses (Ringrose 2008).

My research began with one-on-one interviews followed by textual analysis of interviewees' vlogs as well as vlogs by other Muslim women living in other non-Muslim majority countries. Conducting my analysis across both sets of data enabled me to include larger cultural, national and trans-national narratives about Muslim women's gender identities in my study. In my project, I took the "small story" approach, incorporating individual narratives from Muslim women vloggers into the study of contexts that influence their narratives. This approach is useful as it focuses on the micro experiences that highlight specific local dynamics, practices and the temporal frames within which specific identities are produced. It also takes into account the parts of the women's narratives that do not fit neatly into a clear storyline but which are crucial building blocks in understanding Muslim women's experiences. Facets of Muslim women vloggers' identities are articulated through multiple vlogs that address disparate topics. Focusing on individual narratives is thus particularly important in my study of the women vloggers whose subjectivities are tied up in narratives that are diachronic and distributed across multiple small stories.

Contesting narratives on the practice of hijab by Muslim women demands an investigation of the epistemology of Muslim women's notions of gendered identities. Their negotiation with contesting narratives and their articulation of identities are internal phenomena articulated externally through their vlogs. The small story approach allowed me to situate the vloggers' narratives within the context of dominant narratives surrounding Muslim women's gender identity. The interviews with the vloggers provided insights into how their personal stories' illustrate their social agency. Furthermore, focusing on trends of the vlogging community highlighted the movement and sharing of ideas and the women's agency.

Hijab as Subjectivity

Much of Western feminism assumes that a Muslim woman who covers her body out of religious observance is uneducated, and disempowered in her decision to cover. Bullock and Jafri (2000) observe the correlation between the Muslim woman, particularly ones who wear the hijab, and the state of being oppressed or disempowered manifest in mainstream media discourses that shape ideas around "Canadian" values. Bullock and Jafri (2000) argue that in mainstream media discourses Muslim women, particularly ones who wear the hijab, often signify oppression and victimhood and are positioned in opposition to the "Canadian woman" who idealizes Canadian values.

The "Canadian woman" is all that the third-world woman is not: progressive, modern, liberated, free, educated, autonomous, and so on. Since Muslim women in Canada are usually seen as coming from the third world, practices associated with Islam (especially visible ones like wearing a headscarf) can be seen as the importation of "backward" third world values to Canada, rather than being viewed as "Canadian" practices in their own unique way (Bullock and Jafri 2000, pp. 35–40).

The three vloggers push back on these representations. They articulate a strong sense of belonging in Canada that correlates with Saunders' (2012) observation of Muslims' integration into mainstream cultures of Western countries like the U.K., U.S. and Canada.[3] The vloggers, Fatima, Amina and Sarah state that they are more comfortable identifying as Canadian rather than as Caribbean, South Asian or Arabic because they were born here and grew up within what they term "Canadian culture". All three participants say they either feel and/or maintain a connection to their ethnic cultures through their parents. Sarah explains, "I'm actually born in Canada, so I'm Canadian. My parents are from Lebanon. So, I do associate myself with being Lebanese". The vloggers demonstrate Saunders's argument in *The Myth of the Muslim Tide*. Saunders suggests that for younger generations of Muslims with immigrant roots, their loyalties are not simply tied to geography. Younger generations of Muslims with immigrant roots prefer to identify themselves as Muslims rather than as Pakistanis, Indians, Egyptian or Lebanese as their parents did; they identify as part of the native population, and thus hold similar values that are largely common to the mainstream culture.

Children of immigrants are especially adept at co-opting their immigrant parents' roots into the culture in which they live, or vice versa (Saunders 2012, p. 161). However, for the participants, affective tensions and relations are complex between Canadian culture and their ethno-religious cultures of their parents. Each vlogger was conflicted when responding to the question of identifying as Canadian or South Asian/Caribbean/Arabic. Amina is more comfortable identifying simply as Canadian, but she also feels that doing so is disloyal to her parents. Borrowing from Margo Badran's work, Abu-Lughod subsequently argues for an "escape [from] the binary thinking that posits a rigidly distinct West and East and assumes, therefore, a crude dynamic that correspond to this division" (Abu-Lughod 2002, p. 27). Vlogger Amina struggles with escaping from these binary logics of East/West or Canadian/other binary framework of identity, as she cannot fully and comfortably express herself as Canadian or Jamaican.

Amina also exemplifies Abu-Lughod's logic; her religion ties her to the Muslim *ummah*[4] but her Caribbean background sets her apart from it because she is neither Arab nor South Asian, as are the majority of Muslims in Canada. Nevertheless, Amina feels unaffected by the influences of dominant Muslim cultures; rather, she feels most influenced by "Western culture"—a term used by Amina that I understand to mean an amalgam of diverse cultures within Canada. It is worth noting that both Fatima and Sarah come from two of the largest Muslim demographics in Canada while Amina does not. Both Fatima and Sarah pivot around their ethno-religious communities' collective values when discussing their practice of the hijab and their identities as Muslim women.

The values surrounding the significance of the hijab informed Fatima's decision to wear it. For Sarah, her ethno-religious community presented barriers in her vlogging practices as a hijabi. In stark contrast, Amina was slow to articulate a particular source of influence that shaped her motivations to dress modestly and to vlog on the topics that she feels passionate about. It is, therefore, perhaps a consequence that—different from Amina—Fatima and Sarah both feel adversely effected by their own ethno-religious communities. The two participants' testimonies illustrate how their gender is defined, performed and policed in the public spheres of their communities where ethno- and religio-centric ideologies pertaining to women's gender identities operate. Fatima says negative reactions from close friends and family towards her hijab placed her in a double bind: "If you're not wearing hijab, you can't do this; if you're wearing hijab, you can't do that. It was a lot of judging, I found, by Muslim sisters." This quote reveals the complex layers of meaning attached to the hijab and how it is taken up as a part of Muslim woman's gendered subjectivity. Attitudes towards the hijab within Fatima's community are similarly divided along religious and cultural lines. In East Asian cultures, Fatima explains, older women primarily wear the hijab; a young woman in hijab connotes backwardness and religious conservatism.

This difficult negotiation can also be found in Muslim lifestyle magazines as sites of struggle in "representing the human form and, in particular, [dealing] with competing definitions of female modesty and concerns about the depiction of female bodies" (Lewis 2010, pp. 211–219). Bullock and Jafri's study of the hijab among Canadian Muslim women confirms the multi-layered meanings of religious coverings: "Issues of class are also involved, with some women in favour of covering, but feeling impeded by their upper-class heritage which emphasized the backward nature of covering" (Bullock and Jafri 2000, p. 37). In other words, in particular ethno-cultural communities, the hijab functions as "socio-cultural construct and a semiotic apparatus, a system of representation which assigns meaning (identity, value, prestige, location in kinship, status in the social hierarchy, etc.) to individuals within the society" (de Lauretis 1987, p. 5). Consequently, Fatima feels relegated to the lower strata of her community and alienated by both the older generation, as well as, young women who cover in her community.

Fatima's testimony demonstrates how gender is a tool by which Muslim women are located within their ethno-religious and cultural community, particularly in relation to class. She recalls how she lost her confidence when she was in a predominantly non-Muslim environment, such as her workplace; she felt so unconfident that she struggled to speak in meetings and presentations. This transmission of individual affect from one sphere to another mirrors Byng's observation on the negative consequences of dominant representations of Muslim women. Byng states that "when media create the common sense understanding that veiled Muslim women will not be a part of the American public sphere it has significant implications for how religion informs minorities' participation in American public life" (Byng 2010, p. 124). Muslim communities that face stigmatization eventually internalize the stigma and form negative perceptions of themselves in relation to mainstream society and consequently withdraw from healthy civic engagement.

This transference of negative feelings and attitudes towards the hijab from media representations to Muslim communities and individual experiences was evident among all three vloggers. For Sarah, her Muslim community actively prescribed what it means to be a 'Muslim woman'. According to Jasmine Zine (2008), this prescriptiveness towards women's behaviours and bodies stems from *izzat*—notions around family honour. Husain, Waheed and Husain (2006) explain *izzat* as a concept related to family honour and respect most prevalent in Asian Muslim communities. The concept of *izzat* places an undue burden on mothers, wives and daughters to maintain their family's honour, resulting in heightened policing of their bodies and behaviours (Husain et al. 2006,

p. 4). Just as Western feminism battles against Islam's perceived backwardness on the bodies of Muslim women and girls, so do Muslim communities through norms that "effectively regulate the behaviour and actions of young Muslim women so as not to compromise family honour" (Zine 2008, p. 41).

In surveying a wide range of Muslim women vloggers, it becomes clear that many wear the hijab for a variety of reasons—as a fulfilment of religious obligation or collective cultural expectation, as an expression of their faith, as a marker of their religious and/or ethno-cultural identities, as a political statement, or any combination of these reasons. As Freedman observed from public debates that emerged following France's ban on the hijab within public schools in 2004, many young Muslim women there feel strongly about their French identity *and* their Muslim identity, which is affirmed in the practice of hijab. For women in the U.K., Freedman notes, wearing the hijab helped them to challenge popular meanings attached to different dress styles and in the imagining of alternative identities (2007). In Canada, according to Amina, wearing the hijab is a highly personal choice that helps her to get closer to God. Furthermore, it helps her to feel "comfortable, happy, respected". This personal sense of fulfilment gleaned by Muslim women from the hijab is often overlooked in universal rights discourses which tend to privilege Western models of rights over the women's own lived experiences. Furthermore, as Freedman argues, the universalization of women's right obscures Muslim women's individual agency and the cultural differences that function as modes through which this agency is realized (Freedman 2007, p. 32). My interviews with Canadian Muslim women vloggers reveal that their agency, identity and cultural differences are reflected in their practices of hijab and in vlogging.

Hijab as Narrative

There is no single common narrative that applies to all Muslim women. This is a fact demonstrated by the myriad stories embedded in YouTube videos by women who wear the hijab across the globe and one that continues to be ignored by mainstream media. The subjectivities of the vloggers expressed through the vlogs I analysed are shaped by multiple social, political and ethno-religious dimensions that consistently overlap and nest within each other. Amina produced eleven vlogs, with seven of them discussing fashion, make-up and skincare while the remaining four vlogs focused on her ethnic background, family and culture. She discusses her favourite foods, drinks, and the accent with which her family speaks in elaborate detail, which are all informed by her parents' country of origin. This is an important point to note; Amina reveals that she has never visited her parents' country of origin, but she nevertheless maintains a strong connection to the culture. In one vlog she raises funds for a charity she supports, and in another Amina speaks candidly about what beauty means to her while critically unpacking popular standards of beauty. Amina effectively disrupts mainstream stereotypes about Muslim women by not only vlogging about on fashion, make-up and hijabs, but also by using her channel and audience to focus a spotlight on issues that matter to her.

A scan of the current popular hijabi vloggers on YouTube reveals that Muslim women come from diverse ethno-religious cultural, educational, and professional backgrounds. All three vloggers I interviewed expressed identities informed by hybrids of cultures—Lebanese-Canadian, Pakistani-Canadian, Jamaican-Canadian—that are informed by their families' cultures of origin, Canada and the global Muslim culture. All three firmly identified as Canadian first and felt uncomfortable identifying as culturally Lebanese or Pakistani, even when prodded. Although they are strongly informed by these cultures, their upbringing in Canada creates a distance from those cultures. Their discomfort illustrates the complex relationship the vloggers have with Lebanese, Pakistani or Jamaican culture; furthermore, vlogging allows these granular facets of their identities to bubble to the surface of public discourse.

The women also subvert the notion of Muslim women as a monolithic group through vlogging. They each demonstrate a firm sense of individuality which they exhibit in vlogs with a high degree of satisfaction. Fatima says, "I'm really myself when I'm in front of the camera. So, the videos that I post, and what people may think my personality is based on those videos—that's totally who I am." As Amina became more active in vlogging, she found herself producing more spoken word poetry, one of her favourite ways of expressing her thoughts. She explains, "I feel like that's a great way to get some things off your chest, in a positive way." For Fatima, vlogging was a handy device when she needed to confront the multiple and often contradictory messages she received regarding what it means to be a hijabi. For Sarah, her vlogs were the space where she overcame her stage fright. Each vlogger adroitly pivoted their vlogging practice to serve their individual needs; here, the sense that one can "say whatever you want" is productive in amplifying the diversity of stories among Muslim women vloggers.

The young women also draw their uniqueness from the mix of cultural influences in their backgrounds, their interests and the topics they vlog about. As earlier demonstrated, the majority of mainstream representations of Muslim women feature those from North African or South Asian descent. Amina's background as a Canadian-Jamaican Muslim is rarely seen or heard. Although all three women cover, the vloggers have individual interpretations and practices of modest dress as Muslim women. Fatima explains that she no longer feels pressured to dress according to her culture's interpretation of modesty, rather, she practises dressing modestly according to her comfort level and what she feels Islam requires of her as an individual. In her analysis of Danish Muslim women's sartorial strategies in engaging with the public sphere, Christiansen made a similar observation about the women's practice of modest dressing; she states that there isn't a clear pattern of a political agenda signalled by the women's clothing because "some women may switch from one to the other strategy or move from a phase in which the distinct Muslim style is emphasized to another in which an ambiguous one is presented" (Christiansen 2011, p. 340). Indeed, one of Fatima's oft-received criticisms from her YouTube viewers was that her turban-style is not appropriate because it is similar to the Sikh turban. This clearly points to the fluidity of Fatima's practice of the hijab, which informs her individuality as a Muslim woman.

Hijab as Commercial Practice

The logics and rhythms of consumer culture are embedded in the vlogging practices of young Muslim women. The content of the videos I analysed primarily discussed fashion and make-up, while the majority of videos by the vloggers in this research feature consumer items either explicitly or implicitly. This includes shopping hauls, product reviews, "get ready with me" and "hijabi outfit of the day" (HOOTD) videos. The vloggers' engagement with consumer culture is what makes the Muslim women vlogging trend an interesting and important study. The vloggers are being subversive by rereading dominant cultural trends through their individual Muslim perspective. However, engaging with these trends also subject the vloggers to the logics of consumer culture. Muslim women vloggers' gender identities are therefore consequently shaped by rhythms of consumer culture. In her study of the "Muslim Barbie", Yaqin found that North American Muslims altered their consumer behaviour significantly following the 9/11 attacks. The author observed that the rise of online marketing enabled the trend of "transnational consumerism" to transcend geopolitical boundaries, finding similar patterns in other countries where Muslims live as minorities (Yaqin 2015, p. 174). This study found that Muslim women vloggers' consumption of material goods, as part of their identity articulation, situates them firmly within this homogenizing transnational culture of consumerism. The conspicuous consumption of modest clothing, scarves, make-up and other goods not only contribute to the larger scheme of capitalism, but also shapes the identities they express through their vlogs.

A closer look at the architecture of the internet and social media platforms—and that of YouTube in particular—shows how the global Muslim *ummah* can be subject to a homogeneity of consumer culture (El-Nawawy and Khamis 2012, p. 42).[5] As McChesney observes, "the digital revolution has been compromised by capitalist appropriation" (McChesney 2013, p.97). The accumulation of capital and profits are the main goals for Facebook, Twitter, Instagram, and Google, which owns YouTube. In fact, YouTube explicitly states that it "acts as a distribution platform for original content creators and advertisers large and small". YouTube's description of itself reinforces a metaphor of the Internet as a cyber marketplace where ideas are traded and sold, and where actors compete with one another to sell their best ideas. El-Nawawy and Khamis's analysis of the global cyber Muslim *ummah* follows a similar line of thinking when they likened it to a *souq* (market); they state, "the large number of Islamic websites available today constitutes a virtual community that is similar to 'a bustling marketplace [souq] in which diverse 'goods'—in the form of ideas and concepts about Islam and Muslims—are exchanged, bought and sold'" (as quoted in El-Nawawy and Khamis 2012, pp. 32–33). This drive for profit is woven into YouTube's structure and how its users are indirectly engaged in profit generation.

Two of the vloggers are implicated in the market logics of YouTube. Sarah vlogs primarily to promote her business as a make-up artist and bridal stylist. Vlogging allows her to tap into YouTube's billions of users and reach potential clients. She explains, "I had my business but it was more like within Ottawa or within Canada [...]. So, I thought YouTube exposure would really help with that and it did." Indeed, her instincts are right; YouTube boasts over one billion unique users every month. Further, YouTube's Monetization programme allows Google Ads to play prior to a vloggers videos. The programme allows users to gain income from advertisements. Therefore, the impetus for producing vlogs is not only altruistic—"to help other Muslim women"—but also to increase viewership, which increases a vlogger's income from ad revenues. Sarah also vlogs to help other smaller businesses gain more exposure in her product review vlogs where she discusses products she received from other businesses. A general observation of hijab vloggers indicate that this is a pre-arranged mode of exchange between vloggers and businesses. Viewers are encouraged to purchase the products, usually through links to the business's website on the vlog's description. Vloggers sometimes receive their own discount codes, which they give to their viewers to use in their purchases; this helps the business to track how many of the vlogger's viewers purchased the product as a result of watching the "product review" vlog.

Product reviews are a staple for vloggers. A common example are the hijab tutorial videos where vloggers demonstrate how to wear a hijab using scarves sent to them by Muslim-owned businesses such as Haute Hijab and Vela Scarves. The vloggers would demonstrate different ways of styling the hijab and comment on the qualities they like about the particular hijab. A content analysis of Sarah's blogs showed that one-third of them included hijab reviews or hijab tutorials using a particular brand of hijab. In contrast, Amina does product reviews without material incentives; she explains, "I wanted to review something and I felt, 'Oh, why not help someone because I'm curious about this stuff.'" Nevertheless, the current sample of Amina's vlogs show that products are still indirectly reviewed and/or recommended in her vlogs. This demonstrates how the logics of consumer culture inform Amina's vlogging practices when she is intentionally promoting a product as well as when she is vlogging about other topics. Although most "product review" videos are on cosmetics, clothes and hijabs, they sometimes include food, electronic gadgets, personal care and household items. These videos are more accurately described as "product endorsements"—they generally discuss what the vloggers like about a product and why viewers should purchase them. Rarely does a vlogger—at least none of the three young women I interviewed—find something they do not like about a product.

The genre of "product reviews" illustrates the limits of online free expression. The vloggers' identities as Muslim women are shaped by the logics of the marketplace and the push for material consumption. However, the vloggers view it as a mutual exchange of resources. Amina simply wanted to share her experience of a product so that her viewers can make informed choices as consumers. Following Sarah's review of products sent to her by a fellow Muslim woman, the owner reported increased activity on its Instagram account. Although it is unclear whether the increase translated into more commerce, the cross-platform impact of one vlogger on a business's social media channel is evident. Sarah also feels that these product reviews serve her goal to inspire Muslim women's creativity in fashion.

The vloggers borrow from popular YouTube genre "outfit of the day" videos, commonly known by its abbreviation "OOTD". For Muslim vloggers these videos are also sometimes specified as "HOOTD" or "hijabi outfit of the day" videos. These videos can also be called "Lookbook," a term borrowed from the popular social platform lookbook.nu which is specifically designed for users share photos of their outfits. Vloggers will model outfits based on themes, such as weddings, a day of shopping or for a night out. They can also be seasonal, such as "WINTER LOOKBOOK!" by DinaTokio. HOOTD videos also carry details of each outfit that appear as text interwoven with narrated voice-overs. In the "October-November Lookbook!", Amina posed in five different ensembles; Islamic *nasheed* music played in video's background and text signifying each ensemble's items and brands. "Quick OOTD #2" was fairly brief; the video featured only one ensemble with a voice-over introduction of the video and text overlays with details of the ensemble similar to the first video. These videos highlight Amina's identity as a Muslim woman. In this particular instance, that identity comprises particular clothes (skirt, belt, top, hijab) from particular brands such as Forever21, Call It Spring, and Garage. In this sense, material consumption is entangled with Amina's identity as a Muslim woman and articulates her subjectivity. In other words, her Muslim subjectivity is experienced within the context of the capitalist market system. As such, the "hijab outfit of the day" genre of videos within the vlogging phenomenon amongst Muslim women visually connect Muslim woman's identity to consumer culture.

Conclusion

When I first set out to explore hijabi vlogging, I was highly optimistic about the Internet and social media platforms' potential as tools for the women's self-expression and liberation from oppressive mainstream narratives. Indeed, the continued vilification of Muslims by Western mainstream media and the misrepresentation of Muslim women in particular have necessitated new means of expression that are free of anti-Muslim biases. To that effect, vlogs are particularly effective as alternative channels through which the often-silenced voices of Muslim women can be heard. The effectiveness of YouTube as a platform is proven by the popularity of many Muslim women vloggers who command hundreds of thousands of subscribers on their YouTube channels and similarly large and devoted followings across social media platforms. Devoid of adequate representation in print, TV and other broadcast media, these Muslim women vloggers fill a critical void for young Muslim women looking for inspiration and a reflection of themselves.

The three hijabi vloggers interviewed in this research prove that they are effectively appropriating YouTube to challenge misrepresentations of Muslim women in Western non-Muslim majority countries. Their vlogging practices show that they are both diverse in their backgrounds, interests, and religio-cultural influences. They draw inspiration from a variety of sources—besides religious inspirations like the Quran—such as other vloggers and OOTD videos. They also have highly individual approaches to being a Muslim woman, something that directly contradicts mainstream narratives about Muslim women as uniformly oppressed, and about Islam as a monolithic religion. This is most evident in their individual approaches to practising the hijab, articulated in their creative take on fashion and modesty in their vlogs. Most importantly, the vloggers exhibited a high level of affective agency using YouTube to express themselves. They vlog about issues that interest them personally, they utilize other social media platforms to engage with their audiences and they are adept at tailoring their vlogs according to their audiences' feedback. Vlogging has allowed these three young Muslim women vloggers to challenge common misconceptions about themselves. It was heartening for me, a Muslim woman, to observe these positive outcomes that vlogging has had on these women. Despite this, having turned a critical eye to this phenomenon, I have also unearthed several observations that deserve attention and criticism.

This research shows that despite their freedom of expression on YouTube the Muslim women's identities that are being expressed through vlogging are strongly circumscribed by consumer culture. A brief look at the more popular vloggers will show that the majority of them vlog about clothes, make-up, and hijabs. Shopping hauls, product reviews and gift swaps between vloggers are some of the most common genres of vlogs. It's useful to note that this trend in vlogging is not unique to Muslim women; the same can be observed of the general vlogging trend on YouTube. Thus, this raises the question, "What is the utility of Muslim women's vlogging if they are merely replicating the general trend in YouTube vlogging?" It is also important to note that only one of the vloggers interviewed for this research strongly reflected this underlying consumer culture in her vlogging practices. The vloggers I interviewed for this research represent a diverse array of motivations and utilize multiple forms of vlogging. They use YouTube in ways that reflect their individuality, agency, and diversity of thought and identities. This research clearly demonstrates the immense potential of digital platforms as tools of self-expression. Although young Muslim women have made a lot of progress in getting their voices heard by using these digital tools, there remains to be ample opportunity for these tools to be more effective and used in robust and meaningful ways beyond discussing fashion, hijab, and make-up.

Notes

1. "Vlogger" is a common term referring to people who produce blogs in video from, which are hosted primarily on YouTube but can be disseminated across multiple social media platforms.
2. "Hijabi" is common term referring to women who wear the hijab.
3. For a complete analysis on Muslim diasporic identities in the global west, see Saunders (2012).
4. "Ummah" is a common Arabic term referring to a global Muslim community.
5. El-Nawawy and Khamis (2012), p. 42.

References

Abu-Lughod, Leila. 2002. Do Muslim women really need saving? Anthropological reflections on cultural relativism and its others. *American Anthropologist* 104 (3): 783–790.

Bullock, Kathy, and Gul Joya Jafri. 2000. Media (mis)representations: Muslim women in the Canadian nation. *Canadian Women Studies* 20 (2): 35–40.

Byng, Michelle. 2010. Symbolically Muslim: Media, hijab, and the West. *Critical Sociology* 36 (1): 109–129.

Christiansen, Connie Carøe. 2011. Contesting visibilities: Sartorial strategies among Muslim women in Danish media. *Journal of Intercultural Studies* 32 (4): 335–353.

de Lauretis, Theresa. 1987. *Technologies of gender: Essays on theory, film, and fiction*. Bloomington and Indianapolis, IN: Indiana University Press.

El-Nawawy, Mohammad, and Sahar Khamis. 2012. Divergent identities in the virtual Islamic public sphere: A case study of the English discussion forum 'Islamonline'. *Journal of Arab & Muslim Media Research* 5 (1): 31–48.

Freedman, Jane. 2007. Women, Islam and rights in Europe: Beyond a universalist/culturalist dichotomy. *Review of International Studies* 33 (1): 29–44.

Husain, Meher I., Waquas Waheed, and Nusrat Husan. 2006. Self-harm in British South Asian women: Psychosocial correlates and strategies for prevention. *Annals of General Psychiatry* 5 (7): 1–7.

Lewis, Reina. 2010. Marketing Muslim lifestyle: A new media genre. *Journal of Middle East Women's Studies* 6 (3): 58–90.

McChesney, Robert W. 2013. *Digital disconnect: How capitalism is turning the internet against democracy*. New York: The New Press.

Ringrose, Jessica. 2008. 'Every time she bends over she pulls up her thong': Teen girls negotiating discourses of competitive. *Heterosexualized Aggression. Girlhood Studies* 1 (1): 33–59.

Saunders, Doug. 2012. *The myth of the Muslim tide: Do immigrants threaten the West?* Toronto: Knopff Canada.

Yaqin, Amina. 2015. Islamic Barbie: The politics of gender and performativity. *Fashion Theory* 11 (2–3): 173–188.

Zine, Jasmine. 2008. Honour and identity: An ethnographic account of Muslim girls in a Canadian Islamic school. *Topia* 9: 35–61.

CHAPTER 6

"#YouTuberAnxiety: Anxiety as Emotional Labour and Masquerade in Beauty Vlogs"

Sophie Bishop

Zoella is perhaps the most recognisable beauty vlogger (video blogger) in the United Kingdom, with over 11 million subscribers on her YouTube channel. However, despite her focus on beauty content, it is her discussions of anxiety and panic that have formed the building blocks of her personal brand. Her anxiety has been the focus of magazine features, television segments, and a plot line in her young adult novel, *Girl Online*. She was also announced as the first Digital Ambassador to mental health charity Mind in 2014. The mantra "just say yes!", coined in the first YouTube video about her anxiety, and a subsequent anxiety video entitled "just say yes" is also now central to Zoella's merchandise. The slogan is splashed across phone cases, poster prints, and make-up bags, sold through her own company and riffed off independently on sites such as Etsy. In addition, GIFs and memes circulate on the internet, featuring Zoella's smiling image positioned next to the slogan. The GIF, with its amplified colours, repetition, and stickiness, lends itself to a sharply magnified affective response (Ash 2015).

This chapter will draw from an extended online ethnography of the most popular beauty vloggers in the UK and examine the proliferation of

S. Bishop (✉)
Arts Technology and Innovation, University of East London, Bristol, UK

S. Driver and N. Coulter (eds.), *Youth Mediations and Affective Relations*,
https://doi.org/10.1007/978-3-319-98971-6_6

'anxiety' as a central theme in this beauty vlogging genre. The majority of beauty vlogging channels in my sample feature at least one video on personal experiences of anxiety, stress, and depression. I argue this theme can be read as a negotiation and investment in authentic and feminine performances. This chapter will consider how anxiety videos can be utilized to restore a vlogger's brand when it is in jeopardy, and to pathologize instances of so-called negativity. I do not suggest that these young women on YouTube are not experiencing anxiety, or even an anxiety disorder. However, as Tyler et al. point out, "affect is channeled within and across media with political consequences and we need to theorize these affects as not only unpredictable (which it can be) but also as strategic, and performed" (2008, p. 89). The anxiety video genre can thus provide a lens to examine the affective and emotional labour undertaken by vloggers, when building a successful brand on YouTube.

The 'A List' Beauty Vlogger

In the United Kingdom, the most popular male vloggers adhere to diverse (albeit masculine) genres. They document their travels, pranks, release comedy music videos, make gaming videos, and lecture their viewers about science and technology. However, the most popular female vloggers are almost exclusively beauty vloggers. Beauty vloggers individually operate cosmetic and fashion themed YouTube channels, often supported by a textual blog and a coordinated social media presence. They parse a performance of girl-next-door likeability into make-up tutorials and an amalgamation of other highly feminized video content, including fashion look-books, boy-related chat, 'lifestyle' guidance, healthy eating, and baking demonstrations. However, the popular beauty vlogging video genre considered in this chapter is the 'anxiety video'. The anxiety video is essentially a documented reflection on one's own mental health, almost exclusively performed by female beauty vloggers, in the domestic space of the bedroom. The anxiety video genre fits neatly within a feminized neoliberal "self-help culture" (Ringrose and Walkerdine 2008, p. 235). Often, in anxiety videos, the vlogger reveals their own struggles with anxiety as a means to help their viewers with similar issues.

The most successful and visible female vloggers are overwhelmingly beauty vloggers. They are often young, middle class, and white; a reality that reflects gender and racial inequalities that span many creative and tech industries (Gill 2002, 2010; Hesmondhalgh and Baker 2015;

McRobbie 2015; Neff 2012; Wissinger 2012). A very small fraction of beauty vloggers have successfully gained millions of loyal subscribers on YouTube; the majority of hopeful vloggers are rendered invisible, amassing very few views (Duffy 2017). Ultimately, video distribution on the platform is highly unequal, with very few vloggers attracting the majority of videos. The majority of vloggers are relegated to the 'long tail' of backwater search results (Adamic and Huberman 2001). For the lucky few, beauty vlogging can be a full-time job. Vloggers can earn advertising revenue through the YouTube Partnership Program and through valuable sponsorship deals with brands. The vloggers are eloquent, poised and meticulously groomed, evocative of McRobbie's earlier writing on "A1" girls, defined as "subjects *par excellence* and also subjects of excellence" (2009). Building on the term "A1 girls" and the celebrity implications of highly visible vlogging, I term these successful full-time vloggers the 'A List'. The 'A List' beauty vloggers have a high number of followers; appear in beauty and fashion magazines; have merchandise, including book deals and make-up lines; and are represented by high-profile digital talent agencies. This chapter will focus on the anxiety videos made by two highly visible UK based 'A List' beauty vloggers; Zoella and Gabriella Rose.

The content-creation practices undertaken by beauty vloggers could be considered in terms of a self-branding strategy. Alice Marwick defines self-branding as "the strategic promotion of an identity to be promoted and sold to others" (2013, p. 120); self-branding is also contingent on a performance of authenticity, in other words "comparing current actions against past [actions] for consistency" (Marwick 2013, p. 120). To ensure this consistency, prominent beauty vloggers are carefully managed by cultural intermediaries, such as personal management, talent agencies, and YouTube itself. Beauty vloggers also undertake strict self-monitoring and regulation. Duffy (2017) has observed this level of scrutiny often amounts to high-profile vloggers being "always on" and having to adhere to a fixed self-branding at all times, whether on or offline.

A List beauty vloggers often have overwhelmingly young teenage audiences. Like tween-targeted boy bands and Disney stars before them, the vloggers are often in their twenties yet invested in self-presentation within an un-placeable temporality (Wald 2002). In a similar fashion to 'teeny bopper' boy band music videos and Disney channel movies, vlogs are often filmed in age-neutral locations, including the mall, the coffee shop, and the bedroom. Indeed, the majority of highly visible vloggers draw from what McRobbie has previously defined as teenage "bedroom culture" (2000): they use an age-neutral bedroom as a vlogging set, despite living in their own flats and apartments. We see them in their bedrooms, hosting friends, getting ready to go out, trying out different types of make-up.

A List beauty vloggers are also invested in constructing their self-brands in opposition to 'hyper-sexualized' celebrities and reality television stars. They are often awarded the highly gendered honour of being role models. In this vein, they are carefully scrutinized for moral transgression by news media and audiences alike. One recent media-storm surrounded 'A List' vlogger Zoella's 'pants selfie'. She posted a photo of herself to her followers on Snapchat in 2016, in which she was wearing a pyjama top and underwear. This snap caused UK gossip mags to race to herald the death of her vlogging career. British tabloid rag *The Sun*,[1] for example, shrieked "the YouTube sensation, who's made MILLIONS appealing to young girls and tweens, cast off her squeaky clean image to pose in her knickers" (Jenkins 2016). In addition to the press attention, viewers addressed the controversy in the comments sections of the YouTube video, and on fan message boards such as Guru Gossip. A thread about Zoella's underwear selfie on Guru Gossip titled "Knickerella" features damning comments about Zoella's behaviour, for example, the following post: "why does this bitch feel like she is above it all???? If it were me, I'd be mortified, and let my fans know they don't need to post shots in solidarity" (Guru Gossip 2016). This post, and many others, highlighted what they believed to be Zoella's responsibility to set an example for her young viewers. In this vein, vlogging viewers are consistently monitoring the behaviour of their favourite vloggers, and as we will see later, the smallest transgression can cause a significant backlash.

The Anxiety Video

In response to controversies such as 'Knickerall', many content creators utilise a video performance that I term the 'anxiety video'. This is a popular vlogging genre, performed by many A List beauty vloggers in the UK, some more than once. In the anxiety video, the beauty vlogger discusses their personal experiences of generalized anxiety disorder, social anxiety, or depression. Some videos clearly signpost this content by featuring "anxiety" in the title; examples include "Dealing with Panic Attacks and Anxiety" (Zoella 2012) and "Anxiety Chat!" (Tanya

Burr 2015). Other vloggers reveal their anxiety disorder under more cryptic titles including "STUFF YOU DON'T KNOW ABOUT ME" (Estée Lalonde 2016) and "The Big Chat" (Sprinkleofglitter 2010).

The anxiety video is often stripped back, playing homage to an established YouTube genre 'the coming out video'. Writing on YouTube's coming out videos, Alexander and Losh note;

> An emphasis on revealing a long-hidden, essential truth of unchanging and fixed identity, as opposed to an emphasis on sexual agency and play, may be a reaction to perceptions of flux, instability, and constant change associated with a postmodern, multicultural era. (Alexander and Losh 2010, p. 29)

Here, Alexander and Losh pick up on the theme of consistency within YouTube self-branding practices. The coming out video is identified as a disavowing of past identity performances and setting a strict tone for the vloggers' future self-brand. Like the coming out video, the anxiety video features the vlogger protagonist addressing their audiences directly, often from private domestic space, predominately the bedroom. In both video genres, the vlogger signals the abject collapse of their performed identity, a true and *stable* inner self is ostensibly revealed. In the coming out video, this true self is gay or bisexual. In the anxiety genre, the vlogger signals that their 'confident' self was performed, and the 'true' self is someone anxious, with many struggles and doubts. Both anxiety and coming out performances have value that lies in a positioning as oppositional to behaviours by mainstream celebrities in 'traditional' star industries such as film, television, and music. The vulnerability and amateur quality within these genres trade on a performed binary opposition to representations of confidence, opulence, wealth, and glamour. Indeed, a performance of ordinariness and accessibility, often referred to as authenticity, is extremely important in social media celebrity industries (Marwick 2015; Abidin 2015; Senft 2008). Anxiety videos are humanizing and vulnerable. Therefore, beauty vloggers borrow from the aesthetic of the coming out video in the anxiety video, perhaps in the hope of amplifying and strengthening a performance of authenticity. Their deployment could also be read as strategic, as the anxiety video is often utilised against a charge of 'fakeness', a high-risk accusation that can deflate a channel's popularity. Beauty vloggers are consistently at risk of being charged with fakeness for diverse actions, including working consistently with brands, releasing a ghost-written book, or tactically filming videos with higher status vloggers than themselves. Managing this risk involves numerous self-presentation strategies and labours.

Anxiety and Post-feminism

Many beauty vloggers celebrate their opportunities to produce videos on YouTube, they describe vlogging as a tool for female empowerment. Zoella (2017) has suggested that in the context of YouTube "more women are absolutely bossing it and choosing not to follow society's rules." Similarly, A List beauty vlogger Louise Pentland tells her audiences "you have the same opportunities that I have, just get going with it" (*Blogosphere Magazine* 2017). Although the participatory nature of beauty vlogging is a common narrative, scholars have observed that successful participation is contingent on highly gendered norms of behaviour and consumption (Banet-Weiser 2016; Duffy 2017; Marwick 2015). Therefore, beauty vlogging can be read as "postfeminist" media, often manifesting as "constraining new forms of gender power which operate through the granting of capacity to young women" (McRobbie 2009, p. 7). Most beauty vlogs adopt a post-feminist sensibility that suggest structural inequalities are irrelevant.

As Ros Gill observes, the centring of the female body is symptomatic of a "postfeminist sensibility" in which "femininity is defined as a bodily property rather than (say) social structural or psychological" (2007, p. 5). In this vein, anxiety is positioned by some beauty vloggers as something for all (young women) to negotiate, as both a natural and naturally restricting force to be negotiated by the individual. Zoella's anxiety videos normalize the experience of panic and anxiety. She introduces each 'anxiety' video by stating there has been significant interest in this particular vlogging topic, citing many questions and emails submitted by her viewers. The videos also appear to invite viewers to redefine their own experiences as generalized anxiety disorder and panic. Zoella says, "it's a common thing, a lot of people suffer with [anxiety]", describing panic attacks as "just your body's way of trying to protect you…" and reassuring the viewer "you are not the only person who feels this way" (Zoella 2012).

Anxiety and panic introduce a bio-political threat, the possibility of loss of control at any moment. The typicality of generalized anxiety disorder becomes a point of refrain, even a touchstone that is casually mentioned within non-anxiety content, a reason to not go somewhere, a reason to stay at home. Anxiety vlogs function to imbue the occasional visit to public space, for example, visiting a shopping mall, as a moral achievement. However, representations of anxiety disorders overwhelmingly link femininity with domestic isolation – the retreat into the home, the limitation of participation in public life. In these domestic spaces the vloggers apply cosmetics in pursuit of 'self-confidence'. Contemporary neoliberal society "advocates consumerism as a panacea for anxiety and an expression of good citizenship" (Negra 2009, p. 51). Indeed, for high-profile female beauty vloggers, their videos are largely set within the safety of domestic space; beauty vloggers are rarely beautifying themselves to *go anywhere*, rather they apply make-up to feel better, to feel less anxious. This chapter addresses how the themes and conventions of the anxiety video genre work to situate vloggers within feminized domestic space, whilst simultaneously underpinning this self-presentation as true and authentic.

Visibility Labour and Authenticity Labour

The precarity of A List vloggers on YouTube requires the undertaking of "visibility labour" defined as "the work individuals do when they self-posture and curate their self- presentations so as to be noticeable and positively prominent" (Abidin 2016, p. 5). In her work on social media influencers, Abidin focuses on the example of fans, who labour to become visible to their favourite influencers through strategically commenting on Instagram accounts. The concept of 'visibility' labour is equally apt to apply to influencers, or vloggers, themselves. This work positions influencers to achieve the maximum number of viewers possible, undertaken to negotiate the anxiety of invisibility, and underpinning entrepreneurial participation in online platforms. YouTube videos encompass some visibility labour; they are entrepreneurial outputs that are contingent on vloggers' understandings of trends in the hopes of attracting the views of their "imagined audiences" (Marwick and boyd 2011). This labour is both highly affective and often corporeal, dictating speech patterns, video themes, self-presentation, and grooming decisions, as vloggers ensure they are findable within the noise of online platforms. Vloggers strategically and deliberately participate in popular online genres, such as the anxiety video genre, with entrepreneurial intent. The anxiety video could be seen as a deliberate strategy to generate visibility, as these videos often acquire a higher than average percentage of views.

Indeed, for many vloggers, creating videos to fit within an existing genre is a tactic used to increase search traffic to a vlogging channel, which increases the chances they will be promoted by the YouTube algorithm, and solidifies their positioning within their community (Postigo 2014). Tagging and labelling a video as part of an existing genre will increase the likelihood of the videos being included in a playlist or shared by popular vloggers. Therefore, rather than considering each anxiety video as a standalone text, analysis of the generic themes and tropes can be a starting point for unpacking the emotional labour involved in creating such a video, and the strategic and entrepreneurial intent that underpins participation within this online genre. Building on the idea of 'visibility labour', a specific strain of focussed work is undertaken in the anxiety video, in an attempt to build a representation as real, relatable, and true to one's self. I have termed this 'authenticity labour' defined as a dedicated form of work used strategically to appear amateur and 'real'. Authenticity labour can take the form of purposefully clunky editing, minimal cosmetic use, natural and uneven lighting, and audible background noise. One example of such authenticity labour is in a video by popular beauty vlogger, Gabriella Rose (2015), a mid-sized UK beauty vlogger with just under 1 million subscribers. In Rose's video, simply entitled "Honesty", Rose is set directly in front of an open window using natural lighting that fluctuates throughout the video, sunlight illuminating her face one minute, as she is plunged into darkness the next. Her bed is clearly in shot as she speaks over the loud noise from a busy street, a window intentionally left open, as Gabby suggests she is "clammy." In this vein authenticity is performed as the binary opposite of professionalism, of 'selling out'. Deploying such markers of authenticity is work undertaken to reassure the audience that what is being said is 'real', unscripted, and untinged by brand collaborations and sponsorships.

Anxiety Video in the Personal Brand of Female YouTubers

The first iteration of the anxiety video that will be considered here, is the anxiety video as self-branding strategy. As described earlier, beauty vlogger Zoella has a coherent and legible 'self brand' as the 'good girl'. A recent cover feature in *Cosmopolitan* magazine, she is portrayed as a relatable friend from school, in that she is largely unexceptional and unthreatening;

> Is she beautiful? Yes. But no more so than the prettiest girl in your English class. Is she charming? Polite is the better word, with the sort of quiet confidence and impeccable manners of a good head girl. (Lumsden 2016, p. 36)

This 'goodness' identified by *Cosmopolitan* is central to Zoella's brand. She *is* good; she is a good consumer, she adheres to established gender roles and she has a clean image (with the exception of one non-repeated underwear selfie). Zoella's first anxiety video was published in 2012 and coincided with her meteoric rise to vlogging stardom. At the time, Zoella had a total of 150,000 subscribers on YouTube, now Zoella is the most followed female YouTuber in the UK, with over 11 million subscribers. In her introductory anxiety video entitled "Dealing with Panic Attacks and Anxiety", she sits cross legged on a pink bedspread, fairy lights twinkling in the background. Zoella opens the video with the affirmation that this video is of a different oeuvre to 'normal'. In a similar tactic to the coming out video genre, there is the promise of a reveal of a 'truer' identity than the viewer has been privy to. Zoella states:

> As you are watching this now, you know me as Zoe, I write my blog, I go on my Twitter a lot.. and I like all things materialistic. But what you don't often see is a different side of me, which I will begin to describe in this video. (Zoella 2012)

The video draws viewers in with a mystery but withholds the big reveal for a few minutes: her true identity as someone struggling with generalized anxiety disorder. In a series of anxiety videos, consumerism is suggested to be the cure for her anxiety. Responding to a question about how to negotiate social anxiety, Zoella states "really pamper yourself, take a bit longer picking out your outfit... I always say, like, makeup is amazing because it gives that little bit more confidence that they might not have had before..." (Zoella 2016a). Moreover, anxiety themes also appear in videos otherwise concerned with shopping hauls and grooming practices. Zoella cites specific brands of cosmetics, smoothies, bath products, and candles as having helped her to manage her stress and anxiety. Often the pain described is caused by a barrier to participation within certain kinds of consumption; at one point, Zoella cries that she wishes to be 'normal' defined by her as not having anxiety, so she can attend busy shopping destinations and restaurants. Furthermore, anxiety functions as a plot line in Zoella's romance narrative with her boyfriend Alfie, also a popular vlogger. Alfie is regularly seen 'rescuing' Zoella from anxiety and panic. Describing their first date in the "Boyfriend Tag" video, Alfie talks about how he specifically booked aisle tickets for a surprise trip to the theatre, so Zoella could leave if she felt anxious (Zoella 2016b). Such activity is read as extremely romantic by her viewers, who often compare their relationship to that of a Disney film: Alfie as the white knight or Prince Charming and Zoella as the princess.

Other videos advise the viewer on how to negotiate anxiety without breaking social mores or appearing impolite. In the video "Anxiety Q&A", Zoella notes "if it is a person who is making you anxious, just get away from that person, without being rude... just quietly slip away" (Zoella 2015). Suggesting her viewer acts graciously, even when threatened, could be read as deep emotional labour both performed and advocated by Zoella. Eilleen Hochschild refers to service workers "bowing from the heart", defined as the act of suppressing or conjuring up emotions, to exchange with other social actors in a given social situation (Hochschild 2012, p. 82). Zoella suggests using strategic performances of feeling to negotiate social disjuncture. In telling her audience to ensure they are not rude, she promotes a suppression of feeling as a gesture to relieve the possibility of social awkwardness born from their experiences of anxiety. This discourse rests on the implicit assumption that those experiencing anxiety are not in danger, that the anxiety experienced is irrational, and the responsibility of the actor experiencing it is to ensure social interactions continue uninterrupted by the abject excess of anxiety.

While a debilitating and serious mental illness, anxiety disorder can be represented as 'socially acceptable', when experienced by white middle-class social actors. This is especially true of young white middle-class women, who experience intense media and societal scrutiny on their levels of 'confidence' (Gill and Elias 2014). Anxiety is normalized, perhaps even idealized, when experienced by white middle-class bodies who have the luxury of time and resources to treat it. In fact, for these bodies, the only goal is to ensure that anxiety disorder does not escalate to more serious and perceived to be an *ugly* mental illness, recognized in the bodies of the other (Ahmed 2004). Zoella describes how she improved her experiences of panic and anxiety by simply willing it away, assuming such transformative power is available to all social actors. She advises:

> Just think the same thing as me... I decided to say yes to things that I would not normally say yes to... if you just decide to say yes to the opportunities you are given then you will get more out of life. (Zoella 2012)

Zoella's utterances in this video, firstly asserting her experience of anxiety and then immediately curing it through the mantra "just say yes" are performative speech acts that actively work to forge her identity; it is as a white, middle-class woman that she has the moral authority to transmute speech into a performative act (Butler 1996). That she is designated believable, and sanctioned by mainstream media, is due to the power imbued in her positioning as a white middle-class subject, and underpinned by the desirability of her symptoms in her specific body. In this vein, Beverley Skeggs proposes:

> Only from the position of, and with access to, the resources of the middle-class, can a presumption be made that there is a possibility first, to tell a story, second, to assume the power to re-define and, third, to assume a significance to the story. (Skeggs 2003)

Zoella has the power to define her experience, to diagnose herself, she is not diagnosed by a doctor. She is a privileged subject and in control of her own narrative, free to present her experience as simultaneously authentic and compatible with the themes of the anxiety video genre, which can be unquestioned and neatly packaged to be decoded and promoted by YouTube's algorithms.

Anxiety Video as a Tool to Restore Morality

In the instance of a public transgression, beauty vloggers such as Zoella and Gabriella Rose, draw on the anxiety video to signpost their authenticity, and signal a justification for negative behaviours. The fragility and domesticity evoked by white middle-class female anxiety are the ultimate retroaction to days of more acceptable femininity. Indeed, the anxiety video pathologizes, thus justifies and neutralizes, failings and transgressions that can threaten a beauty vlogger's designation as "good" and entrepreneurial. An anxiety video can restore the vlogger's 'authenticity', likeability and morality following a beauty vlogger's public transgression. Here, I will return to the example of Gabriella Rose. In 2013, Gabriella Rose participated in collaborations with Zoella, thrusting Rose into the spotlight, with more followers and opportunities for lucrative brand deals. However, Rose's success was soon jeopardized by her designation as an online bully, as she often replied to negative comments on her social media platforms and blocked her viewers who were posting them. Audiences publically performed their disappointment with her actions through posts on forums and social media. This was a high-risk moment for Rose, whose carefully built brand was in jeopardy.

As young women often act to determine the morality of those in the public eye, as punishment, Gabby's followers attacked the brands she was working with, such as Primark, by flooding them with complaints about Gabby's online conduct. Readers hurled a barrage of negative comments at a *Daily Mail* article about her Primark collaboration, describing Gabby as an inappropriate choice. In one example she is both unfavourably compared to Zoella (who is described as a 'positive role model'), and designated a bully:

> Of all the youtubers (sic) Primark could have picked they picked Gabriella? Only reason why I can think is that Primark could't get Zoe so they chose Gab before they had fell out. By no means am I a fan of Zoella, Tanya etc., but at least they are positive role models for young girls unlike this idiot. (Barns 2015)

This comment, and many others like it, rest on a belief that Gabby's behaviour was inappropriate and a form of bullying that should not be condoned by a deal with Primark. Audiences here are actively labouring to prohibit brands from working with vloggers they deem to be inappropriate, whilst protecting vloggers who they assess to be good role models.

Rather than being concerned by the (often undisclosed) advertising deals negotiated by vloggers, they undertake considerable emotional and immaterial labour to ensure the 'good' vloggers are rewarded with sponsorship opportunities. This vitriolic response from audiences, and the real possibilities of considerable harm to a vloggers' brand, demonstrates the risk involved when a vlogger speaks out critically, or performs anything other than an authentic femininity that also conforms to industry norms, prioritising the protection of brands. The anxiety genre provides opportunities to reset, to reposition the beauty vlogger as a point of identification, and to remind her viewers 'I'm just like you'.

Gabriella's anxiety video (entitled "Honesty") was published shortly after the negative backlash she experienced, in a direct attempt to address her transgressions (Gabriella ♡ 2015). Gabriella used the anxiety video as an attempt redeem her personal brand from that of being a bully to one as an authentic and flawed, woman. This can be described as a mobilization of the "post-feminist masquerade" to address Gabby's designation as aggressive. In defining this post-feminist masquerade, McRobbie writes:

> The post-feminist (anti-feminist) masquerade comes to the young women's rescue, a throwback from the past, and she adopts this style (assuming for example the air of being 'foolish and bewildered') to help her navigate the terms of hegemonic masculinity... she fears being considered aggressively unfeminine... she fears being mistaken for a feminist. (McRobbie 2009, p. 66)

In keeping with this illustration of the masquerade, Gabby begs for forgiveness for being outspoken and critical, she apologizes profusely for 'calling out' people using Instagram and Twitter, saying "I had a lot of strong opinions... much stronger than I do now... and I was so unhappy within myself." Gabby apologizes for posting her negative emotions online, expressing guilt about burdening her fan base with her depressive thoughts. She says "I'm trying to be a lot happier.... I'm trying to control things that I say and how I do things on the internet."

As is typical for a video of this genre, Gabby begins the video with an allusion to reveal a true identity; however, she is explicit about the ends she is hoping to achieve. She states "I don't want to keep things in anymore... I would rather you just know things... and then hopefully you can get back to liking me" (Gabriella ♡ 2015). Here, she makes explicit the performance she is required to do as a beauty vlogger, with the intention of reinstating her authentic self. She makes clear that she has to labour to present herself in the manner that is required for her job as a vlogger. However, ultimately the negative feelings alluded to behind this surface are described as unnatural and dark; it is only someone who was in a *bad* place that would speak out against negative comments. Indeed, Gabby states she is on a quest to improve herself. She states "I don't want that in my life, I'm trying to do things to make myself happy, I just want to live a healthy lifestyle and be happy with what I do again" (Gabriella ♡ 2015). Gabby's anxiety and depression are inscribed as an individual burden, as her own problem and responsibility, without referring to the collective issues or environment that caused the backlash against her, namely the "powerfulness of regulatory, moralising discourses of femininity and sexuality," encouraging young women to sanction and shame those who they believe to have transgressed these values (Jackson and Vares 2015, p. 16). In this scenario, Gabby normalizes the emotional labour necessary in beauty vlogging, and ultimately discusses her experiences with mental illness to explain her failings in what can be viewed as a strategic deployment of affect.

Conclusion

To conclude, anxiety videos by high-profile beauty vloggers in the UK make visible the strategic performances of affect (Tyler et al. 2008). Vloggers are beholden to the algorithm of an online platform, an unstable environment that lends itself to panic and anxiety. Yet, the pervasiveness of the anxiety video genre and its deployment as a self-branding strategy can highlight the emotional labour, as it intersects with visibility labour, demanded of young women on YouTube. Beauty vloggers' brands are intertwined with anxiety and domesticity in their merchandise and mainstream media, assisting in their inscription as role models and pathologizing transgressions that threaten to jeopardize their brands. High-profile beauty vloggers are invested in their designations as role models (required to possess limitless positivity), thus, the anxiety video serves as a self-reflexive performance of panic, a shifting of blame, and a will to change. However, the genre simultaneously cements the idea that both deployment of a masquerade and significant emotional labour are required to justify the emotional transgressions that are made along the way.

Note

1. As a researcher looking at beauty vloggers, I was even contacted by a newspaper and asked to give a quote about how such poor behaviour encourages young girls to become escorts (I declined, obviously).

References

Abidin, Crystal. 2015. Communicative ♥ intimacies: Influencers and perceived interconnectedness. *A Journal of Gender, New Media, & Technology* 8. https://www.academia.edu/16366449/Abidin_Crystal._2015._Communicative_Intimacies_Influencers_and_Perceived_Interconnectedness._Ada_A_Journal_of_Gender_New_Media_and_Technology_8.

Abidin, Crystal. 2016. Visibility labour: Engaging with influencers' fashion brands and #OOTD advertorial campaigns on Instagram. *Media International Australia* 161 (1): 86–100.

Adamic, Lada A., and Bernardo A. Huberman. 2001. The web's hidden order. *Communications of the ACM* 44 (9): 55–60.

Ahmed, Sara. 2004. Affective economies. *Social Text* 2 (2): 117–139.

Alexander, Jonathan, and Elizabeth Losh. 2010. A YouTube of one's own? Coming out videos as rhetorical action. In *LGBT identity and online new media*, 37–50. New York: Routledge.

Ash, James. 2015. Sensation, networks, and the GIF: Toward an allotropic account of affect. In *Networked affect*, 119–133. Cambridge: MIT Press.

Banet-Weiser, Sarah. 2016. "I"m beautiful the way I am': Empowerment, beauty, and aesthetic labour. In *Aesthetic labour*, eds. Ana Sofia Elias, Rosalind Gill, and Christina Scharff, 265–282. New York, NY: Springer.

Barns, Sarah. 2015. Primark launch homeware range with YouTube star Velvet Ghost. *Mail Online*, July 24. http://www.dailymail.co.uk/femail/article-3172023/Primark-launches-homeware-range-YouTube-star-Velvet-Ghost.html.

Blogosphere Magazine. 2017. Louise Pentland: Blogosphere Magazine Issue 13. https://www.youtube.com/watch?v=AcVDcRiHuss.

Butler, Judith. 1996. Burning acts: Injurious speech. *University of Chicago Law School Roundtable* 3: 199.

Duffy, Brooke Erin. 2017. *(Not) getting paid to do what you love: Gender, social media, and aspirational work*. New Haven, CT: Yale University Press.

Estée Lalonde. 2016. Stuff you don't know about me/Estée Lalonde. https://www.youtube.com/watch?v=9EOU5qLrBSU.

Gill, R. 2007. Postfeminist media culture: Elements of a sensibility. *European Journal of Cultural Studies* 10 (2): 147–166. https://doi.org/10.1177/1367549407075898.

Gill, Rosalind. 2002. Cool, creative and egalitarian? Exploring gender in project-based new media work in Europe. *Information, Communication & Society* 5 (1): 70–89.

Gill, Rosalind. 2010. Life is a pitch: Managing the self in new media work. In *Managing media work*, ed. Mark Deuze, 249–262. London: Sage. https://www.researchgate.net/profile/Rosalind_Gill/publication/265045026_Life_is_a_pitch_Managing_the_self_in_new_media_work/links/556f207108aeccd777410af3.pdf.

Gill, Rosalind, and Ana Sofia Elias. 2014. "Awaken your incredible": Love your body discourses and postfeminist contradictions. *International Journal of Media & Cultural Politics* 10 (2): 179–188. https://doi.org/10.1386/macp.10.2.179_1.

Guru Gossip. 2016. Guru gossip • View topic—Knickerella: 280390 Days of laziness part 40, March 17. http://gurugossiper.com/viewtopic.php?cache=1&f=141&t=27283&start=25.

Hesmondhalgh, David, and Sarah Baker. 2015. Sex, gender and work segregation in the cultural industries. In *Gender and creative labour*, ed. Bridget Conor, 1st ed., 23–37. Sociological Review Monographs. Malden: Wiley-Blackwell.

Hochschild, Arlie Russell. 2012. *The managed heart: Commercialization of human feeling*, updated ed. Berkeley: University of California Press.

Jackson, S., and T. Vares. 2015. "Too many bad role models for us girls": Girls, female pop celebrities and "sexualization". *Sexualities* 18 (4): 480–498. https://doi.org/10.1177/1363460714550905.

Jenkins, Kelly. 2016. YouTube star Zoella poses in her knickers for bedtime Snapchat. *The Sun* (blog), March 22. https://www.thesun.co.uk/archives/tv/1096425/youtube-star-zoella-ditches-wholesome-image-with-bedtime-snapchat-of-her-in-her-knickers/.

Lumsden, Lottie. 2016. The secret life of Zoella. *Cosmopolitan*, November 2016.

Marwick, Alice E. 2013. *Status update: Celebrity, publicity, and branding in the social media age*. New Haven: Yale University Press.

Marwick, Alice E. 2015. You may know me from YouTube. In *A companion to celebrity*, eds Sean Redmond and P. David Marshall, 333–349. Chichester: Wiley Blackwell.

Marwick, Alice E., and danah boyd. 2011. I tweet honestly, I tweet passionately: Twitter users, context collapse, and the imagined audience. *New Media & Society* 13 (1): 114–133. https://doi.org/10.1177/1461444810365313.

McRobbie, Angela. 2000. *Feminism and youth culture*, 2nd ed. Houndmills, Basingstoke, Hampshire, and London: Palgrave Macmillan.

McRobbie, Angela. 2009. *The aftermath of feminism: Gender, culture and social change*. Los Angeles and London: Sage.

McRobbie, Angela. 2015. *Be creative: Making a living in the new culture industries*. Cambridge and Malden, MA: Polity Press.

Neff, Gina. 2012. *Venture labor: Work and the burden of risk in innovative industries*. Cambridge, MA: MIT Press.

Negra, Diane. 2009. *What a girl wants? Fantasizing the reclamation of self in postfeminism*. London and New York: Routledge.

Postigo, Hector. 2014. The socio-technical architecture of digital labor: Converting play into YouTube money. *New Media & Society*. https://doi.org/10.1177/1461444814541527.

Ringrose, Jessica, and Valerie Walkerdine. 2008. Regulating the abject: The TV make-over as site of neo-liberal reinvention toward bourgeois femininity. *Feminist Media Studies* 8 (3): 227–246. https://doi.org/10.1080/14680770802217279.

Rose, Gabriella ♡. 2015. *Honesty*. https://www.youtube.com/watch?v=X4qdIzfWAgA.

Senft, Theresa M. 2008. *Camgirls: Celebrity and community in the age of social networks* (Digital Formations, vol. 4). New York: Lang.

Skeggs, Beverley. 2003. *Class, self, culture*. London: Routledge.

Sprinkleofglitter. 2010. *The big chat | Sprinkle of glitter*. https://www.youtube.com/watch?v=zHsLV8SqT2M. Accessed 3 Jan 2017.

Tanya Burr. 2015. *Anxiety chat! | Vlogmas days 5 & 6*. https://www.youtube.com/watch?v=JVft4hBoEvQ.

Tyler, Imogen, Rebecca Coleman, and Debra Ferreday. 2008. Commentary and criticism. *Feminist Media Studies* 8 (1): 85–99. https://doi.org/10.1080/14680770801899226.

Wald, Gayle. 2002. "I want it that way": Teeny bopper music and the girling of boy bands. *Genders* 35. http://www.academia.edu/download/37010376/Wald_Genders_Teenybopper_Music_and_the_Girling_of_Boy_Bands.pdf.

Wissinger, Elizabeth. 2012. Managing the semiotics of skin tone: Race and aesthetic labor in the fashion modeling industry. *Economic and Industrial Democracy* 33 (1): 125–143. https://doi.org/10.1177/0143831X11427591.

Zoella. 2012. Dealing with panic attacks & anxiety | *Zoella*. https://www.youtube.com/watch?v=7-iNOFD27G4.

Zoella. 2015. Anxiety Q&A | *Zoella*. https://www.youtube.com/watch?v=Sjuk3WMZByo.

Zoella. 2016a. Social anxiety & prank call | *#AskZoella*. https://www.youtube.com/watch?v=h1FY1RXWSlw&t=215s.

Zoella. 2016b. The boyfriend tag | *Zoella*. https://www.youtube.com/watch?v=YMZape3gW-k.

Zoella. 2017. Who run the world? *Zoella* (blog), March 8. https://www.zoella.co.uk/2017/03/who-run-the-world.html.

CHAPTER 7

My Moshi Monster Is "Desolate": Digital Games and Affect in Neoliberal Capitalism

Natalie Coulter

My virtual pet monster named SillySoul, is "desolate", according to the online game *Moshi Monsters*. Her health rating is low, mostly because I have forgotten to feed her for months, her happiness rating is negligible and since she has no "friends" her popularity rating is at zero. All of this means that my Moshi Monster is "desolate" as the game tells me. Of course, SillySoul has also been "apathetic", "lugubrious", "despondent" and even "woebegone". My monster avatar has feelings, she has lots of feelings; complex feelings. Many of my monster's feelings are negative (unhappy) mostly because I ignore my monster, I forget to feed her and I regularly disregard opportunities to redecorate her room or buy her new items, which means I am not working towards improving her health or happiness scores. Nor does her popularity rating ever improve as I fail to connect with other players in the game.

N. Coulter (✉)
Department of Communication Studies, York University,
Toronto, ON, Canada
e-mail: ncoulter@yorku.ca

S. Driver and N. Coulter (eds.), *Youth Mediations and Affective Relations*,
https://doi.org/10.1007/978-3-319-98971-6_7

The game itself tells me regularly that I can "buy items and decorate my room to make [my] monster happy", activities that allow a player to keep their avatar's health and happiness scores up, ideally to 999. I can do this by playing games, winning points (called "Rox") and then purchasing items. One of the goals of the game is to maintain a good mood by keeping these ratings high, and if I don't my Moshi monster will be in a bad mood, "desolate" or "bleak". If I do buy items I can make my monster, "chirpy", "fantabulous" and even "elated". Essentially SillySoul becomes the thesaurus entry for happy.

Worrying about the emotional state of a pet monster avatar may seem like a frivolous endeavour, but I would like to suggest that it allows for an entry point into the affective modalities of children's digital cultures. This paper will use *Moshi Monsters*, as form of children's media, to question the mediatized and affective pedagogies that are embedded within the online game. The purpose of this paper is to extend the theorization of the affective spaces of tween girls in the current moment of neoliberal capitalism.

Moshi Monsters: A Children's Entertainment Brand

I am not alone in my quest for my monster's happiness. Since its creation in 2007 by the entertainment company Mind Candy, *Moshi Monsters* became one of the world's most popular online games for 6- to 14-year olds in 2013, with over 90 million registered players in over 150 territories worldwide (Mind Candy 2013). The creator of *Moshi Monsters*, Michael Acton Smith's hope was "to build the largest entertainment brand in the world for this new digital generation of kids" (Blanchard 2011). Since 2013, the game has declined and the company faced receivership, but in late 2017 was trying to rebound with a new digital strategy with the development of a mobile app called Egg Hunt. It is unclear at the time of writing this paper if this will be a successful rebound.

The game-themed virtual world is a massively multiplayer online game (MMOG). *Moshi Monsters* has spanned a series of other media properties; a top children's magazine, a series of books, a movie released in 2013. There was a whole slew of character licenses, toys and collectibles, along with licensing deals with both McDonalds and Kinder Surprise. At its height in 2013, Moshi Monsters had more than 130 licensing partners worldwide and had sold 80 million collectable Moshi figurines produced by licensing partner Vivid (Mind Candy 2013). The company generates income in a myriad of ways beyond these products; there are the premium memberships through monthly subscriptions fees that allow players to upgrade in order to gain access to more digital spaces in the game and there are also the lucrative possibilities to sell data to third-party users.

The quick rise in its popularity and its even quicker fall, follows a similar trajectory to other child centred MMOGs such as *Neopets, Webkinz* or *Club Penguin*. It would be easy to dismiss *Moshi Monsters* as simply a fad, and not worthy of study, but such an approach undervalues young people's digital cultures. *Moshi Monsters* does offer insight into the affective spaces of children's digital capitalism, as the marketplace ebbs and flows. As an intellectual property, *Moshi Monsters* is fairly gendered and aged. While the company does not overtly claim that it is geared to girls. It does have a girl aesthetic and fits within tween girl culture targeting girls in the age range of 6- to 14-years old. The tween is an aged-based market segment lodged in the liminal spaces between the child and the teenager (Coulter 2014).

The goals of the game are ultimately to be a successful monster; one at a high level (achieved by playing games), with a high "Monstar" rating (based on popularity and engagement with other Monsters), a highly decorated room and with lots of pets called Moshlings (these can be bought with points/Rox), a high number of Rox available to spend which all lead to high happiness and health ratings which means my monster will be in a good mood—"buoyant", "ebullient" and "genial". Sentiments as "desolation", "lugubriousness" and "apathy" are tantamount to losing. While the game does not have overt signifiers of winning such as a live/die goal or a ranking of being in first place, the purpose of the game is to avoid negative feelings, which can be done, the game tells me regularly on a pop-up reminder over my low score, by buying things to decorate my Moshi Monster's room or buying food at the "grossery" store it to improve my monster's health.

While Moshi is not specifically a girl's game, it is clearly orientated to a feminine consuming subject, and as the company who owns *Moshi Monsters*, Mind Candy, indicates in its promotional literature it is a largely girl audience. The aesthetics of the game are coded as feminine; the colours, for example, are bright and vibrant, with lots of splashes of pink. Most of the accessories that can be "bought" in the game are coded as female; necklaces, high heel shoes, feather boas. The girliness of the game is sticky. The girl is an affective state. It is an embodied knowledge, an experience and a "collective of feelings" (Swiddle 2011, para. 10). It "sticks" to objects and people as it circulates. *Moshi Monsters* is a node in the circulation of girliness and as a node the sticky girliness is stuck to the imagined player of the game, who is imagined as a post-feminist subject. Post-feminist subjectivity is premised on relentless individualism, sense of self entitlement and modes of self expression through the consumer marketplace (Banet-Wiser 2015; Gill 2017).

Moshi Monsters: Neoliberal Capitalism in Disguise

In playing this game, I am struck by how much the "owning a monster" actually looks like the mundane practices of neoliberal capitalism. The purpose of the game is for the player to own her/his own monster and perform tasks to acquire "Rox", which are the currency of the game. To acquire Rox, the player must perform games or tasks that pay out a certain number of Rox. An example of these tasks include making pizza in the food factory complete with eyeball toppings, and live "yeasties" in the crust. Or serving "ice scream" cones at the Ice Scream shop. A description of this game is given by the owner of the shop who proclaims "You must make Ice Screams for my customers as fast as you can! Meet your target to earn a portion of the takings and proceed to the next day!" Such tasks clearly mimic the deskilled labour of capitalism. In some instances, part of the gamification of the task is intensified in ways that imitate the perpetual exploitations of labour by neoliberal capitalist demands where more and more work is expected of the worker. The pizza machine may speed up too fast, or in the case of the Ice Scream shop, the customer's demands become more intense without any help from other employees/players. The player as a worker, is expected to make ice screams faster and faster until they can no longer keep up, and they fail, with the game ending, and Rox are accumulated, the owner gets most of them, but the player gets to keep a small per cent. This is not such a different scenario from the neoliberal workplace in which workers are pressured to perform labour under increasingly exploitative demands with little reward.

In *Moshi Monsters*, it is not the game play (or work) that improves the happiness and health scores, it is the purchasing of items from stores which are cute takes on the real marketplace, stores such as like "Yukea" (a play on Ikea) and "Horrods" (Harrods) Store". It's the purchasing and using/collecting the item (the consumption) that instantly increases a monster's happiness and health ratings to high, and thus improves the overall mood of the monster. Unlike other more adult MMOGs where players can trade items for in game profit, *Moshi Monsters* follows the pattern of many other children's MMOGs in that players cannot make in game trades (Grimes 2015). Thus, the purchasing of virtual items is more about collecting and accumulation than participating in the virtual economy of the game. The game provides ample opportunities to showcase these accumulations in the monster's virtual spaces. Virtual commodities can be moved, reorganized, and reconfigured as part of game play. In such play, *Moshi Monster's* like other children's MMOGs, encourage players to "participate in the celebration of the commodity form through a collaborative enactment, and performance of consumer subjectivities" (Grimes 2015, p. 127). I will return to this performance of consumer subjectivity later in the chapter.

The seemingly ludic play for the game requires a constant vigilance of my moshi's ratings which are always in flux. Every game I play, every task I undertake, every new friend I add to my *Moshi* network immediately impacts my ratings, which in turn change SillySoul's mood. My ratings are listed at the side of my homepage in the game, and I am reminded of them often as I play. My monster, like the self that Gidden's references in late modernity, is a project which requires constant self-surveillance, to be continuously reflected upon and worked upon. Giddens suggests that self-identity is not a complex set of traits or characteristics that can be revealed, but instead is a reflexive understanding of one's own biography (Giddens 1991, p. 53). The game, in essence, continually reveals SillySoul's biography in the form of ratings. And the solutions to improve the biography/ratings come from the marketplace, forged within the logics of consumer capitalism, to "buy more goods to make [me] happy", as the game dictates. As such, *Moshi Monsters* is this further extension of selfhood in neoliberal capitalism. The self is perpetually monitored, to be worked upon, but only within the confines of the games structures.

This focus on the self, is part of a broader trend in which media, like the Moshi Monsters game, "have become increasingly central to the biopolitical operations of neoliberalism in intimate, commercial, and public life, where structures of individualization have produced the *self* as 'subject of interest'" (Gill and Kanai 2018, p. 318). The monster self is a subject of interest, and an individualized subject. The desolation of my monster is only experienced by my individual monster, there is no option for social misery, nor are there options for resistance. The 90 million monsters living in MonstroCity (the virtual city of the game) do not work together, nor do they share affective experiences. They are isolated individuals who can connect as Monster friends and increase each other's popularity, but they never work together to complete the capitalistic goals of participating in the Monster economy of MonstroCity, such as by buying more food and buying new room decorations. Thus, the socialness of this game is an illusion. It is an example, of how the logics of capitalism undercut social bonds (Berlant 2011). The game appears to be social, it calls itself a social game in its promotional material. And yet, what is social, is really not social at all, nor is it a commitment to the communal, instead it is a neoliberalized version of social, where the social is really an interest in the self. Seemingly social bonds are instead avenues for accumulation of connections (that translate into popularity points) and opportunities for comparison. The intense individualism of the game tied to self-surveillance and the power of the marketplace allow for the game to be read as a form of post-feminist media.

Moshi Monsters: Digital Affect Culture

Moshi Monsters reveals how emotion is a discursively constructed cultural practice. The emotions registered in the game are not extensions of the emotions of the players, but instead are the prescribed moods that correlate to high ratings. In the game, emotional sensations are rooted in the affects of material conditions that can easily be changed with the simple actions of buying food and buying items to decorate my monster's room. The emotional sensations are also rooted in raising my Monstar rating,—essentially my popularity rating based on how many friends I have.

Moshi Monsters is part of what Döverling, Harju and Sommer (2018) call "digital affect cultures", which are "characterized by the emotional alignment that gives rise to feelings of belonging". In this paper, I am not exploring the feeling of belonging that is experienced by the player, but instead how it is articulated as located within the virtual character. The feeling of belonging attached to the avatar is "a simulacrum" to use Baudrillard's term, of feeling. Recognizing the post-humanist logics of such a perspective, this paper is interested in how emotion is harnessed as affective articulations of game play. Since affect is a cultural practice, that is beyond the individual and is instead an embodied practice of moving within the world (Döverling, Harju and Sommer 2018). The game positions emotion at the core.

Affective capitalism "is a mode of production where systems of organizing production and distribution rely on the capacities of *different bodies*, human and non-human, to encounter each other. These encounters and the relations that emerge are surrounded by a vast array of technologies that produce, capture valourise, commodify and eventually attempt to transform them into different modes of capital" (Karppi 2016, p. 10).

Moshi Monsters and the Quest for Happiness

The goals of the game for a successful life for my monster can be read through Sara Ahmed's work "Queer Phenomenology" (2006). Ahmed explains that "for a life to count as a good life, it must return the debt of life by taking on the direction promised as a social good, which means imagining one's futurity in terms of reaching certain points along a life course" (2006, p. 554)—marriage, children, etc. While the Moshi Monster life course is not so neatly laid out along a temporal line; a "path well-trodden" as Ahmed suggests, as the steps do not need to be taken in a linear order. Instead, the player must make their monster complete a multitude of tasks that the game offers, such as playing mini-games solving puzzles, completing digital art and finding secret codes, that all achieve the signifiers of "a good life" (to use Ahmed's terminology) as outlined above.

The promise, that the game offers, if the tasks are completed, is to have high scores and ratings—high levels, high popularity ratings, and most importantly high health and happiness ratings. There is no room in the game for deviation, or to queer this path by "disturbing the order of things" (Ahmed 2006, p. 565). Instead, the game offers the promise of happiness if the player follows the game's narrow choices. Happiness, Ahmed suggests is a "promise that directs us towards certain life choices" (2010, p. 29). It is promised to those "who live their lives in the right way" (2010, p. 29). The game is essentially a literal translation of this. To follow the game's directions, in essence to "live the right way", is to have the monster's happiness ratings increase and overall mood to improve.

What is so fascinating about the Moshi Monster game is how happiness is one of the main goals of the game. The quest for happiness occurs in two ways, first each monster has a happiness rating that needs to constantly be kept up, or it slides down to zero, it does not quite die, but it is idle until being rebooted. This can be done through buying virtual commodities such as a “slime rickey”, acquiring pets called “moshlings”, and sending gifts to friends. The quest for happiness also figures in that one of the goals of the game is for the monster to be in a perpetually positive (happy) mood. Having happiness as a goal of play, at the heart of a digital game for girls, is not a surprise. *Moshi Monsters* is part of the broader structures of girls’ cultural industries in which happiness, often embodied as fun, is the only affective possibility for girls. The girl must be in a state of constant happiness or fun, or else she disrupts the balance of the status quo.

Sara Ahmed’s work *Promise of Happiness* provides a provocative lens to explore the cultural demands to be happy. “Happiness is a duty,” Ahmed writes (2010, p. 59). The duty is to avoid unhappiness by articulating disappointment with the status quo. Maintaining one’s own happiness, allows others to maintain theirs. Ahmed explores how the duty of the child is to perform happiness for their parents. This is the logics of deferral, in which the parents give up their happiness to ensure the future happiness of their children. “I just want you to be happy”, parents tell their children. The child’s duty is to then make the parents happy by performing happiness (Ahmed 2010, p. 59). The duty to perform happiness can be a conditional tool used to justify social oppression. Happiness is an affective acquiescence to the current social and political conditions.

Building on feminist cultural studies, Ahmed argues that happiness is promised to those who commit to living their life in an unchallenging way that does not upset the status quo (2010). It is the promise that is important here. Happiness is promised to those who maintain the status quo. The promise of happiness is political in that it reinforces and retains current political systems of exploitation. Ahmed uses the figure of the happy housewife as a means to maintain patriarchal capitalism. The housewife, she suggests, is a fantasy figure that “erases the signs of labour under the signs of happiness” (Ahmed 2010, p. 50). Her happiness “functions to justify gendered forms of labour, not as products of nature, law or duty, but as an expression of a collective wish and desire” (Ahmed 2010, p. 50). “How better”, she asks “then to justify the unequal division of labour than to say that such labour makes people happy?” (Ahmed 2010, p. 50). The feminists who call out the unhappiness of this inequality kill joy and become the feminist killjoy.

Ahmed’s reading of these figures of the happy housewife and feminist killjoy is useful in understanding *Moshi Monsters* as part of a girl’s cultural industry that expects girls to constantly perform the affective and moral work of happiness. As I argue elsewhere, the perpetual media discourse for girls to be happy, to constantly perform the embodiment of happiness, laughing and smiling, functions as a means to depoliticize girlhood and frame girls as ideal neoliberal subjects (Coulter forthcoming).

My *Moshi Monster's* desolation is sign a failure, that I am losing in the game. Each time the ratings slide low, the game reminds me that I can improve this rating by buying things to make my monster happy. The overt logics of the affective features of capitalism could not be more obvious. The virtual commodities provide direct and immediate emotional impacts on my monster, and solve the problem of my Monster's unhappiness, which is a problem that needs to be solved.

This fits within the logics of neoliberal capitalism, the game problems are solved through individual actions. My monster, like the postfeminist subject describe by Rosalind Gill, is solely responsible for creating her own happiness (2017). Monster's in the game do not work together. They are no adventures or problems to be solve by a group of monsters. The monsters live alone, and have their own gardens. The social components of the game are really only chatting with each other through a social media type of interface. Or visiting each other's rooms, and seeing each other's ratings, levels and, of course, moods. The social connections are mostly to compare with each other and not to work together. This is the basis of the neoliberal subject, of individualism tied to market fundamentalism, where the boundaries between civil society and the market have been dissolved. Not only does the monster work as an independent subject but it is the marketplace that provides solutions.

Ahmed asks us to consider how "claims to happiness make certain forms of personhood valuable" (Ahmed 2010, p. 11). It is happiness that makes girls' personhood valuable. Happiness validates the girls being and her happiness is to make others happy. "Smile", girls are constantly told as a happy girl is a pretty girl. We can recall Audrey Hepburn's famous quote "happy girls are the prettiest girls" that is reiterated in the post-feminist marketplace on t-shirts, pillow cases and the shiny covers of paper journals. And, of course, it is also surfaces as a meme, a pinterest board and a tumblr. Prettiness for girls is what renders the girl into being. It gives her subjectivity. Other girls are invisible and not present. It is only the pretty girl that has legitimacy and is allowed to take up space. The affective state of prettiness is happy. Unhappy girls are not to be pretty, and unpretty girls are not to be happy.

Feelings of anger, frustration or desolation are political sentiments. Ahmed writes that "the freedom to be unhappy would be the freedom to be affected by what is unhappy, and to live a life that might affect others unhappily" (Ahmed 2010, p. 195). These are feelings that register the "injurious nature of neoliberal capitalism" (Gill 2017, p. 619) and in doing inhibit the happiness of others who rely the girl's happiness; the same girls for whom happiness is duty. Unhappiness, or complaint as Lauren Berlant has shown, is ugly (Berlant 2008). It is both "psychologically and aesthetically unappealing" (Gill 2017, p. 619). Unhappiness deviates from the post-feminist script in which women, who are responsible for their own happiness and emancipation, need to think positively and be inspired to make change. In the game, it is even simpler for my monster. There is no need to think positively, or to find sources of empowerment from the marketplace, all my monster needs to do is to simply purchase virtual commodities. The solution is direct, immediate, simple and easily available to all monsters.

The game offers what Lauren Berlant might call a "cluster of promises" for my monster; the promise of an easily achieved good life, the promise of happiness through the hedonistic accumulation of commodities, and the promise that individualism and neoliberal subjectivity is tantamount to winning, to name a few. The clusters of promises weave themselves into the haptic spaces of the game. The cruel optimism of *Moshi Monsters* is that it offers a virtual promise of a good life that is not possible outside of the game. For Berlant, a "cruel optimism exists when something you desire is actually an obstacle to your flourishing" (Berlant 2010, p. 94). Heather Latimer offers an eloquent explanation of Berlant's cruel optimism. It is that we "attach ourselves to promises of future happiness through the institutions and practices that diminish us" (Latimer 2013, p. 23). Moshi Monsters is part of the pedagogical structures of neoliberal capitalism, that offer promises of happiness, but in the end are really narratives of individualism and acquiescence to the status quo.

As I write this, my monster SillySoul sits there, alone in her game space, waiting for me to show up and feed her, and take her to the store, so she can improve her ratings and levels. She is desolate, and lonely, but I don't have time for her. Her desolation reveals the affective pedagogies of *Moshi Monsters* that naturalize and reify the post-feminist imperatives of neoliberal capitalism. I highly doubt that this was the vision of Michael Acton Smith, when he had a vision of designing the next great children's entertainment property. But that is how neoliberal capitalism functions. Its logics and rhythms are baked into the machinations of seemingly frivolous cultural spaces.

Bibliography

Ahmed, Sara. 2006. *Queer phenomenology: Orientations, objects, others*. Durham, NC: Duke University Press.

Ahmed, Sara. 2010. *The promise of happiness*. Durham, NC: Duke University Press.

Banet-Weiser, Sarah. 2015. 'Confidence you can carry!': Girls in crisis and the market for girls' empowerment organizations. *Continuum: Journal of Media and Cultural Studies* 29 (2): 182–193.

Berlant, Lauren. 2008. *The female complaint: The unfinished business of sentimentality in American culture*. Durham, NC: Duke University Press.

Berlant, Lauren. 2010. Cruel optimism. In *The affect theory reader*, ed. Melissa Gregg and Gregory J. Seigworth. London and Durham, NC: Duke University Press.

Berlant, Lauren. 2011. *Cruel optimism*. Durham, NC: Duke University Press.

Blanchard, Tamsin. 2011. The man who gave birth to Moshi Monsters. *The Daily Telegraph*, July 15. http://subscriber.telegraph.co.uk/technology/8637342/The-man-who-gave-birth-to-Moshi-Monsters.html.

Coulter, Natalie. 2014. *Tweening the girl: The crystallization of the tween market*. New York, NY: Peter Lang.

Coulter, Natalie. forthcoming. Frappés, friends and fun. Affective labour and the cultural industries of girlhood. *Journal of Consumer Culture*.

Döverling, Katrin, Any Harju, and Denise Sommer. 2018. From mediatized emotion to digital affect cultures: New technologies and global flows of emotion. *Social Media + Society* (January–March): 1–11.

Giddens, Anthony. 1991. *Modernity and self-identity: Self and society in the late modern age*. Stanford: *Stanford University Press*.

Gill, Rosalind. 2017. The affective, cultural and psychic life of postfeminism: A postfeminist sensibility 10 years on. *European Journal of Cultural Studies* 20 (6): 606–626.

Gill, Rosalind, and Akane Kanai. 2018. Mediating neoliberal capitalism: Affect, subjectivity and inequality. *Journal of Communication* 68 (2): 318–326.

Grimes, Sara. 2015. Playing by the market rules: Promotional priorities and commercialization in children's virtual worlds. *Journal of Consumer Culture* 15 (1): 110–134.

Hutchins, Robert. 2017. The comeback kings: Mind Candy and the return of Moshi Monsters. *Licensing Biz*. http://www.licensing.biz/big-interviews/read/the-comeback-kings-mind-candy-and-the-return-of-moshi-monsters/046345.

Karppi, Tero, et al. 2016. Affective capitalism: Investments and investigation. *Ephemera: Theory & Politics in Organization* 16 (4). http://www.ephemera-journal.org/sites/default/files/pdfs/contribution/16-4editorial.pdf.
Latimer, Heather. 2013. The straight line: Sexuality, futurity and the politics of austerity. *English Studies in Canada* 39 (December 4): 21–34.
Mind Candy. 2013. Moshi Monsters fast facts. http://mindcandy.com/blog.
Swindle, Monica. 2011. Feeling girl, girling feeling: An examination of 'girl' as affect. *Rhizomes* 22. http://www.rhizomes.net/issue22/swindle.html.

CHAPTER 8

Queer Girls and Mashups: Archiving Ephemerality

Whitney Monaghan

Queer teen characters have long occupied a position of marginality in film and television. However, the development of new technologies has created an expanse of new spaces for queer audiences to both find representation and represent themselves. No longer limited to traditional screen spaces (cinema or television), screen queerness now seems abundant on video-sharing websites including YouTube, Tumblr and Vimeo where new forms including mashup, remix and vlog are particularly popular amongst youth audiences.

To explore the representation of queer girlhood within this new media landscape, this chapter examines a series of queer-themed mashup videos sourced from YouTube. These videos, all titled "Lesbians from TV/Film," are constructed entirely from pre-existing footage and are described by their creator as "a compilation of girl-on-girl scenes" from television and film. In each video, scenes featuring the queer girl characters of films and television series from the 1990s to the early 2000s are edited together with music to convey a particular narrative or theme. Though source screen materials vary, many of the videos include fan-favourite scenes from

W. Monaghan (✉)
Film and Screen Studies, Monash University, Melbourne, VIC, Australia

S. Driver and N. Coulter (eds.), *Youth Mediations and Affective Relations*,
https://doi.org/10.1007/978-3-319-98971-6_8

Bad Girls (1999–2006), *Buffy the Vampire Slayer* (1997–2013), *But I'm a Cheerleader* (Jamie Babbit, 1999), *D.E.B.S* (Angela Robinson, 2004), *Fingersmith* (Aisling Walsh, 2005), *If These Walls Could Talk* 2 (Jane Anderson, Martha Coolidge, and Anne Heche, 2000), *Lost and Delirious* (Léa Pool, 2001) and *The L Word* (2004–2009).

To illuminate how mashup practices including video compilation can shed new light on personal investments in queer screen representation, in this chapter, I propose reading these video texts through Ann Cvetkovich's theory of "archives of feeling" (2002, 2003). As I demonstrate through this chapter, such a reading can highlight the power of mashup videos as a fan-led archive and a means of holding on to fleeting moments of screen teen queerness.

Queer Teens on Screen

The teen genre is well known for its combination of affect-driven drama and cutting social criticism. Through this, the teen-oriented media can provide a unique perspective on the world and function as a "means to interrogate contemporary cultural ideologies" (Bolte 2008, p. 94). The teen genre thus holds "great promise" for screening "lives, desires and issues that are often ignored, stymied or cursorily treated" by screen media (Davis 2004, p. 131). Davis (2004) asserts that the teen genre is especially apt for the representation of queer youth. However, for as long as I can remember, I have been aware of the marginal and ephemeral place occupied by queer youth on screen.

The Gay and Lesbian Alliance Against Defamation (GLAAD) regularly conduct research on queer TV culture in the United States. Their annual *Where We Are on TV Report* provides one of the most comprehensive content analyses of queer representation on television. Though focusing on a North American context, their reports, for the past decade, have found that queer representation is increasing—approximately 3–4% of regular/recurring characters on broadcast primetime television are explicitly identified as gay, lesbian or bisexual, and that cable and streaming series contain more LGBT representations. Despite these increases, trans and gender diverse characters remain rarities within the contemporary media landscape (GLAAD 2016b).

LGBT figures continue to be marginalised within other Western screen cultures. While Canada's *Media Action Media* (2012) highlighted that "non-stereotypical portrayals and constructions of gay/lesbian/bisexual/

transgender characters are beginning to emerge in Canadian dramatic television programs," Cumberbatch et al. (2014) study of diversity on UK television noted just 1% of the figures on TV were identified as lesbian, gay or bisexual. In Australia, *Screen Australia* has also sought to quantify gender and sexual diversity on screen. Their *Seeing Ourselves* report of 2016 identified 88 characters from the LGBTI spectrum in television drama programs broadcast between 2011 and 2015 (Screen Australia 2016, pp. 17–18). This made up 5% of broadcast characters. The majority of these were gay male characters (62 of 88 characters) and, for many, their LGBT status was "incidental rather than pivotal to the storyline."

Queer adolescent characters make up only a small fraction of these numbers because, historically, televisual representations of queer sexuality have been limited to adult characters. While representations of gender and sexual diversity have increased from the 1970s onwards, there were only four major queer adolescent characters on U.S. network television between 1980 and 2000 (Monaghan 2012). This is discussed at length in studies that trace developments in televisual representations of sexual and gender diversity (Becker 2006; Capsuto 2001; Chambers 2009; Gross 2001; Tropiano 2002).

Queer cinema is a little more difficult to comment on, as it is less often subject to the same type of systematic content analysis. In addition, many queer films are independently produced and distributed, achieving brief festival release and generating little critical buzz afterwards. Of course, adding to this is the fact that the term "queer cinema" has multiple meanings. A film's queerness could arise from its content, authorship, or spectatorship.

Since 2013, GLAAD has reported on the quality and diversity of LGBT representation in mainstream cinema. Their *2016 Studio Responsibility Index* found that 17.5% of films released by the major U.S. studios (Warner Brothers, Twentieth Century Fox, Lionsgate Entertainment, Paramount Pictures, Universal Pictures, Sony Columbia Pictures and The Walt Disney Studio) included characters that were identified as lesbian, gay or bisexual, but that the majority of these were minor characters or cameos (GLAAD 2016a). As with television, queer youth make up only a small fraction of these figures. Rebecca Beirne's study (2012) of representation in international lesbian cinema also reflects this. Writing in 2012, Beirne identifies an increasing volume of queer films while simultaneously pointing to the marginality of youth representation. Despite noting clear increases in cinematic representation, Beirne only locates 27 feature films focusing on same-sex-attracted female adolescents in the period spanning 1931–2007.

By all accounts, when queer youth are depicted via film and television, their sexuality and gender identity is made visible through narrow stereotypes and brief storylines. Queer characters are typically depicted as sidekicks rather than protagonists, and in series such as *Degrassi Junior High* (1987–1989), *Dawson's Creek* (1998–2003), *The OC* (2003–2007), *One Tree Hill* (2003–2012) and *Neighbours* (1985–present), they are introduced as an issue to be dealt with and are forgotten soon after. These characters operate almost exclusively within the coming-out narrative, a mode that represents little of gay life beyond the confessional climax (Allen 1995; Davis 2004; Driver 2007; McCarthy 2001; Monaghan 2016). Historically, such characters have been written out of their respective series at the conclusion of their storylines.

In other examples, queer romances are nostalgically remembered, but long lost as in the "memorial mode of representation" discussed in Fran Martin's *Backward Glances: Contemporary Chinese Cultures and the Female Homoerotic Imaginary* (2010). In this mode, queerness is accessed via memory and can only ever exist in the past. When queer desire does exist in the narrative present, as in films such as *Cruel Intentions* (Roger Kumble, 1999), it is represented as part of an experiment or "phase," where same-sex desire is positioned as "just practise" for heterosexual desire. In other cases, it is a product of youthful rebellion and fuelled by drug or alcohol intoxication—as in the films *Thirteen* (Catherine Hardwicke, 2003) and *The Runaways* (Floria Sigismondi, 2010). Then again, queerness can also emerge as a simple distraction from the elongated temporality of teenage boredom as in *My Summer of Love* (Pawel Pawlikowski, 2004).

Drawing attention to the marginality of queer characters, Beirne argues, "when we sit down to watch…entertainment [media], we hope to see some element of our lives reflected, responded to, turned into news or comedy or melodrama for our collective consumption and catharsis" (2008, p. 2). Overwhelmingly, this does not occur for queer viewers, leading Beirne to lament a lack of queer representation. Yet, as queer theorist Jose Muñoz emphasises, the ephemerality of representation forms the very core of queer culture. In fact, Muñoz locates ephemerality as one of the defining features of queerness itself, writing the following:

> Instead of being clearly available as visible evidence, queerness has instead existed as innuendo, gossip, fleeting moments, and performances that are

> meant to be interacted with by those within its epistemological sphere – while evaporating at the touch of those who would eliminate queer possibility. (1996, p. 6)

The importance of representation, ephemeral or not, cannot be understated. All audiences want access to representations that reflect their desires and identities, but queer audiences in particular have been known for their passionate consumption of screen content. As Beirne suggests, "the relative absence of queer characters… has made queer representations, when they do occur, all the more significant, sparking a profound investment in these images" (2008, p. 2).

Mashup

With the development of new technologies, once marginalised queer characters are no longer limited to traditional screens. Representations now seem abundant on video-sharing websites and other digital spaces. The mashup is an emerging form of queer video in these subaltern digital arenas. Julie Levin Russo highlights the proliferation of Internet video in the millennial era, drawing attention to this form, as part of a boom in "user-generated media" (2009, p. 125). Russo (2009) attributes this to an increased "ease of posting, finding, watching, and sharing videos," the popularity of native video capture and editing tools, and finally, the digitisation of mass media, which has enabled users to appropriate and manipulate commercial texts. In many cases, mashup videos contain a queer theme (creating narratives of same-sex romance); however, Russo also draws attention to the innate queerness of this form. She argues that "whatever their explicit themes and narratives, they represent a queer form of production that mates supposedly incompatible parents… to spawn hybrid offspring" (2009, p. 126). A series of YouTube videos titled "Lesbians from TV/Film," created in 2007 by the user Pezza87, provide a good example of this. Described by their creator as "a compilation of girl-on-girl scenes," they harness the form to interrogate queer representation in film and television from the 1990s onward.

The first volume of the "Lesbians from TV/Film" series is described as "a compilation of girl-on-girl scenes" from television and film. The video begins with an archetypal image from the teen genre; a shot of two girls standing at a row of lockers in a high school. After a brief dialogue, the girls laugh and walk off screen, as the image pixelates and dissolves into a shot of one woman massaging another. With this transition, the soundtrack commences. Constructed around an acoustic pop song titled "A Kiss Without Commitment," performed by the artist Daniel Bedingfield, this video spans three minutes in duration and consists entirely of short clips featuring girls and women kissing. While there are adult figures throughout the video, the visual materials are sourced primarily from the teen genre.

In creating "Lesbians from TV/Film," the user Pezza87 has edited and reassembled a vast array of existing screen content. The process of re-editing has long been examined by the disciplines of both media and film studies. Key approaches of these two critical paradigms are surveyed in *Queer Girls, Temporality and Screen Media: Not 'Just a Phase'*, but to briefly summarise, both media and film theory approach digitally re-edited content through existing forms of cultural production, aesthetic traditions, and practices (Monaghan 2016). Within media criticism, re-edited videos are often considered in relation to fan and fandom studies. Following the work of Henry Jenkins and other media studies scholars, re-edited video works have been read as examples of fandom practice. Viewed as an extension of fan-fiction, made possible by more recent digital and media convergence, the practice of editing clips from film and television to music is referred to within such frameworks as "vidding," and has been discussed extensively within media criticism as a fan-driven activity. This term was coined by Jenkins in 1992, when he described groups of television fans using VCRS to appropriate footage, "and re-edit it to express their particular slant on the program, linking series images to music similarly appropriated from commercial culture" (p. 230). More recently, Francesca Coppa (2008) has located vids as visual essays, arguing that each "stages an argument." As Tisha Turk and Joshua Johnson (2012) point out, this argument exists in relation to a vast ecology of "multiple overlapping discourse communities" that constitute fandom. Drawing attention to their creation and consumption, Tisha Turk locates such videos as a means of "collaborative interpretation" of media texts (2010, p. 89). Re-edited videos have also been considered through Jay David Bolter and Richard Grusin's concept of "remediation," as they are composed of refashioned or "re-mediated" fragments of screen media (1999, p. 45). As Turk and Johnson (2012) argue, though media scholarship has tended to focus on the idea of "fans as spectators," rather than producers of such content. The result, as Deborah Kaplan observes, is a field of inquiry that often "elides the texts in favor of the community" (2006, p. 135).

Considered through the lens of film and screen theory, the focus shifts away from communities towards analysis of texts. Within film studies, re-edited videos are often theorised via the practices of the avant-garde and subsequently read as experimental films. Such videos are viewed as products of an artist's creative treatment of found footage or as works that experiment with both form and content. What has most interested me about videos, such as Pezza87's "Lesbians from TV/Film" series, is that their creator seems to occupy the positions of fan and filmmaker simultaneously. From these positions, creators engage with screen media in unique ways. Within these videos, visual data are removed from the original context, re-edited and re-contextualised. The music plays a vital role, providing a means of constructing new queer narratives around the source content. Paul Booth argues that videos of this nature should not be viewed as re-writings of existing media objects, but instead as re-imaginings (2010, p. 35). If we are to follow his lead, it is imperative that we question what is being imagined by "Lesbians from TV/Film" and other mashup videos.

Screen and Queer Archives

The "Lesbians from TV/Film" series highlights how mashup provides a means of holding on to important cultural information and, thus, operates as a form of queer archival practice. For instance, in the first video, the video pixelates after the opening archetypal teen image and dissolves through a range of "girl-on-girl scenes" from television and film.

Significantly, the two girls from the opening shot are sourced from the third season of *Once and Again* (1999–2002), a series that featured one of television's first ongoing queer girl storylines. Other segments within this video are sourced from *Bad Girls* (1999–2006), *Buffy the Vampire Slayer* (1997–2013), *But I'm a Cheerleader* (Jamie Babbit, 1999), *D.E.B.S* (Angela Robinson, 2004), *Fingersmith* (Aisling Walsh, 2005), *If These Walls Could Talk* 2 (Jane Anderson, Martha Coolidge, and Anne Heche, 2000), *Lost and Delirious* (Léa Pool, 2001) and *The L Word* (2004–2009). The soundtrack is simple, containing only the warm sounds of Bedingfield's voice and an acoustic guitar. In each of the clips, the figures come together in the centre of the frame, before they begin to kiss. This set up is repeated throughout the video, with the editing emphasising the kiss and the moment beforehand. This repeated rhythmic movement perfectly matches the tempo of the music. The fragments are not assembled according to a discernible logic, chronological, linear, or otherwise. Instead, they move along with the melody of the soundtrack, providing a broad, non-linear history of queer girls and women on screen, according to the creator.

The second volume in this series shifts the focus to eroticism, and is described as "a collection of girl-on-girl action." This video begins with a moment of darkness that quickly cuts to a group of college-aged girls walking together through a corridor. Following the format of the previous video, a short segment of dialogue precedes the compilation of clips and frames the mashup. After this dialogue, the image fades to white and an electric guitar emerges on the soundtrack. This video is constructed around a punk pop song titled "Dirty Little Secret" by The All American Rejects. Despite the similarities in form, the soundtrack renders this mashup distinctive from the previous video by emphasising the eroticism of queer girlhood as a primary theme. Throughout the video, images from popular film and television are fragmented, as hands grasp other hands, faces, bodies; tears and sweat and rain all combine as lips are forcefully and passionately pressed against other lips.

Mid-way through this video, *The OC*'s Marissa and Alex share a slowed down, extended kiss. A few moments later, several seasons worth of subtext between Xena and Gabrielle in *Xena* is forced to the surface when it is coupled with the lyric, "I'll keep you my dirty little secret." Through this, the mashup transforms the singular and fleeting queer moments from each of the source materials into one extended, sexually charged moment, interrogating the "dirty little secret" of queer desire from numerous angles.

This mashup contains a stronger narrative than the previous video in the series, concluding with several shots of secret queer relationships being revealed. Again and again, the video presents images of girls kissing and then being caught by a friend, a parent, or a bystander. Exposing and emphasising queer desire, this mashup makes visible the silenced, hidden from view and inaccessible experiences of queer girls in contemporary screen culture. There is, however, another desire at play within this video; a desire to hold on to, to collect and to archive film and television's ephemeral images of queer girls and women.

In her examination of cinematic time, Mary Ann Doane (2002) discusses a similar archival desire within early cinematic forms. Discussing early films, including the famous footage of workers leaving the Lumiere factory, Doane argues:

> While photography could fix a moment, the cinema made archivable duration itself. In that sense it was perceived as a prophylactic against death, ensuring the ability to "see one's loved ones" gesture and smile long after their deaths. (p. 16)

As Doane highlights, film was considered valuable because it was perceived as an inscription of time itself, a record of what happens in front of the camera, as cinema could capture "a once-present and unique moment, the signature of temporality" (p. 16). While screen media has undoubtedly evolved from the early moments that Doane discusses, there is a lot to be gained in considering the future of media forms through their past. Considered through Doane's work on film, time and archive, mashup can be viewed as a collection of fragments and symbols of media, memory, sound, image and time. Although digital video no longer inscribes temporality in the same manner as early cinema, mashup is based upon an archival desire to hold on to moments of screen time that have already passed.

Catherine Russell (1999) explores a similar relation between experimental filmmaking and temporality. She describes found footage films (made from pre-existing content) as having "an aesthetic of ruins" because their "intertextuality is always also an allegory of history, a montage of memory traces, by which the filmmaker engages with the past through recall, retrieval, and recycling" (p. 238). These impulses are also present in the "Lesbians from Film/TV" series (and other videos of this nature), in the way that the video creators use the mashup as a medium for holding on to, collecting, and storing (and also playing with) representations that are typically characterised by transience.

Queer theorist Ann Cvetkovich positions this form of engagement with media content as a model for queer archival practice. She argues that the queer archivist "must proceed like the fan or collector whose attachment to objects is often fetishistic, idiosyncratic, or obsessional" (2002, p. 116, 2003). Similarly, Alexis Lothian draws attention to the archival nature of the practices of fans. However, Lothian (2011) argues that "although the online world of creative media fandom is a series of archives," there is risk in valorising the archive as the only model for understanding the practices of fandom because "we risk losing sight of the ephemeral practices that can work transformatively."

Cvetkovich's theorisation of archives counters this by calling, as Muñoz does, for an archive of the ephemeral. Cvetkovich theorises this as a *queer* archive, rather than simply a set of "queer-themed" content that has been archived or collected. In her research on archives of lesbian feeling, Cvetkovich explains the archive as a "ritual space within which cultural memory and history are preserved" (2002, p. 109). As such, her work emphasises that archives are not limited to existing physical spaces but can take on "innovative and unusual forms of appearance" (2002, p. 109). Cvetkovich argues that an archive of queer culture "must preserve and produce not just knowledge but feeling" (2002, p. 110), and thus develops the idea of an "archive of feeling" (2002, p. 112). She writes,

> The archive of feelings is both material and immaterial, at once incorporating objects that might not ordinarily be considered archival and at the same time resisting documentation because sex and feelings are too personal or too ephemeral to leave records. (2002, p. 112)

Foregrounding affect and ephemera, Cvetkovich theorises the archive as a repository of feelings and locates it as a queer space. She argues that the archive of feelings exists, not only in institutional settings, such as museums and libraries, but also in "more personal and intimate spaces and... within cultural genres" (2002, p. 112). Cvetkovich locates film as a significant genre of the archive, drawing attention to the way that archives can be visualised in film and emphasising "the power of the moving image to conjure and preserve emotion" (2002, p. 112).

Located as a prime example of an archive of feelings are the works of filmmaker Sadie Benning. Cvetkovich argues that Benning's collective works are "an innovative archive of lesbian life" (2002, p. 130), that demonstrate "a new language of feminism" (2002, p. 134). Discussing her videos at length, Cvetkovich draws attention to the way that Benning "reappropriates cultural constructions of girlhood that often seem denigrating and infantilising... and converts them into a powerful repository" (2002, p. 134). Mashup acts in a similar manner, reassembling screen content in a way that confronts the historical absence and ephemerality of queer girls in screen media. Through the "Lesbians from TV/Film" series, Pezza87 rewrites contemporary screen culture, appropriating and experimenting with the representation of queer girls and women. In collecting and re-editing these images, an archive is constructed. This is an archive of queer feelings, as Cvetkovich theorises it, reflecting the creator's powerful attachment to queer screen culture.

Questions of the archive are significant for queer theory, because as Danielle Clarke (2004, p. 82) argues, reformulating our understandings of what the archive is and how it operates allow us to reformulate questions of the queer subject. In addition to this, as Helen Hok-Sze Leung demonstrates, theories of the archive allow us to "re-examine what is worthy of research and what counts as knowledge" (2007, p. 561). It is important to note, as Jack Halberstam does, that the "archive is not simply a repository" (2005, p. 169). Rather, Halberstam argues that it can be considered in three overlapping ways; the queer archive is simultaneously a complex record of queer activity, a construction of collective memory and means of theorising cultural relevance (2005, pp. 160–170). When considered as an archival practice, mashup videos such as the "Lesbians from TV/Film" series, not only work to document the representation of queer desire and experience, but also construct collective memory around these images. In addition to this, they offer a means of embedding the ephemeral images of queer girlhood with cultural value and relevance.

Considered in this way, mashup mobilises a quality that Doane locates within early cinema, when she emphasises how the form was perceived as a "prophylactic against death," ensuring the ability to "see one's loved ones gesture and smile long after their deaths" (2002). In the same way, mashup ensures the ability to see much loved characters long after they disappear from film or television screens. Each video is an archive of feeling, of personal investments with temporal fragments that have been collected and reassembled, manipulated and melded into new forms. Considered as a whole, a series of videos such as Pezza87's "Lesbians from TV/Film" accentuate this, expressing new relations to time and new modes of figuring queer girlhood.

Queer Potential and the Incomplete Archive

Though mashup provides a means of holding on to important cultural information, there is a central paradox to this practice. This paradox emerges between the archival desire to preserve, the fleeting nature of queer ephemera and the unpredictable lifespan of content online.

One of the utopian promises of digital culture is that the Internet provides endless spaces for content (and culture) to be preserved and to endure against all odds. As Paul Grainge argues in his introduction to *Ephemeral Media: Transitory Screen Culture from Television to YouTube*, because websites such as YouTube act as a database, they demonstrate "the potential of the web to offer a permanent archive of digital material" (2011, p. 8). However, in many cases, in terms of actual viewer and user experiences, Grainge argues, "YouTube, like the web more generally, is defined by the constant threat of materials disappearing as specific links 'rot' and pages are taken down" (2011, p. 8). For this reason, Kirsten Foot argues that the web is "a unique mixture of the ephemeral and the permanent" (2010, p. 13).

On one level, the archival desire to preserve is disrupted by websites and online platforms, such as YouTube, because they are repeatedly erased when they are updated. Beyond this, however, the archival function of mashup is also disrupted (and often terminated) as a result of corporate control and copyright enforcement. Julie Levin Russo and Francesca Coppa (2012) draw attention to this when they note that vid creators must distribute their projects via "corporate portals" such as YouTube that "disavow all copyrighted material, with little recourse for transformative works." Drawing on Alexandra Juhazs's *Learning from YouTube*, published as a video-book in 2011, Russo and Coppa note the paradoxical nature of YouTube, by highlighting that the popularity of the platform for sharing and mashing video has also led it to prioritise commercial interests. Commenting on this further, they explain:

> Although YouTube has been the milieu for much of the vibrant creativity of video remix, it also has the most highly developed infrastructure for pre-emptively and indiscriminately blocking content flagged by automated filters. (2012)

As a decade-old case study, Pezza87's video series highlights this particularly well. First published online in 2007, the videos illuminate an important tension between permanence and ephemerality that is inherent to all web-based video. It is not clear how many mashups existed as part of the original "Lesbians from TV/Film" series, but only three remain at the time of writing. Volume one, two and five are available for viewing, which suggests that at least two videos in the series have been removed. The incomplete nature of Pezza87's archive renders the final video all the more poignant.

Pezza87's final video, "Lesbians from TV/Film part 5," combines the romantic themes and eroticism of the previous videos, consisting of "the best lesbian scenes from film and television." This video begins with a lengthy scene involving two girls sitting in a high school bathroom.

One girl muses, "checkin' out chicks… maybe that's my problem. Maybe I'm into girls." The other girl smiles slyly and surprises her friend with a kiss before asking if she enjoyed it. "Then you're not into girls," she asserts. "Trust me… I'm a really good kisser and you'd totally be into me right now if you were." At this point, the music and visuals begin. This video is the only one in the series to contain a song from an earlier decade. In this case, the song is "Another Girl, Another Planet," recorded by The Only Ones in 1978. Like the other videos in the series, the visuals consist of short clips of the queer girls from teen film and television, mashing images from *Sugar Rush* (2005–2006), *My Summer of Love*, and *South of Nowhere* (2005–2008), with the repeated lyric "I think I'm on another world with you/I'm on another planet with you." The previous mashups in this series explored moments when queer desires are expressed within film and television, concentrating the climactic kisses of each of the source materials into three-minute videos. This mashup maintains this focus, but employs much longer clips to draw out the moments of queer desire and articulate the feeling of being "on another world, another planet." With its slower, drawn out fragments of representations of queer girls, this video imagines "another world" where queer figures are not represented through transitory storylines, and perhaps where time could be imagined in queer ways.

Queer Teens, Queer Screens

As I have highlighted through this chapter, technological development and the proliferation of new media forms in the digital era have created an expanse of spaces for queer audiences to both find and interact with queer representations. In the past two decades, in particular, accessible video editing software and video-sharing websites such as YouTube and Vimeo have made screen media more malleable than ever before, which has significant implications for queer audiences and creators who seek to actively shape queer representation through new media forms including mashup. Throughout this chapter, Pezza87's "Lesbians From TV/Film" series has been identified as a novel case study that exemplifies this active shaping of queer representation through its repurposing of existing footage to reflect on prior representations of queer girlhood. At this point, it is important to consider what this suggests about the significance of screen media representations for queer youth. What insight does this case study provide into personal investments with queer media representations?

In *Cult Collectors: Nostalgia, Fandom and Collecting Popular Culture*, Lincoln Geraghty argues that video mashups can illustrate both fan creativity and an "emotional connection with popular media texts" (2014, p. 87). However, beyond this sort of personal insight, Pezza87's series of videos also functions along the lines of what Geraghty describes as "communal memory making" (Geraghty 2014, p. 87) around queer screen representation. Discussing the state of queer representation in film and television, Rebecca Beirne argues that the scarcity of queer characters means that "representations, when they do occur, [are] all the more significant" (2008, p. 2). Beirne draws attention to the personal investment of queer audiences in queer representations, arguing that the historical lack of representation sparks "a profound investment" in queer characters, narratives, directors, actors and aesthetics (2008, p. 2).

Mashups such as Pezza87's "Lesbians from TV/Film" series work to illuminate this kind of "profound" investment in screen representation. All volumes of "Lesbians from TV/Film" reflect a deep emotional connection to queer representation across a range of screen forms and texts. However, it is the comments section that best reflects the series impact as a form of communal memory making. Over the decade that this series of videos has been online, many viewers have asked questions about particular moments from the video series. It is common for viewers to comment with questions such as "what is this from?" "How can I find this?" or "I loved this moment. Where can I find the full episode?" which frequently sparks conversation about what each fragment of screen queerness has meant to them. To me, this highlights the continued relevance of such media representations, suggesting that the queer representations of the past are not forgotten or left to gather metaphorical dust. As I have highlighted, mashup creators are regularly taking up earlier representations and remodelling them in ways that destabilise the dominant narratives associated with queer figures. These representations of the past are also engaged with by viewers who reflect on key moments within these digital videos, reminding other viewers of the importance of each and every flash of queerness on screen.

These videos also actively work toward the collation of a queer archive of screen culture. Their creators hold on to representations long out of the public eye, maintaining their importance and pulling them into the present moment. Forged from historical absence, mashup videos such as "Lesbians from TV/Film" experiment with existing queer representation to produce at once a record of queer texts and the powerful feelings attached to queer screen culture, a construction of collective memory around such media forms, and an assertion of their continued relevance. While issues of copyright and corporate control may limit the archival function of mashup and reflect the precarious position of queer texts within broader media contexts, these fan-led archives of queer ephemerality endure.

References

Allen, Dennis. 1995. Homosexuality and narrative. *Modern Fiction Studies* 41 (3–4): 609–634.

Becker, Ron. 2006. *Gay TV and straight America*. New Brunswick: Rutgers University Press.

Beirne, Rebecca. 2008. Introduction: A critical introduction to queer women on television. In *Televising queer women*, ed. Rebecca Beirne, 1–16. New York: Palgrave Macmillan.

Beirne, Rebecca. 2012. Teen lesbian desires and identities in international cinema: 1931–2007. *Journal of Lesbian Studies* 16 (2): 258–272.

Bolte, Caralyn. 2008. 'Normal is the watchword': Exiling cultural anxieties and redefining desire from the margins. In *Teen television: Essays on programming and fandom*, ed. Sharon Marie Ross and Louisa Ellen Stein, 93–113. Jefferson: McFarland.

Bolter, Jay David, and Richard Grusin. 1999. *Remediation: Understanding new media*. Cambridge: MIT Press.

Booth, Paul. 2010. *Digital fandom: New media studies*. New York: Peter Lang.

Capsuto, Steven. 2001. *Alternate channels: The uncensored story of gay and lesbian images on radio and television*. New York: Ballantine Books.

Chambers, Samuel. 2009. *The queer politics of television*. New York: I.B. Taurus.

Clarke, Danielle. 2004. Finding the subject: Queering the archive. *Feminist Theory* 5 (1): 79–83.

Coppa, Francesca. 2008. Women, Star Trek, and the early development of fannish vidding. *Transformative Works and Cultures* 1. http://journal.transformativeworks.org/index.php/twc/article/view/44.

Cumberbatch, G., A. Maguire, V. Lyne, and S. Gauntlett. 2014. *Diversity monitoring: The top TV programmes*. Birmingham: Creative Diversity Network.

Cvetkovich, Ann. 2002. In the archives of lesbian feelings: Documentary and popular culture. *Camera Obscura* 49 (17): 107–147.

Cvetkovich, Ann. 2003. *An archive of feelings: Trauma, sexuality, and lesbian public cultures*. Durham: Duke University Press.

Davis, Glyn. 2004. Saying it out loud: Revealing television's queer teens. In *Teen TV: Genre, consumption and identity*, ed. Glyn Davis and Kay Dickinson, 127–140. London: British Film Institute.

Doane, Mary Ann. 2002. *The emergence of cinematic time: Modernity, contingency, the archive*. Cambridge: Harvard University Press.

Driver, Susan. 2007. *Queer girls and popular culture: Reading, resisting and creating media*. New York: Peter Lang.

Foot, Kirsten. 2010. Web sphere analysis and cybercultural studies. In *The new media and cyber cultures anthology*, ed. Pramod K. Nayar, 11–18. Chichester, West Sussex, U.K.; Malden, MA: Wiley-Blackwell.

Geraghty, Lincoln. 2014. *Cult collectors: Nostalgia, fandom and collecting popular culture*. London and New York: Routledge.

GLAAD.org. 2016a. *2016 studio responsibility index*. http://www.glaad.org/sri/2016.

GLAAD.org. 2016b. *Where we are on TV report 2016*. http://www.glaad.org/whereweareontv16.

Grainge, Paul. 2011. Introduction: Ephemeral media. In *Ephemeral media: Transitory screen culture from television to YouTube*, ed. Paul Grainge, 1–19. New York: Palgrave Macmillan.

Gross, Larry. 2001. *Up from invisibility: Lesbians, gay men and the media*. New York: Columbia University Press.

Halberstam, Judith/Jack. 2005. *In a queer time and place: Transgender bodies, subcultural lives*. New York and London: New York University Press.

Jenkins, Henry. 1992. *Textual poachers: Television fans and participatory culture*. New York: Routlege.

Kaplan, Deborah. 2006. Construction of fan fiction character through narrative. In *Fan fiction and fan communities in the age of the internet*, ed. Karen Hellekson and Kristina Busse, 134–152. Jefferson, NC: McFarland.

Leung, Helen Hok-Sze. 2007. Archiving queer feelings in Hong Kong. *Inter-Asia Cultural Studies* 8 (4): 559–571.

Lothian, Alexis. 2011. An archive of one's own: Subcultural creativity and the politics of conservation. *Transformative Works and Cultures* 6. http://journal.transformativeworks.org/index.php/twc/article/view/267.

Martin, Fran. 2010. *Backward glances: Contemporary Chinese cultures and the female homoerotic imaginary*. Durham: Duke University Press.

McCarthy, Anna. 2001. Ellen: Making queer television history. *GLQ: A Journal of Lesbian and Gay Studies* 7 (4): 593–620.

Media Action Media. 2012. *Representations of diversity in Canadian television entertainment programming*.

Monaghan, Whitney. 2012. Glee: Coming out on US teen television. *Jump Cut* 54. www.ejumpcut.org/archive/jc54.2012/Monaghan-Glee/.

Monaghan, Whitney. 2016. *Queer girls, temporality and screen media: Not 'Just a Phase'*. London: Palgrave Macmillan.

Muñoz, José. 1996. Ephemera as evidence: Introductory notes to queer acts. *Women and Performance* 8 (2): 5–16.

"Pezza87—Watch. Thumb. Subscribe," Youtube.com. https://www.youtube.com/user/pezza87.

Russo, Julie Levin. 2009. User-penetrated content: Fan video in the age of convergence. *Cinema Journal* 48 (4): 125–130.

Russo, Julie Levin, and Francesca Coppa. 2012. Fan/remix video (a remix). In *Fan/remix video*, ed. Francesca Coppa and Julie Levin Russo (special issue of *Transformative Works and Cultures* 9). http://journal.transformativeworks.org/index.php/twc/article/view/431.

Russell, Catherine. 1999. *Experimental ethnography: The work of film in the age of video*. Durham: Duke University Press.

Screen Australia. 2016. *Seeing ourselves: Reflections on diversity in Australian TV drama*.

Tropiano, Stephen. 2002. *The primetime closet: A history of gays and lesbians on TV*. New York: Applause Cinema and Theatre Books.

Turk, Tisha. 2010. 'Your own imagination': Vidding and vidwatching as collaborative interpretation. *Film and Film Culture* 5: 88–110.

Turk, Tisha, and Joshua Johnson. 2012. Toward an ecology of vidding. In *Fan/remix video*, ed. Francesca Coppa and Julie Levin Russo (special issue of *Transformative Works and Cultures* 9). http://journal.transformativeworks.org/index.php/twc/article/view/326/294.

CHAPTER 9

The Queer Potential of *World of Warcraft*: Shame and Desire in the Performance of Gender in Massively Multiplayer Online Roleplaying Games

Johanna Luanne Fraser

Laura Kate Dale, like many other young people, discusses her experiences of gender transition in relation to *World of Warcraft* as an environment where public censure did not impede her ability to experiment with her gender identity. She writes,

> World of Warcraft taught me a lot about transitioning in a space where I didn't have to commit to my future. During a period of my life that I had a huge number of questions about who I was, it taught me things about myself in an environment where, for a long time, I felt safe. And I could walk away from thoughts of transition any time I needed to. (Dale 2014, web)

An increasing body of literature is being developed around the performance of gender in online video games. Not surprisingly, Massive

J. L. Fraser (✉)
York University, Hamilton, ON, Canada
e-mail: jofraser@yorku.ca

S. Driver and N. Coulter (eds.), *Youth Mediations and Affective Relations*,
https://doi.org/10.1007/978-3-319-98971-6_9

Multiplayer Online Role-Playing Games (MMORPGs), have received a great deal of attention in terms of fostering creative explorations of identity and desire. These games provide an online arena where millions of players, young and old, choose and customize an avatar with which to play and interact with other players in relative anonymity. The potential of MMORPGs for identity negotiation and performance, though, has largely been overshadowed by video game and gender research and inquiry that centers on what Eve Sedgewick (drawing on Paul Ricœur) refers to as the "hermeneutics of suspicion and exposure" (2003, p. 140). This hermeneutical approach—which relies on symbolic and systematic interpretation—leads researchers to focus their critical attention on the structures and rules of the games. According to Sedgwick, the tendency to focus on structures makes a subject's experiences of those structures secondary. Because experience cannot always be predicted by structure, an attention to structure alone offers little in terms of explanatory power and excludes dynamic dimensions of embodied and affective experience. In this chapter, I explore how in spite of the visibly gendered and often heterosexist structures of MMORPGs like *World of Warcraft*, gender norms are negotiated in complex and creative ways through game play and interaction with other players. This is most evident when one takes an affective approach—and indeed takes seriously the sensuous relations as well as the feelings, imagination, thoughts and performances of the players. By taking an affective approach to gender inquiry in online gaming, and paying specific attention to the contours of desire and shame in relation to queer and transgender subjects, we can develop a more complex and comprehensive understanding of the queer potentials of these increasingly prevalent media.

Affect After Hermeneutics

A hermeneutics of suspicion is employed by critics of new media, particularly with regard to social media and violent video games, to demonstrate how these technologies can influence and shape the individuals and groups who engage with them (Scannell 2007). The focus of these thinkers is on the structures and scenarios built into the game, overlooking or sidestepping the interactive dimensions of play and subjective desires unfolding in the process of engagement beyond the limitations of the rules (Järvinen 2009). In what follows, I will argue in favour of an alternative approach to understanding new media, which thinks through the subtle contours of affect shaping gender identifications and desires in the context of gaming. I adopt an affirmative and open attention to affect in contrast to a closed hermeneutics of suspicion, in order to take seriously the feelings, motivations, actions, and interactions of diverse and changing players.

Scannell (2007) writes the following:

> [the hermeneutics of suspicion is] certainly the dominant attitude in Cultural and Media Studies as they have developed in the last thirty years or so. It rests on the assumption that you can't or shouldn't take ordinary life and experience at face value because they are deceptive and misleading. (Scannell 2007, p. 11)

This makes some sense given that "the greatest sin of media researchers is to take the innovations at face-value" (Nyre 2009, p. 3). The application of a critical eye to new media is necessary, but it becomes problematic when it comes with hermeneutical rigidity and bias. Hermeneutical bias—that is, when a researcher assumes what they will discover before they discover it—can lead a researcher to ask a question in such a way as to obtain a predictable and desired answer, leaving little room to consider alternatives. Alternatively, Sedgwick proposes a reparative approach. The reparative approach, unlike hermeneutical paranoia, is concerned with addressing the problematics of criticism. Whereas the hermeneutics of suspicion—what Sedgwick calls paranoid reading—places its faith in the exposure of horrors already assumed to exist, reparative readings aim towards adding, rather than taking away. This approach accepts and embraces the messiness, richness, and fullness of culture. Importantly, the reparative impulse, Sedgewick explains is "[n]o less acute than a paranoid position, no less realistic, no less attached to a project of survival, and neither less nor more delusional or fantasmatic" (2003, p. 150). "What we can best learn from such practices", she writes, are "the many ways in which selves and communities succeed in extracting sustenance from the objects of a culture—even of a culture whose avowed desire has often been not to sustain them" (Sedgewick 2003, p. 151). Where hermeneutics seeks to reveal the bare bones of society, a reparative approach addresses society in the flesh, with all its bits and trappings.

The affective approach that I take up herein is reparative in this way. I do not focus on structures and systems. This is because, as Sedgewick (2003) points out, this focus on the largely visible and undeniable existence of structures and systems is very limiting and closes down more dynamic embodied ways of understanding meanings and identifications. "[T]he project of a poststructuralist critical imaginary has become reduced to the search for, and deadening (re)discovery of, prohibition everywhere: prohibition where it appeared there was freedom, prohibition in a space we had not, until now, thought to look" (Hemmings 2005, p. 553). The critical theorist is so concerned with prohibitive structures that it ignores "our qualitative experience of the social world," whereas affect implores the theorist to look deeper into complex and located subjectivities to the "embodied experience that has the capacity to transform as well as exceed social subjection" (Hemmings 2005, p. 549). Affect theory seeks to overcome this problem by addressing what fosters capacities and actions at the individual or group and social levels in the present context. As Hemmings explains, affect theory also encourages us to overcome the limited notion of the individual set forth by traditional ways of thinking. Affect is highly relational, and so the individual, as the focus of affect theory, is better understood in terms of embodied relational selfhood. That is, the subjectivity and identities of the subject are formed and negotiated in relation to her surrounding, and to others. An excellent example of this is offered by Kathleen Stewart in *Ordinary Affects* (2007), which allows us to see affect's visceral relationality at work in 'ordinary' experiences. Her book presents fragments of every-day life, and in the fragment called Relief, she presents the following scene which depicts the ways that the paranoia employed by critical theorists—and the layman—can be disrupted by the affective:

> Unwanted intensities simmer up at the least provocation. And then a tiny act of human kindness, or a moment of shared sardonic humor in public, can set things right again as if any sign of human contact releases an unwanted tension. …
>
> She and Ariana are out walking in the neighborhood. White woman, brown baby. Some teenagers pass them, scowling. Brown boys dressed tough, showing attitude. But as they pass she hears one of the boys say to the others in a sweet boy's voice "did you see that cute baby?" (Stewart 2007, p. 50)

The woman walking along with a baby is wary of the teenaged boys—the scene gives the sense of the paranoia felt by a woman alone in a public place faced with a potential interaction with ethnically diverse young men who, according to the statistics and the stereotypes, may be dangerous. But when paying attention to affect, to her experience, to the experience of the boys, the scene shifts. The woman is no longer in a dangerous situation, a multiplicity of thoughts and feelings unfold that disrupt expectations. The structures of the social world that she inhabits are no longer the sole influence on her behaviour, and on the behaviour of the teen boys. As this example demonstrates, attention to the subtle embodied and embedded dimensions of affect allows us to overcome biases, and negotiate our own actions and reactions. The situation in which the white woman and the baby find themselves in was interpreted initially as dangerous, but the affective moment disrupted the woman's preconceptions. Affect, in this way, can be understood as a force, one which precedes, and undergirds emotions. Throughout the rest of this chapter, I will refer to shame and desire—but we must be careful when blurring the lines between articulable concepts like shame and desire, and the underlying motivating affective capacities or forces that lead or push one to act or react. Shame and desire, because of their deep, visceral nature—rooted in forces of bodily becoming—can be understood affectively, but this does not make them affect. Rather, they are the articulable iterations of felt affect within a subject, and within a group.

Video Games and Gender Performance

When it comes to interrogating the affective contours of video game play, "it's difficult to say with precision *what* the player is feeling, let alone measure it objectively" (Shinkle 2005, p. 2). As such, while thinkers are increasingly noting the value of affect in media studies, limited attention has been paid to the players' own embodiments, feelings, and motivations. For example, Yee's approach (2006) to MMORPGs analyzes the motivations and experiences of game players. Similarly, video game analyst Aki Järvinen (2009) argues that games should be understood in terms of the ways that they illicit and interact with gamers' emotional experiences. Unfortunately, though, while the players' experiences and emotions are taken as central to an understanding of the video game experience, such authors are concerned with game design rather than players varied and changing motivations, interactions, pleasures and emotional investments, and their implications. The games' systems of rules are the central element of analysis.

When structures and systems become the focal point of video games, inquiry researchers tend to seek—and find—a causal relationship between game structures and player behaviours—both in and out of game. For example, those concerned with the impact of video game violence on the behaviour of players outside of the game claim that the narrative of video games justifies violence in the real world. According to these thinkers, violent video games "communicate that violence serves a higher good" and "reward rather than sanction violence" (Hartmann et al. 2014, p. 313). Further, video games are said to distort the consequences of violent acts. The implications of this ranges from a moral dilemma—that is, players find it difficult to make ethical decisions in the game and in the real world—to a moral panic—players of violent video games may become violent themselves (Tamborini et al. 2013). The thesis that violence in video games will result in violence in real life is grounded in the assumption that the rules of a video game make the behaviour of the players predictable. Järvinen (2009) explains,

> Because games with their rules and roles are coercive in nature, the behavior of players tends to be, to a certain extent, more habituated and thus more predictable than in other forms of entertainment. The difference is due to the interactive nature of gameplay: in other media forms, individual interpretations are seldom channeled directly back, via playful behavior, to the media content with which the audience interacts. (Järvinen 2009, p. 88)

So, Järvinen's assertion is that players' behaviours in game is relatively predictable. However, while players' behaviours may be impacted by the structures and rules of the game, the more meaningful decisions they make, those having to do with identity, fantasy, and personal expression, are surprisingly unpredictable. The rules which inhibit and promote certain behaviours do not necessarily impact character choices and enactments in expected ways.

Thinkers concerned with the impact of video game play on players outside of game play would be better served by approaching the problem by investigating the ways that players make decisions and engage with others on multiple levels including specific affective, imaginative, and mediated encounters. *World of Warcraft* is a very gendered game, but its queer potential lies not in its structures, but rather in the way that gamers choose to play within and beyond them. While the behaviour of players may be generally predictable in terms of battle and quest, what is unpredictable is the way that players negotiate differences in role playing, and in identity performance. While ideas of the fluidity of identity construction online has been questioned by contemporary gender and new media theorists, given the representation of traditional gender mores in online arenas—like the gender binary in *WoW*—(see Hayes 2007) new digital technologies like MMORPGs, are still viewed "as a potential path to liberation from these constraints to challenge masculine power place" (Chen 2016, p. 525), given that "[t]hey provide a place in which identity can be explored safely" (Dale 2014, web).

This is because while MMORPGs like *WoW* re-present the systems, values, and mores of everyday life, such games are not simply mimetic, in the sense that these systems, values, and mores might literally reflect those that are found in the world 'behind the screen[1]'—that is, what some might refer to as real or every-day life. Via the fantasy aspect, MMORPGs allow players to play a new role rather than the role they play behind the screen without having to feel constrained by the more obvious structures that dominate their everyday lives—like gender norms, social class, race/ethnicity, or economic status. In this way, I want to argue that a powerful affect such as shame, though still built into the structures of the game (especially given the role of achieving quests, winning battles, and collecting currency) is destabilized as a primary motivating factor for gender choice and attribution. I want to highlight the productive power of diverse desires and identifications among players that are not reducible to shame, but are constituted by a rich and changing array of affective experiences. The choice of gender identity in the game actually becomes quite banal in terms of gender relations, driven by multiple desires—desire for power, beauty, fantasy, or on the opposite end, realism etc. In this way, game play affords an unpredictable and open-ended realm of gender exploration and affective experience.

Shame and Gender Performance

As Massumi (2002) puts it affect is an "intensity corresponding to the passage from one experiential state of the body to another and implying an augmentation or diminution in that body's capacity to act" (p. xvi). Shame, in that it has a direct relationship to the body's 'capacity to act,' is an emotion that has drawn a great deal of attention from affect and gender theorists within the last two decades (see, for example Probyn 2005; Sedgewick 2003; Salamon 2009; among others). Contemporary researchers have tied gender regulations, norms, and embodiments to affective forces of shame. Shame is a strong motivating factor for certain gendered behaviours, particularly among young men (see Salamon 2009). In studies of gender attirbution and choice in everyday life, thinkers have noted the importance of shame in motivating gender choice. As Elspeth Probyn (2005) argues, shame is a powerful feeling that is widely condemned—that is, it is shameful to admit shame. Probyn conceptualizes shame as being tied to human connection—a desire for human connection which, therefore, links shame to a fear of being left out or disconnected from others. Shame, though not prohibitive[2] (Sedgewick 2003), is limiting in that it motivates one's willingness, ability, and desire to be included. It is also powerful given its ability, like other affects, to spread from person to person (Sedgewick 2003)—shame is painted upon the face, and transfers from one person to another in situations where the feeling of not belonging, or of strangeness is felt.

It is not surpising, then, that shame seems to motivate gender choice, especially among young people—the fear of censure from those who adhere to the binary gender norm within Western society leads those who do not fit within the binary to attempt to 'pass.' What is powerful here is not the system itself, but rather, how one's relationship to it produces multiple reactions including feelings of shame. The binary gender system is the norm within a Western social context, and attempts to act beyond the binary are difficult. Betsy Lucal (1999) provides us with insight into how performing outside of the system proves difficult:

> For me, the social processes and structures of gender mean that, in the context of our culture, my appearance will be read as masculine. Given the common conflation of sex and gender I will be assumed to be male. Because of the two and only-two genders rule, I will be classified, perhaps more often than not, as a man—not as an atypical woman, not as a genderless person. I must be one gender or the other; I cannot be neither, nor can I be both. (1999, p. 785)

Betsy Lucal reflects on her inability to get beyond the genders, even as she dresses and acts in such a way as to defy gender norms. In spite of this, she tells us, she is mistaken for a man, not seen as a person without gender or as a woman who is atypical of her feminine sex. Gender is so deeply ingrained in our understandings of one another that we find ourselves, in opposing the binary, simply outwardly expressing one of the two or part of both of the accepted categories. If a female chooses to wear masculine clothes in order to get beyond normative gender categorization, they are read as either male or female in the eyes of others. That said, if one does not sufficiently pass as one or the other binary genders, then there are social consequences—as Miqqi Gilbert (2009) writes, the nonbinary person, or the trans person, "must pass or suffer the consequences of social censure" (Gilbert 2009, p. 96); that social censure comes in the form of humiliation and shaming. "Humiliation and shaming are the frequent consequences meted out for failure to conform to proper gendering" (Salamon 2009, p. 383), and for those who do not fit within the binary norms, this shaming is felt "more acutely to the extent that their transgressions are not momentary but persistent, not correctible errors but ineradicable features of their being" (p. 383).

Desire has the opposite effect of shame—though shame can mediate desire. Judith Butler writes that "desire is always a desire for recognition" and "to persist in one's own being is only possible on the condition that we are engaged in receiving and offering recognition" (Butler 2004, p. 31). This conception of desire is deeply political, but Krystin Gordon's (2008) conception of desire is more personal—yet very complex—in its relationship to recognition. She writes specifically about desire in the context of media—particularly in television, film, and literature. According to Gordon, "desire opens new possibilities and initiates change" (p. 3); but it is more complicated than this, because the concept of recognition that Butler notes still remains within this notion of desire. She writes,

> I want to suggest that desire creates recognition (through identification and the gaze); it marks the narrative; it highlights the moment when lovers' eyes meet; it affects the lives of characters; it marks their bodies, forcing them to move, act or react differently; and it transforms people—radically alters their being-in-the-world. I want to suggest, moreover, that we consider desire as a way of thinking and as a kind of intelligence; as something that supports connections and relations and that produces an expression that is impossible to contain or categorise. (Gordon 2008, p. 29)

It is this transformative- and recognition-oriented notion of desire that I refer to within the rest of this chapter. It is through desire that the rigid relationship of individual to gender binary is challenged in online worlds, where players perform gender in game, and particularly in role-playing arenas where the sex of the player behind the screen is seldom questioned. While the same binary gender norms exist in game as behind the screen, the performance is largely unquestioned in text-based communication. Players seldom reveal their behind the screen identity, unless they partake in voice-chat. In *Second Life, Media, and the Other Society*, Phylis Johnson offers a unique look into the way that queer spaces can be created in MMORPGs, and their potential for impacting social and political change. *Second Life*, an MMORPG wherein subjects create relatively realistic—though often fantastical—lives for their avatars, "becomes a world of possibilities that allows one to experiment with 'sexual ideation and gender mutliplicities'" (Johnson 2010, p. 237). Likewise, in her paper exploring female identity in *World of Warcraft*, Lina Elkund (2011) notes that "[w]hile there are "limitations for female gamers in the form of quite conventional hierarchies, male partners and the heterosexual matrix," (p. 339) games like *World of Warcraft* provide an arena where players can interact with gender identity in relative safety from public censure." The implications of these gender negotiations are highlighted by Elkund as she notes the impact of in-game achievements on the self-image of players. She notes that one of her respondent's "picture of herself as a gamer changed when her avatar became more powerful" (p. 339). MMORPGs provide a unique arena for the troubling of gender norms. Far from being neutral victims of the medium's influence, video game players interact with their avatars and other players often in unexpected ways.

World of Warcraft

World of Warcraft (WoW) is a massively multiplayer online roleplaying game (MMORPG) which since its inception in 2004 has attracted millions of players from across the globe. While its popularity has waned in recent years, there are still more than 5 million *WoW* subscribers (Purchese 2015). It remains one of the most widely played online multiplayer games in the world. As an MMORPG, *WoW* offer players the opportunity to choose a character based on the game's 'lore'. Players can choose to play one of 13 species,[3] which gives them the opportunity to experience a role that is either very similar to, or vastly different than their behind the screen personas. In virtual worlds like Azeroth—the planet on which the game *WoW* takes place—players are able to engage in battles and quests alone or in groups, much like other online multiplayer games. What makes MMORPGs different from other games in that they include an element of role-playing, and players are encouraged to engage with others as their avatar.

While players can choose to engage with others in the game in a myriad of ways, is nonetheless important to note that "[v]irtual gender is not a blank canvas and virtual space remains a discursive arena already shaped by the social and cultural. Whilst it provides a 'safe' space, free from the gaze of adults, it offers no liberation from the material world" (Crowe and Watts 2014, p. 228). That is, Azeroth may be vastly different from earth in terms of species and scientific principles, but gender is still very much binary in game. It is interesting to see how players can overcome the shortcoming of the gender binary through the way they interact affectively and performatively with gender in the game.

Suspension of Disbelief, Fantasy, and Gender Bending

Previous studies in player motivation for gender choice in MMORPGs have indicated that a range of explanations can be offered for choosing to gender swap—that is, play a gender that does not line up with one's behind the screen persona (Paik and Shi 2013). For the majority of players, gender swapping is undertaken to either secure an in game advantage, to defy reality, or, for affective, pragmatic, and aesthetic reasons. For a minority of players, the social relations in their particular online community requires that gender identities are fluidly changed in order to balance the gap between male and female players (Paik and Shi 2013). For players of MMORPGs, one's gender in game appears very often to have little impact on the player, or the way that the player plays the game. Especially in games like *WoW*, where different genders of the same species share the same powers—and gender is largely aesthetic—gender is often secondary to other species' characteristics. As one players writes,

> I generally write the kind of character I want first, and then tack on the gender as an afterthought. However, before I started RP'ing, I pretty much wrote only from a male character perspective in my short stories, and wanted to try something outside my comfort zone. Lo and behold, I learned that gender generally has very little effect on the character unless you decide that it should. (Aureton, Mar 10, 2015, forum post)

Genderbending in games like *WoW* is incredibly common, to the point that it is seldom mentioned in game, except in gest[4] and players rarely ask others whether they are male or female IRL (in real life). Although in ERP (erotic role-playing), the stakes seem much higher and players are more likely to find roleplaying as the opposite sex troubling. Otherwise, one's behind the screen identity, while sometimes important when bonding in game with one's guild-mates, is seldom vital to players who engage in role-playing. This is because it is a fantasy-based game that requires full emersion, without giving clues to one's behind the screen identity.[5]

It appears that some players are more likely to differentiate themselves from their characters than others. As Crowe and Watts demonstrate, the teenage players of another MMORPG, *Runescape*, connect with their characters on a deep level. As one of their 17 year old respondents explains, "Now, as soon as I click ok, I become a girl. I become Sassy" (2014, p. 223). Despite the very structured nature of some roleplaying in *WoW*—in some guilds, rules govern conduct, speech, clothing, and gender—the identity of players behind the screen is seldom questioned. This is easiest when one is using text-based interaction rather than voice chat—because of suspension of disbelief. Until recently, most roleplaying in games like *WoW* took place via text chat, though increasingly with the introduction of team-speak and other group voice chat applications, voice chat has become more common given the ease within which one can communicate with others in game—allowing players to type commands to their characters while speaking aloud. However, a frequently cited explanation for not voice-acting during roleplaying is that, a male individual behind the screen would have difficulty roleplaying a female character convincingly, and vice versa.

Numerous threads exist on the *WoW* forums run by their parent company—Blizzard Entertainment—that address gender swapping in game. Most begin with questions like *why do people play opposite gender characters, why are people annoyed when others play opposite gender characters, and why do you play opposite gender characters?* Though a small minority of respondents seem against persons playing characters that do not line up with their behind the screen identity, the majority of forum respondents see gender swapping as an integral part of the game. As one player writes, "I'm male IRL and all my characters are female. … As far as I've always been concerned, roleplaying is about being someone you're not. So why not change the gender too" (Sevl, Mar 9, 2015, forum post). Other players have found ways to negotiate the issue by delving into the lore of the game, and immersing themselves in the potentialities of fantasy realms. For example, a player writes, "I have a Femsaken [female bodied] warrior that has the brain of a male warrior that was salvaged into a more preserved body, so they ended up being rather uncertain about their current gender" (Gwendi, Mar 13, 2016).

Desire Without Shame

"I don't think anybody actually cares" (Octopusbread, Dec 23, 2012, forum post).

As Probyn argues, shame has to do with the desire to connect with other humans, and results when that connection seems out of reach—as Sedgewick (2003) puts it, "shame both derives from and aims towards sociability" (p. 37). I go further to say that shame results when desire is impeded, and that shame also impedes desire—desire to be what one is, desire to be accepted for what one is, and moreover, desire to be something or someone else than what one appears to be. In *World of Warcraft*, shame is largely absent from gender choice, and from interactions in roleplaying scenarios, in game. While the argument that the relative anonymity of online arenas allows for the performance of identities and behaviours that are hidden by subjects in their lives behind the screen has been disputed by game theorists, MMORPGs do allow for affective freedom from censure. Players' desires to interact with and connect to others, rather than shame, drives player behaviours and identity performance in game, because in game, shame cannot impede the virtual, nor the physical, body's ability to act in virtual worlds. Shame loses its affective power in a world where one can be or perform any number of gender identities—without the shame associated with a lack of connection or acceptance—when one can choose to perform a different gender role than their own and still experience belonging. Shame is less of an impediment when others care less about who you are behind the screen, and engage with you largely as your projected, virtual self.

Demonstrably, Hayes (2007) undertakes a case study of two women playing a single player game and discusses the motivations of the players in choosing their avatars, and performing their role within the game. Her analysis demonstrates the complexity of affective motivations within gaming, and the relationship of the player to their avatar. While her respondents fell within certain gender stereotypes in terms of character choice and development, by interrogating their motivations, Hayes was able to develop a deeper understanding of why these two women chose to develop their characters in the way that they did. For example, one respondent, Joanna, initially chose to build an avatar who uses magic rather than fighting. However, she realized after playing for several hours that performing magic in game required similar skills and dedication as cooking in real life—something she was not interested in. She then decided to develop a character who was a skilled fighter, so that she could kill people in game in order to collect necessary items, and level up. Hayes' analysis also demonstrates the interesting relationship between affect in game and behind the screen. She quotes one of her respondents who says, "That's what I love about these games, is that it really forces you to face down all of your fears" (2007, p. 38). Hayes writes that "the game presented opportunities to enact identities that they valued and were trying to enact in their real life as well" (2007, p. 40). Her respondents created identities in game that reflected ideals behind the screen—and often these ideals were less achievable in their everyday lives than in the game. "My analyses show how each woman used the game not only to engage with familiar practices and identities but also to play with, or project, identities that they desired in real life" (p. 44). But Hayes' analysis is of a single player game—so shame, though at play in the lives of the two women whose experiences she analysed, was not at play in game, as the game was necessarily solitary. Desire, though, did play a role. They chose characters based on traits, skills, and identities they desired in their every day lives.

It is notable, then that in a social game like *WoW* shame is still largely absent. Players are able to remain as anonymous as they please—and more so, gender swapping, and performing unique, challenging identities, is a mainstay of the game itself. As many players have remarked in the online forums, it is completely the norm to play a character that is different in terms of gender and species from one's lived identity behind the screen. Despite the relatively binary and restrictive structures of the game, players choose to develop characters that challenge their own identities—and fly in the face of the norms and structures of the game. Freed from shame—which is such a strong motivator for gender choice and performance in life behind the screen—players are able to act on desires unrelated to the desire for acceptance and belonging associated with gender performance in everyday life. This is demonstrated on the forums for *WoW* where players offer explanations for creating their chosen characters. With diminished pressures towards feeling shame, players choose avatars based on aesthetics, compelling lore, powers and abilities, and customizability: "For me, it's about appearance and actions they perform" (Olumusa, Apr 6, 2015, forum post); "The look, the movement, the lore of the race. Most of my toons are Night Elves, the aesthetics work for me and I love their Lore. Most are female because I like their animations a little better and they have more options for their hair" (Mydnight, Apr 19, 2016, forum post). While others feel more comfortable roleplaying a character with whom they can identify with in terms of gender—"I play male characters because I am male and when I play my character I am the character. I'm not playing Raveintis, I am Raveintis!!!" (Raveintis, Mar 10, 2015, forum post)—most celebrate the freedom of playing a character that allows them to feel powerful, beautiful, interesting, unique, and indeed different than they feel in their lives behind the screen.

While many players see their character in game in the same way that they see Mario (from Mario Brothers) or any other single player game character—as a tool used to reach in game achievements—those who role-play engage more deeply with their character and find pleasure in fulfilling desires to perform roles that would be publicly censured in their everyday lives. Desire to perform different gender roles is not impeded in game by the fear of not belonging, in part because given its text-based nature, one can hide one's identity in *WoW*, but also because desire to connect, to relate, and to belong—which is at the root of shame, according to Probyn and Sedgewick—does not impede one's ability to act: "I will play female characters...and there's nothing that the haters can do about it" (Malora, Mar 30, 2012, forum post).

Gender performance—and players' views towards gender bending—within the online world of *World of Warcraft* can provide insight into how shame and desire operate in relation to gender regulation. Those who commented in the *WoW* forums generally demonstrate an attitude towards gender performance less constrained by the affective force of shame that tends to regulate gender performance in the world behind the screen, and in the everyday lives of the players. Players choose to play a certain character or role in game for a myriad of reasons. More often than not, these choices are made of the grounds of aesthetics, fantasy, or in game goals—like the desire to be a warrior or a healer. On the other hand, for players like Laura Kate Dale, quoted at the beginning of this chapter, this relative freedom from shame, and the ability to play a role that does not line up with one's birth sex, can have very meaningful implications for one's behind the screen identity. As the case of the young player of another MMORPG, *Runescape* demonstrated, one's role-playing of a character can actually immerse oneself into the identity of the character—this player, a boy behind the screen, *became* his avatar, Sassy, when playing the game. This enabled him to interact with players in a way that he was unable to in his life behind the screen (Crowe and Watts 2014). The queer potential of online worlds like *WoW's* Azeroth, may lie in the way they allow us to conceive of a world without shame—where desire, rather than shame, motivates gender performance.

Notes

1. I use the phrase 'behind the screen' purposefully throughout this chapter to refer to what others may consider 'real life' or life outside of a video game. I find it useful to use this terminology for two reasons in particular. First, for some players, game play may represent a significant portion of one's daily social, political, and/or economic interactions. To relegate game play to something other than 'real life' is to undermine the extent to which game play may constitute much of a player's everyday life. Second, referring to game play as something other than 'real life' undermines the significance of the interactions within a game in terms of identity formation, as well as opportunities for social and moral development. Game play, just like life behind the screen, presents players with moral challenges, and opportunities to develop their beliefs, values, and orientations to the world both in an out of game.
2. Sedgewick insists that affect is not prohibitive in the same way that structures and systems are.
3. Human, Orc, Dwarf, Undead, Night Elf, Tauren, Gnome, Troll, Draenei, Blood Elf, Worgen, Goblin, or Panderen.
4. An ongoing joke among commenters on online *WoW* forums is that you can assume that all female characters are middle aged white men, rather than women behind the screen.
5. For example, it is not uncommon for guild rules (rules of conduct for members of a particular group of players, mandated by the group and its leaders) to include the stipulation that personal conversations not take place in the guild chat channel (for an example, see Dark Wolves, web).

References

Butler, Judith. 2004. *Undoing gender*. New York: Routledge.

Chen, Chih-Ping. 2016. Playing with digital gender identity and cultural value. *Gender, Place and Culture* 23 (4): 521–536.

Crowe, Nick, and Mike Watts. 2014. 'When I click "ok" I become Sassy—I become a girl'. Young people and gender identity: Subverting the 'body' in massively multi-player online role-playing games. *International Journal of Adolescence and Youth* 19 (2): 217–231.

Dale, Laura Kate. 2014. How World of Warcraft helped me come out as transgender. *The Guardian*. GamesBlog, January 23. https://www.theguardian.com/technology/gamesblog/2014/jan/23/how-world-of-warcraft-game-helped-me-come-out-transgender. Accessed 28 Sept 2016.

Dark Wolves. n.d. Guild rules. http://www.darkwolves.eu/gwiki/index.php?page_name=Guild_Rules&gid=180473&page_id=21164. Accessed 11 May 2017.

Elkund, Lina. 2011. Doing gender in cyberspace: The performance of gender by female World of Warcraft players. *Convergence: The International Journal of Research into New Media Technologies* 17 (3): 323–342.

Gilbert, Miqqi Alicia. 2009. Defeating bigenderism: Changing gender assumptions in the twenty-first century. *Hypatia* 24 (3): 93–112.

Gordon, Krystin. 2008. *Theorising desire*. New York: Palgrave Macmillan.

Hartmann, Tilo, K. Maya Krakowiak, and Mina Tsay-Vogel. 2014. How violent video games communicate violence: A literature review and content analysis of moral disengagement factors. *Communication Monographs* 81 (3): 310–332.

Hayes, Elisabeth. 2007. Gendered identities at play: Case studies of two women playing Morrowind. *Games and Culture* 2 (1): 23–48.

Hemmings, Clare. 2005. Invoking affect: Cultural theory and the ontological turn. *Cultural Studies* 19 (5): 548–567.

Järvinen, Aki. 2009. Understanding video games as emotional experiences. In *The video game theory reader 2*, ed. B. Perron and M.J.P. Wolf, 85–108. New York, NY: Routledge.

Johnson, Phylis. 2010. *Second life, media, and the other society*. New York, NY: Peter Lange Publishing.

Lucal, Betsy. 1999. What it means to be a gendered me: Life on the boundaries of a dichotomous gender system. *Gender and Society* 13: 781–797.

Massumi, Brian. 2002. *Parables of the virtual*. Durham, NC: Duke University Press.

Nyre, Lars. 2009. Normative media research: Moving from the ivory tower to the control tower. *Nordicom Review* 30 (2): 3–17.

Paik, Paul Chul-ho, and Chung-Kon Shi. 2013. Playful gender swapping: User attitudes toward gender in MMORPG avatar customization. *Digital Creativity* 24 (4): 310–326.

Probyn, Elspeth. 2005. *Blush: Faces of shame*. Minneapolis, MN: University of Minnesota Press.

Purchese, Robert. 2015, Nov. Blizzard will no longer report World of Warcraft subscriber numbers. *Eurogamer.net*. http://www.eurogamer.net/articles/2015-11-04-blizzard-wont-report-world-of-warcraft-subscriber-numbers-anymore. Accessed 5 Jan 2016.

Salamon, Gayle. 2009. Humiliation and transgender regulation: Commentary on paper by Ken Corbett. *Psychoanalytic Dialogues* 19: 376–384.

Scannell, Paddy. 2007. An interview with Professor Paddy Scannell, conducted by T. Sabry. *Westminster Papers in Communication and Culture* 4 (2): 3–23.

Sedgewick, Eve. 2003. *Touching feeling: Affect, pedagogy, performativity.* Durham, NC: Duke University Press.

Shinkle, Eugénie. 2005. Feel it, don't think: The significance of affect in the study of digital games. *Proceedings of DiGRA 2005 Conference: Changing Views—Worlds in Play.*

Stewart, Kathleen. 2007. *Ordinary Affects.* Duke University Press.

Tamborini, Ron, René Weber, Nicholas David Bowman, Allison Eden, and Paul Skalski. 2013. Violence is a many splintered thing: The importance of realism, justification, and graphicness in understanding perceptions of and preference for violent films and video games. *Projections: The Journal for Movies and Mind* 7 (1): 100–118.

Yee, Nick. 2006. The demographics, motivations and derived experiences of users of massively-multiuser online graphical environments. *PRESENCE: Teleoperators and Virtual Environments* 15: 309–329.

CHAPTER 10

The Post and the Grab: Instagram Memes and Affective Labour

Eileen Mary Holowka

This article will approach feminist Instagram art practices by considering, what I term, "platform subjectivities" in relation to affective labor and the conditions of power and visibility that influence the user experiences of gender and racially marginalized subjects. By focusing on the feminist meme artist @GothShakira (hereby referred to as Dre), I will consider multiple dimensions of the uses, values, and ethics of online affective labour, critically attending to "which questions are being asked" (boyd and Crawford, 674) within the context of Instagram activist art practices and research about them. I consider how young women and marginalized people create and navigate these social media spaces in multiple ways that indicate possibilities for empowerment as well as exploitation. I argue that Dre's feminist memes[1] are reflexive and politically responsive examples that exist within complex *in-between* spaces—as both public and private, activist and exploited, erased and visible.

I write this essay with an awareness of the ambiguous ways boundaries between public and private spaces are experienced and interpreted on these platforms. As danah boyd and Kate Crawford argue, "[t]he process of evaluating the research ethics cannot be ignored simply

E. M. Holowka (✉)
Communications, Concordia University, Montreal, QC, Canada

S. Driver and N. Coulter (eds.), *Youth Mediations and Affective Relations*,
https://doi.org/10.1007/978-3-319-98971-6_10

because the data are seemingly public" (2012, p. 672). Although users 'consent' to put their content online by agreeing to a platform's Terms of Service, they do so only because otherwise they are not allowed to use the platform and engage with users, or develop their online reputations as they might like or need. In response to boyd and Crawford's argument, I intend to question my own responsibility regarding the ethics of researching users' 'public' content, including the content I am choosing to look at and the subjects I am exploring as well as those I am excluding. Although I argue that Instagram is an important space that can be amenable to certain kinds of feminist agency and practice, particularly for young women, I am also interested in looking at when that space becomes unsafe for young women and other marginalized bodies because of exploitative forces such as appropriation by social media platforms and the non-consensual recirculation of content. While I am interested in studying "cultures of public feeling" and subversive trends online, there is a risk in clumping together large groups of people who may be acting individually, and may not perceive themselves as working collectively (Cvetkovich and Carland 2014). There is also a danger in projecting the identity of an activist onto someone who may not see themselves as such. As such, I propose an "ethics of care" as important in the process for developing respectful and ethically nuanced research methods that attend to the unique subjectivities, conditions, and power relations of diverse platform users.

@GothShakira

GothShakira (hereby referred to as Dre) is known for her production of intersectional feminist Instagram memes.[2] As a Latinx and a Columbian citizen, Dre's autobiographical memes put into conversation the lived experiences of women of colour in Internet culture. Her work mixes critical theory with popular Internet and meme language alongside images of celebrities in a way that makes complex ideas humorous and accessible. For example, in one image, a picture of Selina Gomez laughing is accompanied by the caption: "when upon realizing ur smarter than him he either sexualizes u for it or tries to mock/put u down for it (or most commonly both) in order to secure his dominance and reaffirm his own feeble sense of masculinity" (Dre, n.d.). The lack of punctuation and the phrase beginning with "when" are both characteristics of Dre's work which have been absorbed by meme culture. Dre often directly references early meme culture in her work by using Internet speak such as "u" instead of "you" as well as by creating intentionally low-res images. By choosing to play into these traditions of meme culture, Dre makes it possible for Instagram users to casually engage with critical thinking and intersectional feminist theory in an easily digestible form, on a popular and fairly accessible platform.

On January 27, 2017 Instagram Dre spoke at Concordia University's Art History Graduate Student Association (AHGSA)'s conference *no neutral art, no neutral art historians.* During this presentation, she called for more subversive, accessible, and diverse Internet art, arguing that the creation of these works offers an alternative archive of lived experience to the otherwise largely male-dominated meme culture. In order to change the politics of online meme culture, she insists on resisting normative visualizations through creative and thoughtful representation: "I don't know what to add, but take up space and keep taking up space" (Dre 2017).

Resisting Dominant Memes

As Dre herself pointed out in her talk, memes are an "art form mainly used by white, cis men on 4chan" (2017). One of the most famous manifestations of dominant meme culture can be traced through the image of "Pepe," an anthropomorphic frog originally created by Matt Furie for a comic series called *Boy's Club.* In 2015, Pepe moved from being a popular meme to becoming a symbol of the alt-right movement, often connected to Donald Trump's campaign, white nationalism, and men's rights activists (PBS Idea Channel 2017). For some time, during the writing of this chapter, Dre used an adapted image of Pepe as her Instagram profile picture, as a way to reflect on her ongoing engagement with, but also resistance to, meme culture. By creating embodied, personal, and aesthetically low-res memes, Dre and other feminist meme artists such as Binny Debbie (@scariest_bug_ever) and shannon (@sensualmemes) take back memes in ways that resist and also provide alternatives to misogyny, racism, and the alt-right.

There are many layers of power that play out in the (re)appropriative art of meme culture and it seems most important to consider *what kind of archive is being created* and *who is benefiting from the work.* Dre's memes not only make visible these issues in their wit, but also in their mere existence—particularly when they are included in galleries or featured on paying social media sites. It is not only necessary to consider which bodies are being seen in online spaces, but also which bodies are being erased *through that act of seeing*. It is important to remain wary when privileged subjects are using their power to, as Donna Haraway writes, "represent while [themselves] escaping representation" (Haraway 1988). During her presentation, Dre argued that art is one way of making visible what is often erased and that these online spaces such as Instagram can serve as forms for public dialogues that resist normative representations.

Affect, Affective Labor, and Community

In order to understand online affective labour through Dre's memes, it is important to first look at the way affect itself manifests in Instagram practices. In her chapter "Happy Objects," Sara Ahmed describes affect as "what sticks, or what sustains or preserves the connection between ideas, values, and objects" (2010, p. 29). Although Ahmed does not look directly at affective labor, understanding affect as something "sticky" allows us to look further at what exactly holds online communities together. However, despite being "sticky," affect is also commonly characterized as messy and "inarticulate" (Grossberg 2010). Likewise, in her edited collection *A Networked Self*, Zizi Papacharissi describes online spaces as a place of inbetweenness and doubling of experiences/identity (2011, p. 308). Affect manifests in many contradictory and complimentary ways, and therefore it is important not to articulate affect theory or social media interactions in a single, definite way. Instead, it is important to look at what these instances *do*—"the effect of affect" (Seigworth and Gregg 2010, p. 24). In other words, *how* are online spaces such as Instagram used and what is their connection to the lived experiences of the people using them?

Dre's memes are affective and effective in exposing the lived experiences of women of colour in emotionally vulnerable ways. In her work, she reveals herself in vulnerable ways in order to talk about what life as a young, woman of colour on the internet is like. But the creation and sharing of that vulnerability is not without its costs, particularly when trolls take to the comments sections. During her presentation at Concordia University, Dre described how she now often takes a step back from these comments because of the affective labor of engaging with them. It also becomes important to consider how many of her fans do this work in her place, even though they themselves are engaging in unpaid labor. Similarly, Dre has commented on the exploitation of her own labour, such as in her "Big Ass Meme" (2016), which was physically hung in galleries. The caption reads,

> when a marketing team comprised mainly of non-poc baby boomers approaches u to create content based on ur highly nuanced and specific personal experiences as a sex-positive latinx millennial for their monetized and syndicated 'lifestyle' clickbait site in order to sell the 'reliability' of ur subversion to ur generational cohort and they expect to pay u in nothing but the social capital u already possess. (Dre, n.d.)

Dre's "Big Ass Meme" pinpoints the dangers of social media platforms such as Instagram structuring themselves around the circulation of affect. Of course, this production of affect can also (and simultaneously) be a function of community, as seen in the case of Dre's fans creating their own memes or joining discussions in the comments sections of her posts.

Jodi Dean (2015) has argued that affective networks only produce "*feelings* of community" as opposed to actual community; however, I would argue that such shared and circulated feeling (or affect) is exactly what constitutes community (2015, p. 91). All of our online interactions today are constructed through users' affective labor, such as continual posting and participation (Pybus 2015, p. 236; Parks 2011). While this work can be voluntary and beneficial, it can also be taxing and even dangerous, as shown by Dre's own memes. Affective labor also tends to be gendered as feminine, which is important to consider when looking at online affective labor's role in the lives of young women, such as Dre, particularly when these activist or self-identifying posts might be used without creators' permission or simply talking about being a woman on the internet garners harassment. Although users are "ostensibly reporting activities and tastes for the knowledge of friends, such practices also provide an intricate archive of cultural preferences for savy marketers to exploit" (Gregg 2009, p. 210).

On Instagram, this exploitation often also manifests when a user's posts are used as data or re-circulated without the author's permission, as was the case with 'artist' Richard Prince who profited by selling screenshots of women's Instagram posts with his comments on them in art galleries (Plaugic 2015). Unlike Dre's memes which also take already existing images to use alongside her own commentary, Prince's work is unaware of the consequences of whose images he is using and ultimately profits off the work of others. Dre's memes are far more self-conscious about their borrowing and are actively engaged in conversations around meme-making, appropriation, and repurposing visible for all kinds of audiences. Exploitative work, whether it be Prince's plagiarism or the less explicit exploitation of data-mining (albeit equally violating), is why it is necessary to look at the different power structures at work in these online communities.

Community and Archives of Feeling

Instagram communities (such as those around Dre's memes) function as an "archive of feelings" that represents not only collected memories, but also feelings and experiences. Here, I use Ann Cvektovich's term "archive of feelings" to describe the affective connectivity taking place within online communities, which comprise their own archived memory and collective history that is not institutionalized. Cvetkovich's book *An Archive of Feelings* (2003) accounts for the often-overlooked experiences of women and queers by considering activism, performance, and other literature as significant cultural archives of these lives. I use her work as a way to consider feminist Instagram art practices as important cultural archives that allow for the visibility of otherwise institutionally-erased bodies. Jennifer Pybus' chapter "Accumulating Affect: Social Networks and Their Archive of Feelings" argues a similar point, "by taking into account how online archives *depend upon* the circulation of our data as enacted by affective labour and constructed within archives of feeling" (2015, p. 242). Pybus is careful to look at archives in terms of "[w]ho and what gets remembered" and how those memories accumulate meaning and cultural significance (2015, p. 239). Like the other scholars mentioned above, Pybus understands affect as something that "bridges the gap between our intentions (based on the content we choose to circulate and hence bring into our archives) and what we perceive (how it gets received by others)" (2015, p. 242). What I want to push forward in this chapter is how fundamental affective labor is in structuring these archives of feelings. Although it is important to understand the affective communities behind these practices, it is also necessary to look at who is benefiting from these structures when online platforms and networks are *designed* to work on users' affective social relations. I argue that Instagram art practices need to be understood as *both* empowering *and* exploitative, embodying the ephemeral and unstable contours indicative of affective relations.

In her presentation at Concordia University, Dre called for "Internet Historians." She described how she can no longer see her "cringey Instagram from 2012," because she deleted this content off of the platform in order to make her account less personal and 'become' "GothShakira" (2017). This decision addresses a whole other issue of online archives. Because Instagram's API (application program interface) is closed, it requires a lot of personal and affective labor to try and create one's own archive off of the platform.[3] Although we can build precarious archives of feelings, the actual content and affective labor behind these communities is always at risk of being erased, removed, or going unarchived. Dre's work offers the potential to make visible and remember otherwise erased subjects. Her memes encourage more experimentation on Instagram, and the resulting online archive of feelings allows for groups to form that may not be included in other, more institutional archives. For example, her work often questions the reasoning behind whose voices get heard and why her memes get attention over others. Consider the following text from one of her memes:

> when u realize that although some may consider ur content to be 'good' u have at least in some way received major media attention for it over others who are just as (if not more) deserving of the same recognition because u r white-passing and/or run in mostly white middle-class to upper-middle-class social circles rendering some descriptions of ur personal experiences relatable and appealing to the same people who run those major media outlets in a masturbatory cycle of eurocentrism. (Dre, n.d.)

Even Dre's more accessible and widely distributed intersectional feminist work is always balanced on a precipice of erasure, whether it be through the lack of visibility, commodified hyper-visibility, or the loss of content due to insufficient archives.

Pybus argues that a platform, community, or person's "digital subjectivities are in part reproduced by the act of forgetting" (2015, p. 242). By 'forgetting,' she is arguing that online archives sometimes leave "no means of gathering content that will come together to produce meaning" (2015, p. 244). While it is certainly difficult to track all the content posted online (boyd and Crawford 2012, p. 666), Pybus' argument overlooks the lived experiences of users who *do* produce and ascertain meaning in the content they are reading or archiving, even if their archives lack permanence. I would argue that the more interesting part of the "act of forgetting" considers which bodies are forgotten in our archive-making, or excluded by a particular practice. What is most interesting about these online archives of feelings is their potential for making visible and remembering otherwise devalued and marginalized subjects who may not be included in other, more institutional archives.[4] For example, the video platform Vine became an important space for black culture and comedy, and thus was a place where young black people could explore their identities in a thriving community (Hughes 2016). When Vine shut down its ability to post content, the fear was that this community would lose its space for expression. Just as 4-Chan fosters alt-right politics and Vine housed comedy, different platforms create different kinds of communities. In order to understand the role of online affective labor on Instagram, we must first understand how that labor is influenced by, what I will call, Instagram's *platform subjectivities*.[5]

Platform Subjectivities

Platform subjectivities refer to the different affects, identities, and ideologies that are coded into online platforms. I keep subjectivities plural here because of the many possible desires and identifications that can come out of one platform. Platform subjectivities can refer to the political dimensions of a platform, such as the prominence of black culture on Vine, or Reddit's lean toward libertarian, anti-feminist political views (Massanari 2014) which subsequently influences the kind of affective labour a platform values. Instagram, like most social networking sites, relies on continuous posting and participation which itself feeds into capitalism, however, a platform's subjectivities might run contrary to capitalism, such as when its users post anti-capitalist content. Platform subjectivities are influenced in part by their technical construction and interface, as well as designers and users' intentions, but also out of users' affective labour and how they subvert or shift those subjectivities.

The platform subjectivities of Instagram are based partly on its user base, such as that 90% of Instagram's users are under 35 (Pennsylvania State University 2015), are more likely to be black or Hispanic than white ("Instagram Demographics" 2015), and are more likely to be women than men[6] (Greenwood et al. 2016). It is likely that these demographics feed into why so many Instagram posts focus on self-representation, feminist dialogues, self-expression, the exploration of identity, self-imaging, clever memes, or the creation of alternative archives of experience—all of which have the power to be activist and affective/effective outside of (or within) their personal context.

Platform subjectivities are also constructed based on the structure of a platform, which in Instagram's case is mostly image-based, although it also includes surprisingly generous text boxes. While the image-based design allows for easily-digestible content, the additional text actually does a lot of the critical work. It is within the articulation of written text that users usually describe the images' potential meanings and intentions, whether that be related to self-love, celebration, sadness, an activist call to action, or just fun. Instagram can be a surprisingly good platform for creating conversations because the image-based design allows for easy circulation, while the text offers the chance to communicate more critical or informative ideas, say to educate, organize, or challenge. When users really do not want their words to be missed, they sometimes put text in the image, as seen with Dre's memes. Although not one of the original platforms used for circulating memes, Instagram has become a space for memes to operate away from the usual right-leaning platforms.

If the majority of users on Instagram are young, non-male, people of colour, it is important again to consider the ways that platform subjectivities and affective labor tie into gender and race imbalances. As Lisa Nakamura (2015) writes, "[w]omen perform much of the 'free labor' of social media: they are more likely to use Facebook than men; they use picture-sharing services like Instagram and Pinterest more frequently [...] they populate and generate original and unique content for fan bulletin boards; and they produce and share fan fiction" (2015, p. 223). It becomes important to consider the users of a particular platform in order to understand the ways in which users are exploited. If affective labor has typically been gendered, in what ways has this been reinforced through social media practices, particularly on Instagram? In order to understand the ways in which users are exploited, we need to first understand the history of how surveillance can lead to control and erasure, and how this shapes Instagram's platform subjectivities.

Erasure

I use the term "erasure" as a way of characterizing the marginalization and dehumanization of certain subjects and their art through under and over-representation as well as appropriation. Nakamura describes in her article "Blaming, Shaming, and the Feminization of Social Media" how "women and people of color are still overwhelmingly the objects of the biometric and surveillance gaze, as they always have been" (2015, pp. 223–224). As Andrea Smith words it, "surveillance is not simply about 'seeing' but about 'not-seeing' the settler state" (2015, p. 22). Smith looks at surveillance today and how it reflects a long history of patriarchal and colonial surveillance practices where "[t]he purposeful gaze of the state on some things and peoples serves the purpose of simultaneously making some hypervisible through surveillance while making others invisible" (2015, p. 25). What becomes invisible is "seeing the state as the settler colonial, white supremacist, and heteropatriarchal formation that it is" (2015, p. 38). Nakamura looks more closely at how surveillance effects different bodies, in particular how it "*remakes* the body as a social actor, classifying some bodies as normative and legal, and some as illegal and out of bounds" (2015, p. 221). Likewise, Alexander Cho also points out in his article how queerness is continuously "systematically erased from the public record as a 'private' thing" (2015, p. 48).

What these scholars make apparent is an ongoing history of the control and erasure of certain bodies and communities that has continued into social media practices. Although the majority of Instagram's users may be non-white, there is still a visual prominence of the white body in many Instagram communities. Similarly, internet culture (particularly memes) has long been dominated by white, heteronormative ideologies. In contrast, Dre often uses images of women of color in her memes as a method of increasing the visibility of marginalized bodies while making other aspects of their misrepresentation and erasure apparent. In an interview for *The Fader,* she says she began doing this because she "saw a lot of people of color, especially black people, being used as reaction images in memes" (Raiss 2016). In the case of heteronormative memes, as opposed to Dre's subversions, the visualization of marginalized bodies is used as a way to further erase a group's humanity. However, she also questions her own use of paparazzi-taken images of J-Lo and Selena Gomez in her memes. On the one hand, she is attempting to represent more women of color, but on the other, she is conscious that she may be reproducing their images in questionable or appropriative ways. There are constant and very serious risks to engaging in affective labor that are not often considered in regards to gazing, grabbing, or researching social media artists, especially when hyper-visibility can become another act of erasure due to appropriation or harassment.

Value, Celebrity, and the 'Grab'

Which sort of posts (and which kinds of affective labor) get valued and which get erased? Power dynamics and platform subjectivities (or platform prejudices) are made explicit when women's nipples are censored and men's are not, for example. This kind of censorship can include the erasure of political viewpoints or bodies that are not as welcome within a platform, but also reveals the capitalistic structuring of who gets valued in terms of money or "social value" (Pybus 2015, p. 236). Instagram emphasizes production, celebrity, and value (in terms of likes, comments, and the social value of affective labor that Pybus posits) (Pybus 2015, p. 236). This emphasis shapes not only the platform's expectations and the users' self-identifications, but also the expectations of all the other laboring 'produsers' in the network (Bruns 2007). Posting becomes expected of users (by the companies at the top, as well as their followers), but that expectation comes without any conscious effort to consider the affective labor those posts might require, especially in the case of users for whom posting is more of a risk (of harassment, surveillance, and more).

Working off of Pybus' argument that what structures a platform's archives of feeling is the continual posting and affective labor of its users and the earlier claims that identity is networked, I turn to Theresa M. Senft's (2008) writing about camgirls as another way to think about Instagram. Senft also makes the claim that "identity is never entirely self-derived" by arguing that identity "results from 'grabs' as it circulates around the various networks through which we associate our family, friends, employers, legal and medical systems, economies, nationalities, and so on" (2008, p. 52). Senft posits the grab in place of Laura Mulvey's (1975) male 'gaze' to characterize the ways in which interactions within social media can be more invasive than just the act of looking, such as in a screen-grab or through circulation (2008, pp. 46–47):

> on the Web, spectatorship functions less as gaze than grab. By 'grab,' I mean to clutch with the hand, to seize for a moment, to command attention, to touch—often inappropriately, sometimes reciprocally. To grab is to grasp, to snatch, to capture. Grabbing occurs over the Web in different ways during each stage of production, consumption, interpretation and circulation. (Senft 2008, p. 46)

Instagram use alone consists of many different kinds of 'grabs,' including the ways that subversive art gets subsumed and normalized back into capitalism for a profit, as well as the more explicit 'grabbing' by 'artists' such as Prince's appropriation or data-mining, as mentioned earlier (Plaugic 2015).

One of the main risks of performing online affective labor and being vulnerable online is the disempowerment of having one's content circulated without permission, whether because of online bullying, the appropriation of the work for other means, or even becoming the target of stalking or physical violence (Senft and Baym 2015, p. 1598). Meme culture tends to be more traditionally anonymous in regard to creation; however, Dre marks all of her memes with her username "@gothshakira" so that her content cannot be easily circulated without reference to her labor. Although meme-making is an art of borrowing and recirculating works, Dre's memes show that there are still socially conscious ways in which this kind of work can be done. She not only remains conscious of the kinds of images she is recirculating, but also engages in these conversations within the memes themselves. She also puts her content forward without hiding behind anonymity, even though that increases the risks for online harassment. Having the username @gothshakira helps casual users find her feminist memes in ways that would be far more difficult without recognizable creators.[7]

Risks of Exploitation/Activism

What remains consistent in looking at the online affective labor of Instagram self-imaging is the complexity of determining whether something is activist or exploited, because both can emerge simultaneously in the case of social media. I draw this boundary between activism and exploitation here, because of the way conversations around social media activism are commonly framed (either as idyllic or pointless). I use exploitation as a way to refer to the misuse or appropriation of marginalized subjects' affective labor or personal information. By activist, I refer to any kind of political participation on Instagram—including ones that involve self-representation, feminist dialogue, self-expression, the exploration of identity, self-imaging, and the creative construction of memes—that has the potential to create alternative images and narratives, change a conversation, or foster new forms of thinking. I also refer to specific social media practices as a form of activism so as to include those who cannot protest in public or physical ways (such as people with disabilities, people who receive a lot of harassment on or offline, or young people who are not allowed out of the house) (Keller 2014). While Instagram communities are often exploited, they also call out exploitation in self-reflexive ways, as seen with Dre's work.

Many scholars have pointed out the ways that the empowerment these platforms can provide is also used to further "objectify and surveil" its users (often women and marginalized groups) (Dubrofsky and Wood 2015, p. 93). No matter how radical a social media post may be, it is still being posted within a space "designed to be exploited" (Ippolita et al. as quoted in Andrejevic 2011, p. 82). It is impossible when posting on Instagram to know if the picture will ever be seen, even by certain followers, or (on the other hand) where it might end up if it is circulated in multiple contexts. As mentioned, there are always risks of harassment and stalking (Senft and Baym 2015, p. 1598) but there are also different kinds of costs that accrue when Instagram labor becomes commercially channelled, such when it is used as a way of promoting artwork or boosting a modeling career. What are the emotional and economic costs of putting oneself on a public platform in the hopes of achieving some kind of view-related value?

Although these questions of exploitation are necessary, it is also true that people still keep posting, despite the risks, because of the affective intensities enabled by the platforms, and there are many instances of empowerment and activism on these platforms. Dre's feminist memes, for example, can be considered activist in their resistance of heteronormative and alt-right Internet culture, introducing young feminists to intersectional feminist ideas, and making space for activist dialogue on Instagram. On one hand, is the fear that social media activism is not legitimate and only serves to produce more content for social media companies, while on the other is the idea that social media provides utopian possibilities for participatory engagements and creativity. I argue that these approaches are not mutually exclusive, and that critical understandings of social media necessarily require an awareness of the limits of one's own theoretical framework and material conditions that enable practice.

Because of the complex interaction between activism and exploitation on social media, I am wary as a researcher to put too strong a label on anyone's work. This may seem to contradict the fact that I have specifically referred to Dre's work as an activist practice, but I am trying to take into account those users for whom her work signifies in this way. It is important to open spaces for other meanings and identifications. Certainly, a user's work can be activist without them intending it to be, and likewise, work that is intended to be activist can be exploited. What I hope to accomplish in this paper is to avoid exploiting the affective labor of these artists I am observing, but instead to honor the complex and often invisible work they do, propose a more ethical way of researching these practices, and acknowledge the ways in which their participation is both extremely valuable in a political sense, while simultaneously being used and valued in multiple and ambiguous ways.

Dre is a somewhat public figure in terms of her meme-making, but her identity is also somewhat masked. Although her memes are quite vulnerable and her account includes selfies and some details about her personal life, she also clearly hides parts of herself from the public. Her meme-work has taken her to a more public place, but her account and identity still exist in complex spaces between the public and the private, which must be considered when talking about her and her work as art or activism. The kind of self-critical work Dre performs on her own memes is the kind of work that should be done when researching social media users:

> when ur looking forward to ugly-singing villancicos and gorging urself on tamales over the holidays with ur family but remember that right now there are tens of thousands of latinx immigrants (including extremely vulnerable unaccompanied minors) being held, abused and exploited in ICE's for-profit detention centres who, bc of an inability to speak the language of power both literally (English) and figuratively (socioeconomic status) will not be able to access the critical immigration resources required to be released and legally live in safety with their loved ones. (Dre, n.d.)

In this example, Dre performs an awareness of her own privilege (the ability to gorge herself on tamales over the holidays with family) while simultaneously questioning the challenges of other latinx-identifying subjects who are often erased by capitalist discourse. Dre constantly questions her privilege and agency in her work. The kind of critical awareness that she performs is what is often missing from conversations and research about social media activism and exploitation. I propose that this research needs to include a consideration for the affective labor of creators and what the costs of 'grabbing' might be.[8]

Responsibility as a Viewer, Witness, and Researcher

In thinking about the exploitation of Instagram users' affective labor, it is, therefore, necessary to question my own intentions and whether I am also being exploitative. boyd and Crawford (2012) write about the ethics of being a researcher in their article "Critical Questions for Big Data: Provocations for a Cultural, Technological, and Scholarly Phenomenon," arguing that "[t]he process of evaluating the research ethics cannot be ignored simply because the data are seemingly public" (2012, p. 672). boyd and Crawford propose a number of related questions in their piece:

> What if someone's 'public' blog is taken out of context and analyzed in a way that the author never imagined? What does it mean for someone to be spotlighted or to be analyzed without knowing it? Who is responsible for making certain that individuals and communities are not hurt by the research process? What does informed consent look like? (2012, p. 672)

I would like to propose some possible answers to these questions. In my research on Instagram art practices, I have found that taking 'public' content out of context is somewhat inevitable. This does not mean the author's intentions cannot or should not be considered, only that these 'public' forms of expression can end up having a life of their own due to their circulation. I propose that this means we need to consider social media posts on many levels. I argue that each post will have multiple effects (or affects) and that our research must attempt to engage with as many of these manifestations as can be traced. It is important to reconsider production in regards to consumption and to understand these producers as authors, bodies, and users themselves.

When considering the rest of boyd and Crawford's (2012) questions, I want to suggest a general method for researching social media posts. I propose that interviews should be conducted with the research users, such as Instagram posters, if possible, and the interviewees should be made aware of how their content is being used and for what purpose. It is also important to consider what exactly 'public' means to the people who are posting. Are they aware of how widely their posts are being viewed or did they click agree to the 'Terms of Service' because otherwise they would be excluded from a platform the rest of their community belongs to? Like boyd and Crawford, I question what "informed consent" looks like in relation to social media posts, where there are many factors influencing someone's decision to click 'agree' or make a public post. As researchers, it is important not to assume that this kind of 'consent' is informed, and to not take the seeming publicness of a post as a sign that it is fair game.

Instead, we must consider how to understand, research, and interpret people's continued use of platforms in a way that is ethical and respectful. In her afterword for the collection *Feminist Surveillance Studies*, Nakamura calls for "a feminist ethics of pedagogy and care" (2015, p. 227). Care ethics or the "ethics of care" focuses on "maintaining the world of, and meeting the needs of, ourself and others," particularly "those who are dependent and vulnerable" (Maureen Sander-Staudt). It is especially important to remain respectful of those who are doing the most affective labour and experience the greatest subjective social and material costs of sharing work, in this case the young and marginalized users constantly posting (often vulnerable) images on Instagram. Although care ethics has a complicated and problematic history of being connected to mothering and femininity, I suggest an ethics of care that challenges this essentialism in order to call for a more complex understanding of who is denied care and how we can perform our research with care. By turning towards care, and away from a reliance entirely based around data, we allow room for marginalized and erased bodies, lived experiences and vulnerabilities, as well as the uncared-for subjects who too often slip through the cracks.

Conclusion

What would an ethics of care look like for social media affective labour research? I argue that this would involve and engaged ethnographic approach to the content that is being researched, one that considers the bodies behind the hashtags, the images, and its data. Based on my analysis up until now, I want to additionally argue for the importance of looking at people's work both inside and outside of intention (as much as that intention can be traced), acknowledging both the potential divisions between their public and private selves as well as the potential lack of clarity between the two (how will an analysis affect their private lives?) while also considering the power imbalances that may put them at risk for exploitation or erasure. How do these different practices shape platform subjectivities? In regard to this paper, who am I excluding by focusing on only one artist and am I framing her work in a way that could be potentially harmful to her? I have explored these questions in the case of one Instagram user in order to argue that these practices of online affective labor exist in complex in-between spaces that are in constant communication with other forms of affective labor and must be researched in detail and with care. Once we consider these complexities, we can begin looking at what is being put into practice by users, considering the ways power mediates social engagements and representations as well as affirm powerful new modes of resistance through image making and storytelling that underlie the possibilities that are being created on these platforms.

*** Portions of this research originated out of a collaborative article published on Pause Button.
Walker, Cody and Eileen Mary Holowka. 2017. "Archives against Instagram: Becoming Our Own Internet Historians." *Pause Button* 2. http://milieux.concordia.ca/portfolio-items/archives-against-instagram-becoming-our-own-internet-historians/.

*** Dre was shown this paper and consulted before publication.

Notes

1. In some cases, "feminist memes" can also refer to memes that make fun of feminists or that are anti-feminist in their ideology. However, in this paper, I use the term "feminist memes" to represent memes that enact a feminist ideology.
2. In this context, "meme" refers metonymically to a specific type of viral phenomenon or meme called an "image macro." Image macros are humorous memes featuring a photograph with text superimposed on top or above the image. For clarity and to consider the Internet culture in which these are situated, I will hereby refer to them as "memes."
3. Recently, this has begun to change when Instagram introduced an archiving function where you can save images or collections of images to your account.
4. It is important to note here that, most users likely do not think of themselves as participating in an archiving process, although they may consider their contributions part of a community or network. This gap is what makes the Instagram archive of feeling distinct from community archive projects (such as the Lesbian Herstory Archives).
5. Credit for this term goes to Dr. Carrie Rentschler, who first suggested it in a class.

6. Unfortunately, I haven't been able to find statistics on non-binary or trans people, which sadly provides yet another example of how these people are erased from institutional archives.
7. There is no singular archive of feminist memes so it becomes difficult to track the content down. Users might be familiar with one user who makes memes, but without that kind of authorship, it is not necessarily easy to find similar kinds of content.
8. This conversation seems particularly significant in regards to the current conversations around cultural appropriation in Canadian Literature that gained steam on social media. Although I have not seen an instance where Dre referred specifically to this conversation, her work often takes up similar issues of cultural appropriation and the erasure of marginalized bodies.

References

Ahmed, Sara. 2010. Happy objects. In *The affect theory reader*, ed. Melissa Gregg and Gregory J. Seigworth, 29–51. Durham: Duke University Press.

Andrejevic, Mark. 2011. Social network exploitation. In *A networked self: Identity, community and culture on social network sites*, ed. Zizi Papacharissi, 82–101. London: Routledge.

boyd, danah, and Kate Crawford. 2012. Critical questions for big data: Provocations for a cultural, technological, and scholarly phenomenon. *Information, Communication & Society* 15 (5): 662–679.

Bruns, Axel. 2007. Produsage: Towards a broader framework for user-led content creation. In *Proceedings creativity & cognition* 6.

Cho, Alexander. 2015. Queer reverb: Tumblr, affect, time. In *Networked affect*, ed. Ken Hillis, Susanna Paasonen, and Michael Petit, 43–57. Cambridge: MIT Press.

Cvetkovich, Ann. 2003. *An archive of feelings*. Durham: Duke University Press.

Cvetkovich, Ann, and Tammy Rae Carland. 2014. Sharing an archive of feelings: A conversation. *Art Journal* 72 (2): 70–77.

Dean, Jodi. 2015. Affect and drive. In *Networked affect*, ed. Ken Hillis, Susanna Paasonen, and Michael Petit, 89–100. Cambridge: MIT Press.

Dre (GothShakira). Instagram account. n.d. https://www.instagram.com/gothshakira/. Accessed 5 Dec 2016.

Dre (GothShakira). 2017. But like I just want to tell Instagram all my secrets without having to worry about 4chan neo-nazis: Autobiography, Intersectionality and Privacy in Political Meme Art. *No neutral art, no neutral art historians*. Concordia University, January 27. Online at: https://www.youtube.com/watch?v=MZBv016hOmU.

Dubrofsky, Rachel E., and Megan M. Wood. 2015. Gender, race, and authenticity: Celebrity women tweeting for the gaze. In *Feminist surveillance studies*, ed. Rachel E. Dubrofsky and Shoshana Amielle Magnet. Durham: Duke University Press.

Greenwood, Shannon, Andrew Perrin, and Maeve Duggan. 2016. *Social media update 2016*. Pew Research Center. http://www.pewinternet.org/2016/11/11/social-media-update-2016/. Accessed 5 Dec 2016.

Gregg, Melissa. 2009. Learning to (love) labour: Production cultures and the affective turn. *Communication and Critical/Cultural Studies* 6 (2): 209–214.

Grossberg, Lawrence. 2010. Affect's future: Rediscovering the virtual in the actual. In *The affect theory reader*. Durham: Duke University Press.

Haraway, Donna. 1988. Situated knowledges: The science question in feminism and the privilege of partial perspective. *Feminist Studies* 14 (3): 574–599.

Hughes, Jazmine. 2016. Vine dries up. Black humor loses a home. *New York Times*. http://www.nytimes.com/2016/11/01/arts/vine-jay-versace-black-culture.html?_r=0. Accessed 13 Dec 2016.

"Instagram Demographics." 2015. *Pew research center*. http://www.pewinternet.org/2016/11/11/social-media-update-2016/. Accessed 5 Dec 2016.

Keller, Jessalynn. 2014. Making activism accessible: Exploring girls' blogs as sites of contemporary feminist activism. In *The politics of place: Contemporary paradigms for research in girlhood studies*, ed. C. Mitchell and C. Rentschler. New York: Berghahn Books.

Massanari, Adrienne. 2014. *Participatory culture, community, and play: Learning from Reddit*. New York: Peter Lang.

Mulvey, Laura. 1975. Visual pleasure and narrative cinema. *Screen* 16 (3): 6–18.

Nakamura, Lisa. 2015. Blaming, shaming, and the feminization of social media. In *Feminist surveillance studies*, ed. Rachel E. Dubrofsky and Shoshana Amielle Magnet. Durham: Duke University Press.

Papacharissi, Zizi. 2011. Conclusion: A networked self. In *Self: Identity, community and culture on social network sites*, 304–318. London: Routledge.

Parks, Malcolm R. 2011. Social network sites as virtual communities. In *Self: Identity, community and culture on social network sites*, 105–123. London: Routledge.

PBS Idea Channel. 2017. Pepe: Rare, racist or both? *YouTube*. https://www.youtube.com/watch?v=9uXYIdvV1CU&t=19s. Accessed 5 Dec 2016.

Pennsylvania State University, College of Information Sciences and Technology. 2015. Instagram behavior for teens different than adults. *ScienceDaily*. https://www.sciencedaily.com/releases/2015/06/150616155028.html. Accessed 5 Dec 2016.

Plaugic, Lizzie. 2015. The story of Richard Prince and his $100,000 Instagram art? *The Verge*. http://www.theverge.com/2015/5/30/8691257/richard-prince-instagram-photos-copyright-law-fair-use. Accessed 14 Oct 2016.

Pybus, Jennifer. 2015. Accumulating affect: Social networks and their archives of feelings. In *Networked affect*, ed. Ken Hillis, Susanna Paasonen, and Michael Petit, 187–202. Cambridge: MIT Press.

Raiss, Liz. 2016. Meet goth shakira, the high priestess of intersectional feminist memes. *Fader*. http://www.thefader.com/2016/06/03/goth-shakira-feminist-memes. Accessed 14 Oct 2016.

Sander-Staudt, Maureen. n.d. Care ethics. *Internet encyclopedia of philosophy: A peer-reviewed academic resource*. http://www.iep.utm.edu/care-eth/. Accessed 5 Dec 2016.

Seigworth, Gregory J., and Melissa Gregg. 2010. An inventory of shimmers. In *The affect theory reader*. Durham: Duke University Press.

Senft, Theresa M. 2008. I'd rather be a camgirl than a cyborg: The future of feminism on the web. In *Camgirls: Celebrity & community in the age of social networks*, 33–54. New York: Peter Lang.

Senft, Theresa M., and Nancy K. Baym. 2015. What does the selfie say? Investigating a global phenomenon. *International Journal of Communication* 9: 1588–1606.

Smith, Andrea. 2015. Not-seeing: State surveillance, settler colonialism, and gender violence. In *Feminist surveillance studies*, ed. Rachel E. Dubrofsky and Shoshana Amielle Magnet. Durham: Duke University Press.

CHAPTER 11

"Filleing" the Cinema Gap: The Precarity of Toronto's Necessary Emerging Network of Feminist Film Critics

Claudia Sicondolfo

Introduction

From Laura Mulvey's influential essay on *Visual Pleasure and Narrative Cinema* (1975) to Sophie Mayer's contemporary take in *Political Animals: The New Feminist Cinema* (2016), feminist film and media scholars have long been grappling with ongoing gender disparities' realities across international film and media industries. Since 2010, in Toronto, there has been a rise of outspoken online, emergent feminist film critics who argue that disparity not only occurs behind the camera, but also within industry mastheads. These feminist critics, Kiva Reardon of *cléo Journal*, Emily Gagne and Michelle Medford of *Cinefilles*, Sîan Melton of The Muff Society (MUFF) and Amy Wood of Drunk Feminist Films (DFF), connect film and media gender disparity within film and media criticism with its industries—the same industries that perpetuate sexist stereotypes onscreen and consistently hire the same sort of white, male, able-bodied, and cis-gendered storytellers offscreen.

C. Sicondolfo (✉)
Cinema and Media Arts, York University, Toronto, ON, Canada

S. Driver and N. Coulter (eds.), *Youth Mediations and Affective Relations*,
https://doi.org/10.1007/978-3-319-98971-6_11

These Toronto-based feminist publications and interactive screening series are founded and led by emerging female creative workers, all under the ages of 35.[1] This chapter documents the lived realities of these four young women who helm each of these groups and demonstrates how each of these women situate their own subjectivities, bodies, and labour within a climate that offers limited opportunities for emerging critical writers and filmmakers, particularly for those who are women-identifying. The critical work of these young creatives is affectively relational: in negotiating their feminist subjectivities, they collectively call for improved structural support, both for youth creative labour and for increased gender parity across film and media industries.[2]

Based on conversations with the women who run these initiatives, I argue that these emergent feminist creative workers produce a combination of online film criticism, along with affective feminist collectives that occur within physical and shared screening spaces—a combined practice I call hybrid film criticism. *cléo*, founded by Reardon in 2012 following the completion of her Master's degree in Cinema Studies in her mid-20s, is an online, open-access "journal of film and feminism" (http://cleojournal.com). It has published 14 issues (as of December 2017) and features an intersectional, all-women editorial masthead. *cléo* is committed to paying contributors equally despite their career-level. *Cinefilles* was founded in 2010 by aspiring film critics Emily Gagne and Michelle Medford following their graduation from Ryerson's Journalism program. Originally, a passion project, *Cinefilles* provided them with a place to publish film writing they could not publish elsewhere, eventually expanding to hire fellow emerging women contributors.

Following *Cinefilles* termination in 2016,[3] Gagne began partnering with Sîan Melton's MUFF (Monthly Underground Female Film) initiative, a feminist screening series founded in 2014 dedicated to building an online and offline network to highlight the work of women in film. The series has a focus on building a community of girl-led filmmaking and audiences. DFF, founded by Amy Wood, Shaunna Bruton, Steph Guthrie, Gillian Goerz in 2012, describe themselves as a "collective of feminists who would rather laugh than cry their way through representations of gender in Hollywood films" (Tersigni 2016). DFF began as a YouTube web series and has expanded into sold-out live screening events where they encourage their boisterous feminist audiences to collectively "yell back." By examining the collective, hybrid networks these women have built, I trace the creation of an alternative, meaningful critical film space.

This chapter, however, also traces the affective un-productivity of their labour. As these four women find themselves struggling against and through their often un(der)paid digital labour, they also find themselves repositioning their livelihoods, labour, and hybrid creative practices within creative precarity cycles.

In uncovering the labour patterns of these feminist publications and screening collectives, I turn directly to the young women to ask them about their experiences. This chapter expands upon three of the primary goals that unfold during our conversations: (1) why these women are moved to produce work; (2) how their work responds to gender imbalances in the field of film and media writing and representation; and (3) how they demonstrate meaningful youth labour practices throughout their creative exchanges. This paper seeks not to essentialize all young creatives or women film critics. It is motived by careful historical and interpretive analysis operating on the belief that human-situatedness in research can illuminate a deeper understanding of relationships in practice (Campbell 2013, p. 21). In centralizing the motivations and struggles of these emergent female film critics and creatives, I provide a nuanced historical and social analysis of how their work responds to their unique social position within history.

Situating Contemporary Youth Creative Labour

While conducting interviews with these four women, the often-underlying question rooting their feminist labour was one which asked *how do we build vital communities to fight the individualizing creative economic model that surrounds us?* In looking at their labour practices and content output, these four feminist creatives challenge production expectations of small-scale creative labour by creating work that is politically meaningful yet also seeks a profit, thereby pushing back on traditional "volunteer" expectations. In considering youth an active phase of life, and youth cultural production as instrumental in transforming, challengeing, and creating within the public sphere (Ares 2010, p. 6), the spaces generated by youth creative labour are constructive places where young people can identify each other and their work in response to influencing social-economic systems.

Miranda Campbell's (2013) research on Canadian youth creatives applies Angela McRobbie's "hobby work" to the micro-economies created by young feminists. Campbell documents how Canadian youth-run alternative, small-scale creative industries remain largely un(der)funded and misunderstood, due to ongoing narrow policy definitions of small-scale and self-generated youth-led creative labour. Campbell also carefully documents the implications of the 2008 industrial economic collapse on pathways for Canadian youth creatives, noting considerable job cuts within the arts. In 2008–2009, as youth increasingly began turning towards the creative industries as a source of employment post-graduation, financial, and structural and polity support for their self-produced emergent initiatives remained unresponsive.[4] While young creatives are acknowledged as "vulnerable" within policy documents, their employment precarity remain misunderstood, structurally supported through outdated post-graduation life course transitions. Campbell notes, for example, the Conservative Government's Budget 2009 suggests it will enact policy to allow "youth [to] later enter the workforce [despite] not currently working," (p. 111) however, there is no acknowledgment on the shifting life practices preventing them from doing so.

The feminist film collectives and critics interviewed for this paper do not view these shifting employment contexts as provisional or momentary, but as tangible and permanent realities, they must maneuver personally and professionally. Along with being the founding editor of *cléo*, Reardon holds various contracts for the Toronto International Film Festival (TIFF) and works as a freelance critic. Gagne worked full-time as a marketing and social media coordinator while she ran *Cinefilles* and continues to program MUFF events. Amy Wood, one of DFF's founders, manages several projects as a marketing and communications freelancer, and Siân Melton ran MUFF from London, England while interning for feminist blog *Women & Hollywood* and holding a day job as a social media manager.

Such dispersed employment realities reflect ongoing changes in Canadian labour market demands. Stats Canada *Labour Force Survey* for November 2016 indicates concerning precarious employment developments in Canada: a rise in part-time employment from November 2015 by 6.4%; an increase in youths (demarcated as 15–25) employed in part-time capacities by 5%; and a 5.4% decline in youths occupying full-time employment (Statistics Canada, November 2016). These four feminist critics work within an accelerating knowledge-driven market economy where direct trajectories from graduation to full-time employment are uncommon. Their reality is that they must sustain themselves financially and emotionally as emerging professionals within a climate of intensifying employment fracturing.

"*Fille*"-ing Space: Building Hybrid Spaces of Feminist Film Criticism

Throughout our conversations, all four feminists situated the meaningfulness of their work within the need to fill—or, rather, *fille*—the lopsided gendered labour gaps within film and media industries. These are spaces rooted in principles propelled by community-led youth work, including: (1) risk-taking; (2) building connectivitiy between offline and online networks; and (3) sharing in meaningful, engaged communities that emotionally and professionally support their feminist identities.

Cléo *and Risk*

After receiving her Master's degree in Cinema Studies in 2012, Kiva Reardon became increasingly discouraged by the gendered reality of trying to establish herself in the world of film criticism. Reardon often found herself as the lone woman film reviewer on the masthead. When she was submitting her reviews that commented on the gender issues onscreen or behind the camera, Reardon's editors often rejected the critique, arguing that the public was "not interested in gender stuff." Reardon "was overwhelmed by the whiteness and maleness of it all" (personal interview, April 2016). Her response was definitive: "what can I do to structurally change the industry I'm trying to work in? I'll create my own jobs and give similar opportunities to the people who are facing a similar experience to try to manifest something with a tangible output."

In launching *cléo*'s tenth issue in April 2016 titled "Risk," Reardon posted on her Facebook wall:

> [w]e've published 77 pieces. Our masthead boasts 58 contributors–and 50 of them are women. This means that 86% of our critics are female. This matters in an industry where women are chronically unrepresented. (In 2013, 78% of the top critics on Rotten Tomatoes were male). The idea behind starting *cléo* was to carve out a space for women writing about film ... to create a platform that will help new voices get a foot in the door and allow them to try out ideas that other publications weren't willing to take risks on.[5]

Reardon points towards a 2016 San Diego State University study about female film critics that found only 27% of the "top critics" on Rotten Tomatoes were women (Lauzen 2016). In Toronto, the stats are equally disparaging. In 2017, the Toronto Film Critics Association (TFCA) (of which Reardon is a member) appointed its 13th female member out of a total of 37. Only two of these 13 are women of colour. Moreover, *Women in View*'s (a Canadian not-for-profit organization dedicated to strengthening gender and cultural diversity in Canadian media), a 2016 research report charts overall Canadian industry imparities– of the 327 directors, writers, and cinematographers from 2013–2014 working in Canada only 57 (17%) of those credits are women (Fraticelli 2015, p. 6).

Reardon's post demonstrates a negotiation with her personal relationship with feminism through a political and public identity she fosters through online self-publishing, a youth-driven media production tool. The title of *cléo*'s tenth issue is not accidental. With a "risky" limited fundraising budget, *cléo*'s editorial team of young women, intersectional from the onset, remained committed to creating their own online, self-publishing practice. Taking very literal *risks* with young and emergent writers, Reardon identifies her project as a systemically important response to lived, industry gaps (Simonpillai 2016). Reardon continues to take "risks" – the journal commits to paying its female contributors, many of whom are just beginning their professional writing careers.

Reardon's Facebook post also illustrates the activist potentials of online social media outreach. Jessalynn Keller (2016) documents the networked identity performances found in the practices of young feminist bloggers within a longstanding history of feminist public writing. While Keller is not the first scholar to lineate connections between female subjectivity and writing (McRobbie and Garber 2006; McRobbie 1994), she argues that contemporary young women foster "risky" political identities when they "go public" online. As Reardon "goes public" as she performs an identity in relation with both her work and her feminist subjectivity, connecting Reardon to a larger feminist network that exists between and among her online and offline worlds.

Cinefilles, *on/and/off/Line*

Cinefilles is rooted in similar motivations to create personal, alternative spaces for emerging female writers. The online blog originally provided Gagne and Medford with a place to publish film writing they could not publish elsewhere, yet they were increasingly provoked by a lack of female film criticism and filmmakers. "Our goal ever since has been to shine a light on women like us, who love writing and making films ... we want to '*fille*' the void in film journalism" (Gagne, personal interview, April 2016). Eventually, Gagne and Medford began publishing fellow young "*cinefilles*," building critical film space to address feminist themes on and off screen.

In giving online visibility to women critics and industry professionals, Gagne provided a tangible outlet to address the systemic difficulties young women—including herself—face when trying to establish themselves across film and media industries. Web operations, however, became increasingly difficult to maintain, so Gagne began sustaining *Cinefilles'* online visibility through live events. Initially partnering with MUFF for a one-off event in October 2015, Gagne and Sîan Melton have now expanded their partnership into a reoccurring film talk-back series called "Reel Girl Talk," housed as a MUFF initiative. "Reel Girl Talk" pairs a film with a roundtable discussion of the feminist issues raised in the film. Gagne explains how the expansion into live events facilitated the creation of a missing and necessary hybrid space where *Cinefilles'* online and offline networks could collaborate through varied spaces, across virtual and physical presences.

There are two important ideas to note in Gagne's emphasis on the importance of live events and how they relate to feminist and youth creative practice. First, as a revenue initiative, the creative shift from online to offline screening space acts as a "micro-economy": a small-scale cultural work practice that grows out of what was previously (mis)understood as personal "hobby work" (Campbell 2013; McRobbie 1989). Micro-economic work, according to McRobbie, is work and is meaningful work that often grows in response to youth employment precarity and dissatisfaction. Gagne reports some of the initial imperatives to move towards live screening events included the possibility of transferring ticket revenue into supporting *Cinefilles'* online operating costs.

Second, her emphasis on sharing "liveness" underscores the importance of sense and meaning making practices deployed by young people wanting to share in lived experiences. The live events, attended by a predominantly youth, women-identifying audience, continue conversations already occurring on the *Cinefilles'* blog and on MUFF's social media networks. These events demonstrate the importance of liveness as an ongoing relational and shared experience, evocative of what Jacqueline Kennelly and Stuart Poyntz explain as youth "living out as a meaningful relationship with the world" (2015, p. 10). This relational, worldly negotiation is particulalry notable in Reel Girl Talk's

January 2017 event dedicated to the theme of "Women in Sport." Gagne programs *Girlfight* (2000), featuring a woman filmmaker of colour and a film featuring a young female athlete of colour, along with a post-screening conversation between Mackenzie Duffy (Creator and Executive Producer of WiSe Talk, a student-led initiative that supports the education of young women in the sport media industry) and Steph "Iron Lioness" (Co-Creator and Creative Director of Iron Lion Training Inc.). Iron Lioness is a West Indian woman boxer who speaks about her bullied childhood and her relationship to sport and the film.[6] Iron Lioness also talks about her need to belong to a women's sporting community, reminds the audience that women's boxing was not recognized as an Olympic sport until 2012. These post-screening discussions situate *Girlfight*, a 2000 film, within a current lived oral history, addressing the underrepresentation of racialized women across the cultural industries—within sport, cinema, and in critical writing. In other words, this programming choice acts out a meaningful relationship with specific socio-economic realities for Gagne and the *Cinefilles* community at large.

The MUFF Society's "Fun" Mentorship

The MUFF Society began in an ad hoc fashion when Melton started programming for a Toronto-based cinema in 2014. MUFF has since evolved into a multi-faceted, feminist community featuring programming that is "socially responsible, with a focus on women filmmakers" (Melton, personal interview, April 2016).[7] Its central event is the bimonthly screening series MUFFxTO, championing women in film, both on and off screen. Every screening has raffle prizes, a pre-show with a pop-up shop featuring local women artisans, a women-centric playlist inspired by the film, and a photobooth with props. Short films are programmed in the mini-MUFF series, which pairs local, women-made films with a MUFFxTO feature. Reel Girl Talk and HER-story are quarterly series that screen women-directed Canadian topical documentaries. The MUFF Blog highlights feminist films and local filmmakers, and profiles local women-centric film crowdfunding campaigns. Building conscious, mentoring communities—particularly among youth audiences—unifies MUFF's offshoot initiatives. Reel Girl Talk is co-presented by a Toronto-based organization called Reel Girls Toronto, whose mandate celebrates the stories of young women aspiring to work in Toronto's arts sectors. Such initiatives prioritize the connectivity of feminist creatives at different levels of their careers.

MUFF's network facilitates the sharing of public feminist presence, and follows the historical continuum of connecting feminists through multi-faceted creative practices. This "consciousness raising"[8] programming is specifically dedicated to providing iterative spaces that both celebrate and explore the conflicting sense-making relationship of being both "girl" and "feminist" within a time of heightened girl-targeted consumerism (Coulter 2014). MUFF's branding, for example, is unbashfully pink, but this consumer-based identification is consistently questioned. In a September 2016 Blog post follow-up to an argumentative Q&A session, for example, Melton challenges MUFFians to express their anger or disagreement with panelists honestly but respectfully (Melton 2016). She does not issue a plea for censorship, rather mentors a space that is supportive and productive for panelists and audience goers alike. Melton's post also demonstrates how MUFF's brand negotiates with the disciplining behavioral paradigms of "girls" within arts and culture sectors.

Within MUFF's hybrid programming model, a celebration of feminism in and around cinema is an embodied and shared expression of participatory feminist "fandom." As the audience is engaged through a brand emphasis on "fun," MUFF's events analogously create visible publics for their spectators and panelists, announcing themselves publically as legitimate cinema-going, youth-oriented audiences who can be both critically feminists and fans.

Playing Critically with DFF

Along with MUFF and *Cinefilles*, DFF has simultaneously tapped into a youth-led phenomenon of building critical and interactive feminist screening series. The popular web and live event series screens popular films with problematic gender representations. Past screenings include *Love, Actually* (2003) and *Bring It On* (2000). DFF's first video analyzed *The Craft* (1996) through feminist criticism, playfully complemented with a drinking game. Following the video's online popularity, DFF evolved the online series into live screening events. One of DFF's founders, Amy Wood explains that DFF envisions both on and offline spaces as outlets for feminists to share their frustrations collectively, energetically, and through public demonstrations of spectatorship defined on their own terms (personal interview, April 2016). DFF's audiences tell Wood that they like the *DFF* series because it is a way for them to have fun while engaging critically and collectively in feminist discourses.

At their screening events, program notes are distributed with prompts for audience member responses through loud call-backs and collective drinking (both alcoholic and non-alcoholic drinks are welcomed), cued by repetitive problematic racist and sexist scenarios and innuendos in the film.

Kristen Cochrane (2016) has traced how DFF's screening spaces reposition traditional masculine rituals (such as drinking game cultures and shouting) in centering visible and vocal intersectional feminist spectatorial positions. This spatial negotiation also occurs within DFF's online spaces. For example, DFF's 2016 National Canadian Film Day[9] video features an analysis of Deepa Mehta's *Bollywood/Hollywood* (2002) and presents commentary by three Canadian-South Asian Toronto creatives, Amil Niazi, Resh Brown, and Scacchi Koul, who watch the film with their spiked Mango Lassis. Niazi sarcastically (and sincerely) honours the film "by eating brown food" (samosas and pakoras). The three women chat about how nice it is to see brown grandmas and aunties on screen. Mehta's film also incites them to share certain annoyances about living as South-Asian young women in Canada, "like when white people talk to me about yoga." At a certain point, Niazi, Brown, and Koul playfully challenge the stereotypical representations of typically dismissive South-Asian female characters, eventually inspiring Koul to call her mother. We're privileged to the phone conversation between Koul and her mom, who eventually scolds her daughter on-air for being a "drunk feminist," thus putting to rest the stereotype of the dismissive South-Asian mother seen in *Bollywood/Hollwood*. Throughout this video, as these women perform their talk-back, the spectatorial subjectivity of Niazi, Brown, and Koul resists a more traditional passive spectator-performer binary of public cinema-going. It also highlights the contradictory affects embodied by many young feminists who might "enjoy" self-identifying within popular, mainstream culture.

DFF's hybrid critically "fun" model seems to be working. DFF charges for their events so they can support the online production of their YouTube series. They have recently expanded into a larger screening venue and due to their YouTube presence, they have gained international attention from young women in Australia interested in launching a local DFF chapter. In combining online digital media criticism with communal experiences, DFF's participatory screening spaces create a overlying of publics which supporte and sustain the other. These are also self-regulated spaces, where the public demonstration of intersectional feminist identities remains safe, where the online trolling many of the DFF founders face consistently is not permitted, and where these young women can collectively "yell back" (Wood, personal interview, April 2016).

Centering Feminist, Youth-Led Creative Workers: Affective and Lived Realities

Through their networked hybrid publics, Reardon, Melton, Gagne, and Wood build what Lucy Bolton (2011) calls a "feminist genealogy"—connecting women and their labour to each other, with the goal of influencing a male-dominated world of film criticism to think differently about cinema—to produce not only a different kind of cinema, but also a different kind of socio-economic space of parity. They also characterize a growing practice by young women who identify with feminist practices through what is increasingly becoming branded as a fourth wave. Recent popular culture and feminist blogs written by millennial feminists classify the fourth wave through digital media technologies (*Untitled Magazine* 2015; Mattil 2013). They emphasize intersectionality and multiple ways to be publicly feminist. Keller's research (2016) on young feminist bloggers notes that while many young feminists do not take the feminist wave metaphor literally, they also do not necessarily identify with the third wave. It is not necessary to uphold a linear and totalizing "wave" metaphor; however, it would be erroneous to ignore the unique temporal-historical understanding of the feminist and professional subjectivities of these four emergent feminist film and media creatives. By centering their unique lived realities, significant insights into labour and media industries are notable. The following sections outline two important youth-centred recommendations situated directly from my interviews with these four women: (1) increased policy responses acknowledging the online situatedness of emerging and women creatives; and (2) improved structural flexibility for digital and hybrid non-fiction and event-based creatives and collectives.

Online Situatedness

Through online self-publishing pathways, Reardon, Gagne, Melton, and Wood work within the growing paradigm of young women and girls who use online networks to produce critical work. These online networks provide space for contemporary young feminists to situate their needs, criticisms, and observations regarding outdated educational policies[10] and inequitable labour and gender standards.[11] Despite this growing web-based trend, following a three-year comprehensive study on Canadian online polity, Jane Bailey and Valerie Steeves (2015) report that policy makers have not yet taken the lived realities of girls and young women online into account, nor have they reflected seriously on how intersecting identities are formed online. DFF, for example, has taken it upon themselves to regulate their online space, turning off commenting from their YouTube videos, thus uninviting public misogyny.[12]

For Reardon, it is very important that *cléo* remains open-access. At the time of our conversation, *Camera Obscura* is the only other international feminist film journal in publication, but high subscription fees make it often inaccessible to critics outside of academia. However, the magazine has struggled to secure both provincial and federal funding largely due to it being online and open-access. *cléo* was rejected from the Magazine Grants section of the Ontario Arts Council (OAC) in 2015. Reardon views the Trillium Foundation grants (another provincial funding agency) as "just for shadowing," given that the revenue for a publication needs to be at minimum, $65 K. "We don't even have a subscription base!" is Reardon's response to this requirement. *cléo* has also been twice denied from Canada Council for the Arts (CCA)[13] grants. The first rejection specified that they were not eligible for any grants since *cléo* did not pay their writers—a flawed rejection, as Reardon applied for funding precisely *to* pay her team of writers. Reardon's second CCA rejection specified that the journal did not feature sufficient Canadian content. Expressing frustrations towards the unsustainable mythos of the Canadian granting narrative, Reardon states, "all of our writers are Canadian and we feature Canadian content in every issue. Maybe the CCA should fund more female industry professionals so we can write about them. Who are we going to write about? Deepa Mehta, ad nauseam?"

cléo eventually received an OAC grant following the restructuring of the Magazines Grants. An OAC officer confirmed that the newly formed category of Publishing Organizations: Projects is a continuation of [the magazines program]. It is effectively the same program with a new name and somewhat broader eligibility criteria. Without specifying what this "somewhat broader eligibility" entails, it demonstrates an inclusive shift within categorization to include online publications. *Cléo* continues to hold a Patreon campaign to pay their editors, who remain unwaged.

According to Reardon and Gagne, granting programs do not reflect the reality that online creatives must pay for the internet. Throughout *Cinefilles'* six-year run, Gagne states they struggled to keep up with their operational costs, expressing frustration in the lack of minimal support they could access for their digital operational costs, such as website hosting fees, online designer fees, website bugs and bandwidth. Gagne explains that sufficient editorial staff and operational demands depend on the other, and *Cinefilles* could not operate without the support of both: "We don't make a lot of profit… but it's definite and real and there is true passion there for me. I've always wanted to get to a space where we can get to more money so we that we don't call it *volunteer*. When we make money, it goes back into the website. But, no, I wouldn't call it volunteer" (personal interview, April 2016). Gagne appreciates that *Cinefilles* filled a journalistic void, yet as a writer herself, not paying her contributors made her uncomfortable, and she terminated the intitiative.

Struggling to keep up with their operational costs, Reardon and Gagne unhappily duplicate conditions of the writing internship models found within larger publications. While an examination of this unsustainable internship structure is beyond the scope of this paper, these examples demonstrate how this model is too easily replicated by micro-economies within a fracturing and self-disciplining political economy. While both Gagne and Reardon are motivated *to* work because of their subjectivities as young feminist creative entrepreneurs, it is this same system that challenges their work from growing beyond unsustainable gendered socio-economic realties. In her book, *Work's Intimacy* (2011), Messila Gregg conveys affective limits as unspoken additional labour pressures attributed to contemporary professional employees, particularly upon women knowledge workers. The increased demands for online, professional co-presence makes visible the impossible narrative of a postfeminist work-life balance (Gregg 2011). Outstanding from Gregg's work, but notable in this project is how this disciplinary affective labour is particularly heightened for emerging women creatives. Gagne and Medford, for example, feel particulalry drained by their own expectations to maintain "hyperactive" workdays to keep *Cinefilles* afloat. In as much as *Cinefilles* is fueled by an affective passion to create visible online alterity for emerging feminist writers, its termination is similarly fueled by limits. The empathy required to maintain a "permanently transitional" networked presence, always "on" and ready to "make a difference" is exhaustive and becomes exhausted.

Gregg centres the affective intimacies of her research subjects through their lived reality to "begin a longer conversation about the better workplaces we might imagine for the future" (2011, p. 18). Similarly, by centering the online situatedness of Gagne and Reardon, a "better" online workplace can be imagined for contemporary youth feminist writers. In 2016, the Online Film Critics Association of Canada (OFCAC), headed by Trisha DeVries, was established. I argue that it is largely due to the affective labouring realities of critics like Gagne and Reardon that the OFCAC operates with significant deviations from the TFCA. Of its ten board members, five are women (albeit a glaring absence of women of colour remains). Gagne was recently invited to join this network despite being a critic who is not always profiting from her writing. Strikingly, the association's mission "welcome[es] new, established and alternative forms of criticism within a professional context." Mentorship and membership is offered to critics, editors, publishers, and podcasters alike, demonstrating how CAOFC's flexible organizational structure begins to respond to the affective limits expressed by online writers like Gagne and Reardon.

Funding Flexibility for Hybrid Models

In a climate of increasingly individualizing cultural industries, McRobbie has demonstrated how youth are targeted through promises of often-impossible combinations for lucrative and self-fulfilling labour. "Work, [now] comes to mean much more than just earning a living; it incorporates and overtakes daily life" (McRobbie 2002, p. 99). "Meaningful" work is often associated with the promise of professional selfhood, and so it is often pursued through limited structural and policy support, resulting in intensive self-disciplining. Reardon and Gagne are no exception. While the cultural industries surge with young creative entrepreneurs online, irregular and insecure livelihoods do not dissipate with this new type workforce culture, but are rather intensified.

These feminist collectives confront this contradiction directly through their hybrid online/offline critical screening. DFF's live performance structure, for example, forces us, as cultural thinkers and policy makers, to confront questions about *how* these types of projects should be funded. Having registered as a for-profit company because they wish to generate self-sustained profit from all "the unpaid hours they put into their work," (Wood, personal interview, April 2016), DFF's for-profit business model eliminates them from qualifying for many municipal, provincial and federal arts grants that require not-for-profit (NFP) registration. Additionally, DFF's performative, ongoing on-and-offline curation does not align with many traditional curatorial grants. The 2016 OAC's "Diverse Curatorial Projects"[14] supports diverse programming and ancillary publications, but the organization must be a registered NFP and events cannot begin prior to the award's receipt, immediately eliminating DFF from eligibility.

DFF's micro-economic, entrepreneurial model solidifies an important narrative: such youth-driven, feminist models do not and often cannot *work* within traditional Canadian tri-level (federal, provincial, municipal) public arts granting structures. Their hybrid labour exists outside many of the granting options noted already in this paper. Their labour calls for more flexible funding of entrepreneurial models. This means increased allocations for emerging community-level start-ups, but it also means a necessary rethinking of the widely instituted NFP requirement. Interestingly, is it within a privately-funded provincial Laidlaw youth-led community initiative grant where a seemingly more-flexible model is located. To remain more "inclusive of youth-led groups in Ontario," this grant does not require NFP registration (Laidlaw 2016). While it is unsurprising that a for-profit company acknowledges the economic benefit of encouraging for-profit registration, it remains equally surprising that following Campbell's comprehensive research, many of Canada's tri-level granting agencies still require rigid NFP-registration for micro-economic labourers along with often rigid delineations of creative work that either lives on *or* off line. As a cautionary clarification, this example underscores Laidlaw as an example of a more flexible rethinking of what qualifies as meaningful paid labour—a rethinking which should be embraced by Canada's tri-level funding structure. It remains somewhat alarming that the private sector maintains more flexible qualifications for youth-led community labour.

Moreover, as DFF's hybrid curatorial and creation model remains disconnected from traditional public funding models, it also responds to a need for improved access to professional mentors vital for emerging women creatives. As a young freelancer, Wood believes, "a support system needs to be created from the ground up. We need structural support: business advisors, marketing consultants." It is important to remember that as MUFF, DFF, and *cléo* continue to respond to structural gaps in networking and community, they take on additional gendered emotional labour (Gregg 2011, p. 13). These feminists, already in precarious positions, becomes increasingly self-disciplined, motived by a *need* to rectify what is missing in structural policy. All four of women, for instance, expressed full support for the recent 2016 and 2017 National Film of Canada (NFB) parity announcements (NFB/ Blog 2017), optimistic these quotas will result not only in the hiring of women filmmakers, but also in increased mentorship opportunities for creatives beyond their already exhausted grassroots initiatives. The move for young women creatives to create networked and hybrid, alternative spaces of connectivity will depend on how societal programs respond.

Conclusions

This paper demonstrates how young and emergent feminist creatives situate their lived socio-economic professional and personal subjectivities within their affective and meaningful labour. As these women create feminist work and space, they strive to build vital communities of connectivity and visibility within an increasingly individualizing creative economic model. In speaking along with their lived realities, I argue these young women challenge policy makers and cultural theorists to respond to the affective and collective labouring gendered realities of young, feminist creatives.

At whose expense must this labour constantly fall to? In 2016, the Canadian Liberal Budget announced an additional $165.4 million in the Youth Employment Strategy. However, Budget 2016 remains disconnected from the disparaging realities of youth creatives. Employment pathways for youth are, once again, demarcated in a traditional sense by helping "young Canadians gain valuable work experience" (Department of Finance Canada 2016). While the need to create "new green jobs" is highlighted, there is no acknowledged focus on the creation of "new" youth-led, creative work. Such a budget as Banks and Hesmondhalgh have argued really just reflects an extension of a neoliberal agenda that aims to "develop workforce skills, stimulate business-oriented education and improve competitive advantage across the creative industry sector" (2009, p. 426). Budget 2016 continues to reflect an outdated top-down employment stimulus policy approach. Its increased investment on the employer remains linked to national economic stimulus, rather than on investments in grassroots entrepreneurial development, social reform, and cultural equity.

As cultural critics interested in understanding the relationships between legislated and systemic policy and the changing socioeconomic lived realities of young creatives, we are being invited by feminist labourers like Reardon, Gagne, Wood, and Melton to listen and respond; to produce qualitative research that places youth and their labour practices in direct conversation with quantitative research and new policy initiatives. This is messy work, but I encourage us as researchers, educators, and policy makers to undergo similar methodological enquiries. This work highlights the affective tensions that root themselves amongst the networks of digital hybridity and imparity currently being exposed by the important labour of critical young feminists.

Notes

1. While the categorization of youth is a discursively-produced, fluid life stage, for this project youth is delineated between the ages of 18–35 to address the social and temporal employment realities contemporary youth cultural workers face.
2. In the "Notes on the Translation and Acknowledgments" section of *A Thousand Plateaus*, the translator defines affect/affection: "Neither word denotes a personal feeling (*sentiment* in Deleuze and Guattari). *L'affect* (Spinoza's *affectus*) is an ability to affect and be affected. It is a prepersonal intensity corresponding to the passage from one experiential state of the body to another and implying an augmentation or diminution in that body's capacity to act" (1987, p. xvi).
3. As of 2017, *Cinefilles* has suspended operations. Their work remains viewable through the Internet Archive Wayback Machine archive: https://web.archive.org/web/20140803094228/www.cinefilles.ca/ (29 captures. August 3, 2014–October 1, 2017).
4. Marc Malgot and Katherine Larose-Hébert (2010) report that following the 2008 industrial economic collapse, the value of information and knowledge economies (Garnham 2005; Banks and Hesmondhalgh 2009) has heightened, encouraging young people to stay in school longer. Their report acknowledges unpredictable and fragmenting contemporary nonlinear youth life paths related to unavailable competition for stable employment, rising and unaffordable housing and few prospects for savings, due to higher debt-loads often incurred from "re-professionalizing" through schooling and re-certification. This contemporary youth life course continues to prolong entry-points into "stable adulthood" beyond the age of 30. See, also, Gaudet 2007 for additional reports on prolonged adulthood.
5. Accessed April 19, 2016. Reprinted with permission.

6. Steph "Iron Lioness" Origin's Story (16 February 2017), http://www.ironliontraining.ca/blog/2017/02/iron-lioness-an-origin-story/.
7. As of November 2017, MUFF has suspended its ongoing screening series citing (unsurprisingly) labour, time, and resources. MUFF remains active online and in partnership with events across Toronto, https://www.muffsociety.com/news-1/2017/11/15/listen-up-super-important-announcement.
8. Keller (2016) has called similar connective spaces "consciousness raising" zones, placed along longstanding feminist art practices from 1920s women's liberation marches to riot grrrl zines in the 1990s to contemporary online social media activism (p. 83).
9. A national initiative that encourages the viewing of a Canadian film by as many Canadians as possible in a single day: https://canadianfilmday.ca/.
10. See the 2015 youth-led #WeGiveConsent campaign by Tessa Hill and Lia Valente: https://www.change.org/p/ontario-ministry-of-education-make-consent-a-topic-in-the-2015-ontario-health-curriculum as one policy-influencing example.
11. See Meghan Murphy's blog *Feminist Current* http://www.feministcurrent.com/about/ for one example of youth-led online feminist criticism in Canada.
12. Wood confirms all members of DFF have been targets of online trolling.
13. In 2017, the CCA established six new funding programs. Replacing a number of discipline-specific specialized funding programs, these changes reflect an acknowledgement of increasing diversification in Canadian arts practices; impacts of new technologies on the arts; young artists working collaboratively with communities and sectors outside of the arts; and the "piecing together" of employment across NFP and for-profit community arts practices: http://canadacouncil.ca/funding/grants.
14. The eligibility guidelines for the grant have been removed. A report of the grant's results is available at http://www.arts.on.ca/grants/general-granting-information/grant-results/2016/october/culturally-diverse-curatorial-projects/. Accessed Nov 2017.

Bibliography

Ares, Nancy. 2010. Introduction. In *Youth-full productions: Cultural practices and constructions of content and social spaces*, ed. Nancy Ares, 1–17. New York: Peter Lang.

Bailey, Jane, and Valarie Steeves (eds.). 2015. *eGirls, eCitizens*. Ottawa: The University of Ottawa Press.

Banks, Mark, and David Hesmondhalgh. 2009. Looking for work in creative industries policy. *International Journal of Cultural Policy* 15 (1): 415–430.

Bolton, Lucy. 2011. *Film and female consciousness: Irigaray, cinema and thinking women*. London: Palgrave Macmillan.

Campbell, Miranda. 2013. *Out of the basement: Youth cultural production in practice and policy*. Montreal: McGill University Press.

Cochrane, Kristen. 2016. The perversity of Drunk Feminist Films. *Canadian Theatre Review* 168 (Fall): 63–67.

Coulter, Natalie. 2014. *Tweening the girl: The crystallization of the tween market*. New York, NY: Peter Lang.

Deleuze, Gilles, and Felix Gauttari. 1987. *A thousand plateaus: Capitalism and schizophrenia*, trans. Brian Massumi. Minneapolis: The University of Minnesota Press.

DECODE. 2007. *Next generation of artistic leaders and arts audience dialogues*. Ottawa: Canada Council for the Arts.

Department of Finance Canada. 2016. Growing the middle class. Tabled by William Francis Morneau (Ottawa), March 22. http://www.budget.gc.ca/2016/docs/plan/budget2016-en.pdf. Accessed Nov 2017.

Drunk Feminist Films. 2016a. Drunk Feminist Films presents: *Bring It On*. Program notes. Review Cinema, February 6.

Drunk Feminist Films. 2016b. Drunk Feminist Films & National Canadian Film Day: Bollywood/Hollywood, April 15. https://www.youtube.com/watch?v=29GaPVRtFHI. Accessed Nov 2017.

Fraticelli, Rina. 2015. *Women in view: On screen: October 2015 report*. Toronto: Women in View. http://womeninview.ca/wp-content/uploads/2016/01/Women-In-View-On-Screen-2015.pdf. Accessed Nov 2017.

Garnham, Nicholas. 2005. From cultural to creative industries: An analysis of the implications of the 'Creative industries' approach to arts and media policy making in the United Kingdom. *Journal of Cultural Policy* 11 (1): 15–29.

Gaudet, Stéphanie. 2007. *Emerging adulthood: A new series in the life course*. Ottawa: Policy Research Initiative, Government of Canada.

Gregg, Melissa. 2011. *Work's intimacy*. Cambridge: Polity.

Hahn-Bleibtreu, Marina, and Marc Molgat (eds.). 2012. *Youth policy in a changing world: From theory to practice*. Opladen, Berlin and Toronto: Barbara Budrich Publishers.

Hastie, Amelie, Lynne Joyrich, Patricia White, and Sharon Willis. 2016. (Re) Inventing *camera obscura*. In *Feminisms: Diversity, difference, and multiplicity in contemporary film cultures*, ed. Laura Mulvey and Anna Backman Rogers, 169–186. Amsterdam: Amsterdam University Press.

Keller, Jessalynn. 2016. *Girls' feminist blogging in a postfeminist age*. New York and London: Routledge.

Kennelly, Jacqueline, and Stuart Poyntz. 2015. Introduction: Lifeworlds and surplus meaning in changing times. In *Phenomenology of youth cultures and globalization*, ed. Stuart Poyntz and Jacqueline Kennelly, 1–19. New York: Routledge.

Laidlaw. 2016. Youth led community change project descriptions. http://laidlawfdn.org/library/past-grants/. Accessed Nov 2017.

Lauzen, Martha M. 2016. *Thumbs down 2016: Top film critics and gender*. San Diego: Centre for the Study of Women in Television & Film, San Diego State University, June. http://womenintvfilm.sdsu.edu/files/2016_Thumbs_Down_Report.pdf. Accessed Nov 2017.

Mattil, Caitlyn. 2013. This is what a millennial feminist looks like. *Identities.mic*, June 21. http://mic.com/articles/48407/this-is-what-a-millennial-feminist-looks-like#.Dz2S2KhkV. Accessed Nov 2017.

Mayer, Sophie. 2016a. *Political animals: The new feminist cinema*. London and New York: I.B. Tauris.

Mayer, Sophie. 2016b. Where we are is here. *Another Gaze*, March 14. http://www.anothergaze.com/where-we-are-is-here-on-the-influence-of-female-filmmakers.

Malgot, Marc, and Katharine Larose-Hébert. 2010. *The values of youth in Canada*. Ottawa: Policy Research Initiative, Government of Canada.

McRobbie, Angela. 1989. Second-hand dresses and the role of the ragmarket. In *Zoot suits and second-hand dresses: An anthology of fashion and music*, ed. Angela McRobbie, 23–49. London: Macmillan.

McRobbie, Angela. 1994. Shut up and dance: Youth culture and changing modes of femininity. In *Postmodernism and popular culture*, 150–171. London: Routledge.

McRobbie, Angela. 2002. From Holloway to Hollywood: Happiness at work in the new cultural economy? In *Cultural economy: Cultural analysis and commercial life*, ed. Paul du Gay and Michael Pryke, 97–114. London: Sage.

McRobbie, Angela, and Jenny Garber. 2006. Girls and subculture. In *Resistance through rituals: Youth subcultures in post-war Britain*, ed. Stuart Hall and Tony Jefferson, 177–188. London: Routledge.

Melton, Sîan. 2016. Listen up: Our first panel and how not to act at it. The MUFF Society Blog, September 22. https://www.muffsociety.com/news-1/2016/9/22/listen-up-our-first-panel-and-how-not-to-act-at-it. Accessed Oct 2017.

The MUFF Society. 2017. Reel Girl Talk Series: *Girlfight*. YouTube, January 29. https://www.youtube.com/watch?v=NYMgzqJ3XCg. Accessed Nov 2017.

Mulvey, Laura. 1975. Visual pleasure and narrative cinema. *Screen* 26 (3): 6–18.

Neroni, Hilary. 2016. *Feminist film theory and cléo from 5 to 7*. New York: Bloomsbury.

NFB/Blog. 2017. International women's day 2017 | NFB to take its commitment to parity even further, March 7. http://blog.nfb.ca/blog/2017/03/07/iwd-2017-nfb-take-commitment-parity-even/. Accessed Nov 2017.

Reardon, Kiva. 2016. 2016's need for female film critics. *TIFF: The Review*, December 16. http://www.tiff.net/the-review/2016-in-female-film-critics/. Accessed Nov 2016.

Simonpillai, Radheyan. 2016. Because it's 2016: The Canadian film industry gender gap. *NOW*, October 5. https://nowtoronto.com/movies/because-it-s-2016-the-gender-gap-in-canadian-film/. Accessed Nov 2017.

Statistics Canada. 2016. Labour Force Survey, November. http://www.statcan.gc.ca/daily-quotidien/161202/dq161202a-eng.htm. Accessed Nov 2017.

Tersigni, Jacqueline. 2016. Drunk feminist film criticism? Toronto groups say bring on the laughs. *The Globe and Mail*, January 28. http://www.theglobeandmail.com/arts/film/drunk-feminist-film-criticism-toronto-groups-say-bring-on-the-laughs/article28437836/. Accessed Oct 2017.

Untitled Magazine. 2015. Millennial feminism: The 4th wave of feminism has officially arrived, September 24. http://untitled-magazine.com/millennial-feminism-the-4th-wave-of-feminism-has-officially-arrived/. Accessed Oct 2017.

CHAPTER 12

Making a Name for Yourself: Neo-identities and Tumblr

Christine Feraday

According to traditional conceptions of attraction, gender, and identity, a person is straight, gay, or bisexual; they are male, or they are female. Within the mainstream, there's little opportunity to openly deviate from these rigid categories. Cisheteronormativity, the hegemonic force that normalizes and rewards cisgender and heterosexual existence, demonizes and pathologizes all non-cisgender,[1] non-straight identities, but provides conditional and superficial acceptance for non-cis/non-straight identities that aren't "too out there." In an interview, Mattilda Bernstein Sycamore calls this the "violence of gay assimilation." Non-straight people are accepted by the mainstream if their existence can be easily understood by straight people, and if they perform their 'sameness' through cultural assimilation. Behind the "glamorous, sweatshop-produced rainbow flags, Tiffany wedding bands [and], Grey Goose Cosmo-tinis" of the assimilationist agenda is a militant "policing of the borders" of gender and sexuality (Ruiz 2008, p. 241) which undercuts the legitimacy of non-straight and non-cis people that don't fit the accepted narrative. Any 'acceptance' in these cases is conditional on the preservation of the status quo.

C. Feraday (✉)
Communication and Culture, Ryerson University, Toronto, ON, Canada

S. Driver and N. Coulter (eds.), *Youth Mediations and Affective Relations*,
https://doi.org/10.1007/978-3-319-98971-6_12

Many non-cis and non-straight people have reacted to these restrictive ideas of gender and desire by developing alternative understandings of what it means to not be straight or cisgender. There is a long history of creating, reclaiming, and redefining words in order to capture the experience of non-cis, non-straight identities. Words like 'butch' and 'femme,' for instance, play an important role in lesbian history, emerging in the 1940s and 1950s as a way of "organiz[ing] lesbian intimacy" outside of strictly heteronormative dynamics (Kennedy and Davis 2014, p. 192). Other identifiers, like 'queer' or 'androgynous,' have gained popularity because they allow non-cis, non-straight people to describe their identities in a way that challenges cisheteronormativity.

Today, much of this language-play and pushback happens online. On the internet, non-cis and non-straight people are creating new words to describe sexual orientation, romantic orientation, and gender identity. These new words, which I refer to in this chapter as "neo-identities," are a reaction to rigid, cisheteronormative conceptions of identity. Rather than describing new experiences or phenomena, neo-identities represent new attempts to describe experiences that have complex and varied histories. The experience that someone describes when they label their gender with the neo-identity 'opscugender' (a gender that is hard to see or grasp) is not necessarily a new experience. The word 'opscugender' simply represents a new attempt to name that experience. In a society that pressures people to identify within very strict confines, neo-identities offer a way of reframing attraction and gender identity; not only to challenge cisheteronormativity, but also to make oneself heard and understood by others. They are often highly specific and personal. Sometimes, they are only used by a handful of people. Some have slowly begun to enter the mainstream, with celebrities like musician Miley Cyrus coming out as pansexual (attracted to all genders), or DJ and actress Ruby Rose identifying as genderfluid (a gender that shifts or changes) (Sieczkowski 2015; Molloy 2015). While terms like pansexual and genderfluid are slowly gaining mainstream recognition, these pop culture examples only provide a small glimpse into the larger movement taking place in youth-oriented internet communities.

The internet allows non-cis and non-straight people to find each other and communicate despite geographical distance. On Tumblr in particular, non-cis and non-straight people are currently engaged in ongoing conversations about new identity labels. Tumblr specifically allows for the rapid spread of information because of its 'reblog' system,[2] which circulates and re-circulates posts quickly and with wide reach. Tumblr's capacity for anonymity and its popularity among young, social justice-oriented people make it an even better platform for unique discussions about identities that fall outside of the mainstream.

Using existing academic research on Tumblr and interviews with Tumbler users, this chapter will examine the ways in which non-cis and non-straight youth are using Tumblr to create a new language of identity. In the chapter, I conceptualize language creation and cataloguing as a way of challenging restrictive conceptions of gender/desire, a method of understanding oneself, and a strategy for creating lasting community and connection. Neo-identities are important, not only because they resist cis-heteronormative understandings of attraction and gender, but also because they represent the way many non-cis and non-straight people are learning to make sense of their own identity and experiences. In examining the recent proliferation of neo-identities in online non-cis and non-straight communities, it is essential to also examine the political and personal significance of the words themselves. I also argue that neo-identities are meaningful and impactful *outside* their intrinsic linguistic significance. Ongoing intra-community conversations about the value of neo-identities are important on an affective level, because they create community and understanding among marginalized people in ways that engage embodied and emotional dimensions of experience. My paper traces some of the affective resonances that work to foster supportive and inclusive relations as a basis for alternative modes of identification and expression.

Challenging "Normal"

Linguists would characterize many neo-identities as nonce words; experimental words created to solve specific, one-off communication problems (e.g., personal neo-pronouns[3] only used by one person). Many other neo-identities would be considered coinages, relatively new words which resonate within isolated social groups, but which are not well-known beyond those circles (e.g., the identity monstergender,[4] which is mostly used on Tumblr). True neologisms (e.g., aromantic, demigirl, explained later in the chapter) and fully lexicalized words (e.g., butch, femme) are rarer on Tumblr, as most neo-identities are yet to emerge in communities external to Tumblr.

To better understand neo-identities and the people who use them, I interviewed nine non-cis and/or non-straight Tumblr users who claimed at least one neo-identity. I posted a call for participants on my research blog and reached out to individual Tumblr users who fit the requirements. The interviews took place over email, and I asked each interviewee questions about their identity words and their experiences on Tumblr. Beyond interviews, I also used content I found by searching Tumblr, but due to the sensitive nature of the topic, I only reference posts that were clearly intended for public consumption and circulation (either because the author specified as much or because the post was not highly personal or identifiable in nature).

Many neo-identities reinforce the idea that gender and attraction do not need to conform to strict categories. Indeed, the majority of the people I interviewed were on the asexual or aromantic spectrum, meaning they either did not experience sexual and/or romantic attraction, or they experienced these types of attractions in non-normative ways. Mainstream narratives about relationships don't often differentiate between the different types of attraction, and many neo-identities respond to this oversight. Identities like idemromantic, for instance, highlight the struggle many people have in differentiating between different types of attraction. People who are idemromantic feel no difference between platonic and romantic attraction. One interviewee, Hyourin, discovered the word idemromantic after doing research on the aromantic spectrum, but before finding that word, they 'tried on' other identities that just didn't seem to fit. "I identified as panromantic[5] for quite a while and it just felt fake," Hyourin told me. "It didn't feel right and I couldn't figure out why. I'd never really separated platonic from romantic, I just hadn't realized it." The word 'idemromantic' helped them to understand their own experiences and feelings.

Recognizing the different types of attraction and one's relationship to each type can make a substantial difference for people who are feeling 'left out' by society's definitions of attraction and desire. Neo-identities that address different types of attraction and desire also help sum up complicated feelings and experiences with a single word. 'Akoiromantic,' for instance, refers to romantic attraction that fades or disappears when reciprocated. Another interviewee, Kay, described to me nir[6] experiences of akoiromanticism:

> As for being akoiromantic, it's like this: To start with, romantic attraction is very rare for me, to the point where I always assumed the people around me were exaggerating how often they had crushes on people. I think I've

> had maybe four crushes in my life? And I'm honestly not sure about the first one, it's possible it was something I pretended so hard that I started believing it myself. Then, on those rare occasions when I do get a crush on someone, if there's any hint at all that the feeling is reciprocated, the attraction goes away. Not instantly, but inside a week or so.

Kay's experience of romantic attraction is different from mainstream narratives about romance. Being able to sum up nir specific, personal experience of romantic attraction with a single word—akoiromantic—makes it easier for Kay to communicate nir feelings and needs to the people around nem.

Neo-identities that relate to gender point to the fact that there are many ways of experiencing gender, far beyond 'maleness' or 'femaleness' (or even 'in-betweenness'). Andy, who is a demigirl, describes herself as mostly a woman, "but part of [her] feels as though [she] could be genderfluid or agender."[7] In this case, Andy's gender identity cannot be wholly described as female, but instead *includes* femaleness, as well as including other experiences of gender. Demigenders like Andy's challenge the idea that all gender can be described with the categories of male and female, instead suggesting that many people have the potential to be multiple genders at the same time, or at different times, and that those multiple gender identities can exist in fluctuating proportions. Similarly, identities like 'agender' account for times where gender, or the feeling of being gendered/inhabiting a gender, is not a factor in a person's identity.

In addition to complicating the categories of maleness and femaleness, some neo-identities present new categories of gender altogether. These identities suggest that gender can be influenced by aspects of the self that are not commonly associated with gender. Neo-identities like this fundamentally challenge mainstream definitions of gender. They enable us to recognize gender as an intensely personal experience of the self and, as such, sometimes denote the ways that personality (or other factors) might influence gender. For Hatch, pronouns are about a larger concept of gender that incorporates aspects of gore personality. Hatch uses go/gore/goreself pronouns, because: "I like gore and horror and I feel that's important enough to have as a part of who I am." Things that Hatch likes, rather than being messily assigned an inherent 'maleness' or 'femaleness,' become important enough to gore that they constitute an entirely new personal category of gender.

Vee, whose gender identity is inherently linked to its[8] identity as 'otherkin',[9] describes the mingling of gender and other aspects of the self like this:

> I don't just feel an absence of gender, but a strong feeling that the thing that should identify me in the world, the label that should be placed on me and the social category into which I should fit, is not male or female, not man or woman, but reptile person. In the way that other people seem to feel male or femaleness is important to their self-image, reptilianness is important to me.

For some people like Vee, understanding gender involves creating an entirely new category. Gender is understood here as a part of identity that can be experienced differently for different people, in that it is not restricted to normative categories. We do not normally think of other aspects of the self as having to conform to strict binaries or distinct types. People don't normally consider there to be only two personality types, for instance; personality is recognized as being diverse and variable across all people. Like all aspects of the self, gender can't be defined in a succinct, uncomplicated way, and there doesn't seem to be any reason that understandings of gender can't be informed by traits associated with personality or other parts of ourselves. If anything, looking at gender identity in a new light can help us uncover limiting or oppressive understandings of gender. At the same time, it's equally valid if a person feels their gender is totally unrelated to their personality, if they have no investment in defining their gender, or if they feel they don't have a gender. Neo-identities broaden our perception of what gender is, or how desire can feel outside of cisheteronormative confines. Gender and attraction can be conceptualized outside of categories that we normally take for granted, which allows us to question normative categories and allows non-cis/non-straight people to better understand their own experiences.

The Relief of Finding the Right Word

Cisheteronormative narratives of 'normal' attraction and gender aren't only damaging because they *ignore* the real experiences of real people—people who don't fit within the categories of gay/straight/bi and male/female, like the people I interviewed—but because they actively harm and other those people. When the only possibility presented to someone doesn't fit with their experience, they internalize negative messages about their own identity and validity. If someone doesn't fit with what is considered 'normal,' then they must be ***abnormal***. It's an easy leap from 'abnormal' to 'wrong' and 'broken.' Neo-identities offer reassurance to people who have grown up thinking they are abnormal, wrong, and broken because they don't fit into societal understandings of attraction and gender.

Again and again, the people I interviewed described how finding their identity words brought them relief and reassurance. When people discover their experiences don't fit into the culturally accepted categories of attraction or gender, they feel out of place. One interviewee, Roe, described it as being "in purgatory," or "neither here nor there." For another, Niamh, the feeling of using the wrong label was like wearing "trousers that are just an inch too short." These are feelings that non-straight and non-cis people have always experienced, and they aren't unique to people using neo-identities. Cisheteronormativity is limiting to everyone. Even with some non-cis and non-straight identities becoming better recognized by the mainstream, non-cis and non-straight people of all identities ('new' or not) are taught implicitly to believe that they don't belong.

For people uncomfortable with mainstream identity language, finding a fitting label often "feels like something has slotted into place," or like "a sigh of relief" (Roe). Hyourin gave a similar description: "When I found a word that fit, a label that made sense, it was satisfying and… comfortable. Like finally cuddling up in a blanket after being outside in the cold." There is a sense of real, physical relief that accompanies finding the right label, like a weight off of the shoulders.

The relief is also about realizing that 'different' does not mean 'wrong.' For Hyourin, recognizing their asexuality meant: "I wasn't broken, I wasn't flawed or undesirable. I was just different. And that was okay." When someone finds the right word to describe their experiences, they are also more likely to discover the existence of a community of other people that share their feelings. "I think with any label the first feeling is relief," Roe wrote. "*Oh this exists. I'm not broken. Other people feel this way too.*" The existence of language that describes you confirms that you aren't alone; that you aren't the only one to feel the way you feel. In a post about discovering their asexuality, Tumblr user anagnori describes these feelings in detail:

> … I did not have the words to describe my experiences, so I could not articulate my identity, even to myself. And trying to reject social norms when you have no clear identity of your own is like trying to hold back the sea with a sandcastle … When I called myself "asexual," my past became meaningful. The blank spaces themselves became important. I observed patterns and preferences in myself that I could not see before. From an "undecided" perspective, my teenage years were a wasted opportunity, a social failure. From an "asexual" perspective, I could see that I hadn't wasted anything - I was being true to myself all along, and my life had been better for it. (2016)

When people have the language to describe their experiences, they are reassured that those experiences aren't deviant or invalid. The first step in articulating identity to others is articulating it to one's own self. According to another research participant, Illya, having the right word to describe one's experience "[makes] it easier to think about," and easier to understand. In this way, affective experiences and representations are intimately articulated within the lives of young people's exploration of neo-identifications.

Challenging cultural norms without meaningful, accurate language really is, as anagnori writes, "like trying to hold back the sea with a sandcastle." Once people have the language to describe how they feel, though, they can more confidently define themselves outside of the confines of cisheteronormativity. More than just being tools for a radical re-organization of cultural norms and assumptions, neo-identities are a life-saving resource for real people in their everyday lives. They are reassuring and life-affirming. Neo-identities remind people that they are not 'wrong' or 'broken' simply because they're different.

The Right Site at the Right Time

Tumblr is at the heart of the neo-identity boom because of its accessibility to non-cis and non-straight people who want to have conversations about identity. The site is built in a way that makes identity exploration easier in some contexts, and it's very different from the other social media platforms that are popular right now (e.g., Twitter, Facebook), because of how information circulates, how communities organize, and the social justice focus of many Tumblr users. All of these elements have made it an indispensable platform for creating, expressing, and discussing identities.

For every interviewee, Tumblr was a useful and entertaining space, and for some, it was an important outlet where they could more easily 'be themselves.' In an article called "A beautiful design and no jerks: how Tumblr did it," Jeff Roberts writes that Tumblr "has grown to tens of millions of users but still retain[s] an intimate, community feel," because it encourages "a more thoughtful form of community engagement" (2012). Roberts attributes Tumblr's communal atmosphere to the reblog system, which makes replying to and commenting on content less anonymous. In reality, though, Tumblr's strength is not that it doesn't allow for anonymity, but that it allows for the right *kind* of anonymity: just enough that users feel free to be more open about their identity, than they are on other social media.

Because Tumblr doesn't require you to link your blog to your 'offline identity' the way a website like Facebook does, people have the opportunity to be anonymous on Tumblr in the sense that their blog will probably never be meaningfully connected to their legal name. This doesn't mean that people on Tumblr use that anonymity as an opportunity to create a fake persona; instead, many of them use it to be more open about aspects of their identity that might receive backlash in their offline life. By now, most Western families are highly connected on Facebook. As Adam Rifkin writes for TechCrunch, "As long as Mom sees you on Facebook occasionally, she isn't going to think to look for you on another site" (2013). Most people don't have relatives following them on Tumblr. The people I interviewed confirmed that part of Tumblr's appeal is the sense of anonymity and privacy it promotes. "I go to Facebook to stay in touch with friends in real life," Roe told me, "I go to Tumblr to escape from real life." Facebook is seen as a space for keeping in touch with 'real life' friends, while Tumblr was a website where users felt like they could express themselves more authentically, without facing repercussions offline. According to Devin: "[Tumblr is] the only place that I can be unapologetically me, because only two people that follow me know me in real life." The anonymity also made it easier not just to express non-normative identities, but also to explore them, thanks to Tumblr's 'anonymous ask' option: "You can ask questions about your sexuality and gender identity without having to be embarrassed" (Devin).

Tumblr is also attractive to non-cis and non-straight people because of its community, which is large and varied. For Hyourin, Tumblr is a particularly good platform for finding community "because everyone comes to Tumblr to be around things they love." While other websites might have more homogenous communities or specific themes, "Tumblr is about blogging. It has no character limit, and is designed around shouting out to the void and seeing if some people shout back" (Hyourin). People can also shape their own experience of the website by only following the types of people they're interested in hearing from, which allows smaller communities to emerge within the website. In addition to being a large and diverse community, Tumblr also has many non-cis and non-straight users, and many people on Tumblr are interested in social justice. Discussions about identity and language naturally develop out of a community with such similar interests. As such, many of the people I interviewed found their identity words through Tumblr. "When I first joined the website, I learned how open a community it was and that there were a lot more gender and sexuality identities than I could've imagined at first," Andy wrote. For Kay, seeing someone ne followed on Tumblr come out as demisexual[10] was what helped nem start to understand nir own identity: "I hadn't ever heard a word that came that close to describing me before." Tumblr provides access to information and community, as well as providing enough anonymity that people feel comfortable using that information and taking part in the community.

Tumblr is very useful for identity exploration, and for promoting conversations about neo-identities in particular. The platform allows for the rapid spread of information due to the reblog system (most posts on Tumblr are reblogs rather than original posts), which means that new ideas for neo-identities and debates around definitions can happen quickly and visibly. Informational blogs on Tumblr catalogue the various new identity words, and moderators of these blogs work to stay up-to-date on the evolving definitions of the new identity words. These blogs also devote themselves to helping people understand and name their identity when they're uncertain of how to label themselves; the safety provided by the anonymous ask system makes it easier for questioning individuals to ask for advice. People can anonymously ask questions, describing their experience of gender or attraction, and then blog moderators will do their best to provide possible identity word options that describe those experiences. Finding these kinds of resources on Tumblr isn't difficult. Most people involved in the non-cis, non-straight communities on Tumblr will come into contact with people who use neo-identities, through the people they follow and the reblogs they see. Tumblr users often display their identity words right on their blog for everyone to see. People come into contact with these unfamiliar words and then investigate them further (going into what Roe called in our interview "a research spiral"). The community and modes of communication present on Tumblr make it ideal for counter-public communication (Renninger 2015). Non-cis and non-straight people can come together to talk about self-naming, seek advice from others like them, share emotional experiences, and explore their own identity. As Nancy Fraser writes of counterpublics; "On the one hand, they function as spaces of withdrawal and regroupment; on the other hand, they also function as bases and training grounds for agitational activities directed toward wider publics" (1990, p. 68). Tumblr is a safe space, where neo-identity users find relief (an escape from the 'real world'), but also a "training ground," where neo-identity users learn strategies for navigating and challenging cisheteronormative society.

The way Tumblr allows users to express their identity also affects how neo-identities are communicated on the platform. While Tumblr doesn't require users to share personal information, many people do so on their main blog page, or on a separate 'about' page. On social networking sites like Tumblr, users have access to a certain amount of visibility and image control that they might not otherwise have in their day-to-day lives. Visibility is important, because "people craft their identities through interaction, in concert with others and out of the diverse contextual resources within their reach" (Tiidenberg 2013, p. 177). This relates in part to the ability to talk to other people in one's community, as mentioned previously, but the simple act of *being seen* is also important to identity development. 'Being seen' as the identity one claims, is validating and reassuring; on Tumblr, users can influence the way they are seen. While it may be difficult to explicitly signify genderfluid identity in an offline context without being misinterpreted, Tumblr users can label their blog as the blog of a genderfluid person and make that aspect of their identity explicit. They can, to some extent, influence the way they're perceived by others. Hilary Thurston suggests that Tumblr gives users the ability to "control the gaze," because "control is achieved by posting items on a blog whose theme is queer identity, style or politics to ensure a queer reading of the posted content" (2013, p. 5). When someone posts a selfie on a blog that explicitly identifies them as a bigender[11] person, for instance, they ensure a queer reading of their image; this is also achieved through the addition of specific tags, like #bigender. It's harder to explicitly advertise one's identity as bigender offline, because clear markers of non-normative identities are hard to come by and often put the wearer in danger.

Tumblr is by no means a utopian environment where non-cis and non-straight people can exist exactly how they want without conflict. The platform has weaknesses, like a lack of moderation, and the communities on Tumblr have their fair share of inter- and intra-community disputes. That said, Tumblr still offers certain features that other social media do not, and these features have made it an ideal environment for the type of identity formation and expression discussed in this chapter.

Affective Dimensions of Neo-identities

Not everyone is convinced that neo-identities have real-world utility and value. When I discuss my research, people often wonder what practical use some of these very obscure, rarely-used words could possibly have as part of a larger social movement. Many highly specific neo-identities won't be integrated into mainstream society. Some will only ever speak to a handful of people; some may only speak to the respective individuals that created them. But to call a nonce word like "goreself" or coinage like "monstergender" successful only if it 'sticks,' is short-sighted. Language change and lexical creation involve continuous processes and continuous conversations; there isn't necessarily a finish line to be reached. It is also a mistake to say that neo-identities are only important as individual words with concrete definitions. The words and definitions themselves are important to non-cis and non-straight people, but neo-identities are also valuable for their emotional and affective significance. While some neo-identities may not gain mainstream acceptance or popularity, they are impactful because they create understanding, connection, capacities, and community between the people that use them. They represent a process of self-discovery and community building that is deeply tied to the emotional resonances produced between diverse subjects. Neo-identity users come to learn more about themselves and others through the process of creating or claiming a neo-identity, and the affective experiences shaped and transformed by neo-identities hold as much importance as the words themselves.

Alexander Cho's article, "Queer Reverb: Tumblr, Affect, Time," provides an excellent explanation of how Tumblr itself is inherently linked to affect. Cho writes that "Tumblr [trades] in affect" (2015, p. 44). Cho makes this claim because Tumblr is a primarily visual medium, featuring,

> … post after post of explanationless images, traded from one anonymous Tumblr user to another. A gorgeous landscape photo of a tropical beach after a photo of a genderqueer boy wearing a three-piece suit after a galactic vision constellated with Lady Gaga in Alexander McQueen heels. (Cho 2015, p. 43)

These images, often presented without captions or credits, are interesting to Tumblr users because they *resonate* with them, often in ways that are difficult to define (Cho 2015, p. 53). Tumblr users reblog things for a variety of reasons, sometimes to make a political point, or to make their followers laugh, or simply because the post resonated with them. These posts can often seem unexceptional to an outsider, but on Tumblr, "[y]ou are the sum of your posts, which are a visualization of your connections to others—a porous, living assemblage" (Cho 2015, p. 45). Reblogging something allows you to communicate something about yourself, as well as your relationship to other people.

Tumblr operates non-linearly, a disconnected stream of text and images from a vast number of different sources, and its communities function in the same way. There is no unified, coherent 'Tumblr community,' and smaller communities on the platform are equally amorphous. Tumblr users may consider themselves members of a few particular communities but have liminal access to many more. There are no boundaries between different communities and no requirements or processes for joining a particular group on Tumblr. A sense of belonging to a community is, instead, mostly based around who follows who and who sees what.

Neo-identities often act as cross-community connectors on Tumblr because they create culture(s), conversation, and vigorous debate. Indeed, the affective dimensions of neo-identities are as meaningful as the linguistic ones; neo-identities have allowed non-cis and non-straight people to engage in meaningful and passionate interaction with one another.

These interactions remain important, even if a person decides not to claim a neo-identity or if a particular neo-identity falls into obscurity. Cho describes Tumblr as "nonlinear, incoherent, and impermanent" (Cho 2015, p. 45), and neo-identities are easily conceptualized in the same way. Neo-identities often change in their meaning or have multiple meanings simultaneously. This incoherence doesn't render neo-identities unimportant or uninfluential, though; they still have a strong affective impact. Sara Ahmed claims that affect is sticky: "Affect is what sticks, or what sustains or preserves the connection between ideas, values, and objects" (Ahmed 2010, p. 29). The affective nature of neo-identities can stick longer even than the neo-identities themselves. Neo-identity users interact with a community that understands them; a community that operates in opposition to cisheteronormativity. The subsequent feelings of belonging and acceptance are easily as important as the meaning of the identity words themselves.

Like the seemingly random, disconnected images shared on Tumblr, neo-identities gain popularity because they resonate with people. Such affective resonances are abstract and hard for other people to understand. There are multiple neo-identity words that describe very similar feelings, and yet different people can be drawn towards different words because those words affect them in a different way. Often, this has nothing to do with strict definitions, but rather a gut feeling. Many neo-identity users *can't* rely on strict definitions, because definitions of neo-identities are so abstract and open to interpretation. What does it mean to be 'gendervoid,' for instance; to have the feeling of a void, where there usually exists a feeling of being gendered? Unless the identity gendervoid resonates with you, it's very difficult to totally comprehend that concept, which is why gut feelings are so important to how neo-identities work.

Rather than dismissing neo-identities as a frivolous fad, it is important to recognize neo-identities as part of a long history of non-cis, non-straight language creation, and it is equally important to consider the value of neo-identities outside of their longevity. The emotional and affective significance of neo-identities has a long-lasting, meaningful impact on the marginalized communities that use them. Communities built around the creation and exploration of neo-identities create a sense of belonging and self-understanding among people who often feel abandoned, excluded, and erased. These moments of connection are easily as important as the words and definitions that emerge from them.

Opening a Seam

For the people I interviewed, and many other people on Tumblr, neo-identities are a way of highlighting and resisting the shortcomings of cisheteronormativity. Neo-identities create conversation. They make people ask questions. Oppressive conceptions of gender and desire are dangerous when they remain unquestioned; when they're taken for granted. Words that describe non-normative experiences of gender and desire expose the damaging nature of constructed cultural norms. Jordana Rosenberg compares these realizations to Alain Badiou's theory of 'the event': "something happens, an 'event,' and it cracks open a seam in the reproduction of the status quo" (2014). Neo-identities crack open a seam; they cause us to re-evaluate ideas that have been presented to us as natural. They cause us to recognize the wide variety of experiences and identities that can, and do, exist. They force us to ask, what does it mean to experience desire? What does it mean to be gendered?

More tangibly, for people who have grown up thinking they are 'broken' or 'wrong,' neo-identities provide intense feelings of comfort, relief, and self-understanding. They allow people to make sense of their own experiences by giving those experiences a name. Some new identity words may become fully lexicalized, like the word 'queer,' but even those that don't leave an impact on the community through their affective significance. Neo-identities inspire important moments of community building and allow non-cis and non-straight people to better understand themselves and connect with supportive peers. In all of these ways, neo-identities contribute to a larger goal of social change, which happens in small, personal steps rather than great, abstract strides.

Notes

1. Cisgender: identifying with the gender one is assigned at birth.
2. 'Reblogging' on Tumblr refers to re-posting a post to your own blog (similar to Facebook's 'share' function). The post is then visible to all of your followers and can be further reblogged by others.
3. Neo-pronouns are new pronouns outside of he/she/they (e.g., ze/hir).
4. Monstergender is a gender that feels monstrous in some way.
5. Panromantic is experiencing romantic attraction to all genders.
6. Kay uses ne/nem/nir/nemself pronouns.
7. Agender; the absence of gender; genderlessness.
8. Vee uses it/it/its pronouns.
9. Otherkin feel that they are, at least partially, non-human. Otherkin often identify with non-human animals and objects, though the experience of inhumanity varies.
10. Demisexual, only feeling sexual attraction once an emotional bond has been formed.
11. Bigender, experiencing two gender identities.

References

Ahmed, Sara. 2010. Happy objects. In *The affect theory reader*, ed. Gregory J. Seigworth and Melissa Gregg, 29–51. London: Duke University Press.

anagnori. 2016. What's in a name? *Tumblr*. anagnori.tumblr.com.

Cho, Alexander. 2015. Queer reverb: Tumblr, affect, time. In *Networked affect*, ed. Ken Hillis, Susanna Paasonen, and Michael Petit, 45–58. Cambridge: MIT Press.

Fraser, Nancy. 1990. Rethinking the public sphere: A contribution to the critique of actually existing democracy. *Social Text* 25 (26): 56–80.

Kennedy, Elizabeth Lapovsky, and Madeline D. Davis. 2014. *Boots of leather, slippers of gold: The history of a lesbian community*. Abingdon: Routledge.

Molloy, Shannon. 2015. Ruby Rose says she doesn't identify as female or male, after releasing a gender-bending short film. *News Limited*. news.com.au.

Renninger, Bryce J. 2015. "Where I can be myself… where I can speak my mind": Networked counterpublics in a polymedia environment. *New Media & Society* 17 (9): 1513–1529.

Rifkin, Adam. 2013. Tumblr is not what you think. *Tech Crunch*. www.techcrunch.com.

Roberts, Jeff. 2012. A beautiful design and no jerks: How Tumblr did it. *Gigaom*. www.gigaom.com.

Rosenberg, Jordana. 2014. Gender grouble on Mother's Day. *Avidly*. www.avidly.lareviewofbooks.org.

Ruiz, Jason. 2008. The violence of assimilation: An interview with Mattilda AKA Matt Bernstein. *Radical History Review* 100: 237–247.

Sieczkowski, Cavan. 2015. Miley Cyrus comes out as pansexual. *The Huffington Post*. www.huffingtonpost.com.

Thurston, Hillary. 2013. Pretty, witty and femme: Negotiations of gender and sex in femme sartorial representations on *Tumblr*. Masters thesis, Simon Fraser University.

Tiidenberg, Katrin. 2013. How does online experience inform our sense of self? NSFW bloggers' identity narratives. In *Change and continuities of lifestyles in transforming societies*, ed. A.A. Allaste, 177–203. New York: Peter Lang.

CHAPTER 13

This Is Why We Can't Have Nice Things: Tumblr Publics, John Green, and Sanctionable Girlhood

Morgan Bimm

Girls who take up space online increasingly find themselves positioned within a frustrating matrix of contradictory cultural expectations and millennial feminist politics. Kevin McDonald, a sociologist writing in the late 1990s, noted that youth are expected to navigate, in ever more sophisticated ways, "the impossible binary construction of young people as either the ideal reflexive subjects of late modernity [or] its passive victims" (as quoted in Harris and Shields Dobson 2015, p. 153). It seems logical to posit that such a binary has become even more exclusionary in the years since McDonald wrote, with the complicating presence of ever-evolving technology and rapidly shifting layers of third wave and post-feminist politics shaping the early political consciousness of so many millennial girls today. The question of how girls take up space online and the conversations that spring up around their interactions with adults and other authority figures is an area of particular cultural contention. Amid anxieties about the Internet-saturated nature of today's youth

M. Bimm (✉)
Gender, Feminist and Women's Studies, York University, Toronto, ON, Canada
e-mail: mbimm@yorku.ca

S. Driver and N. Coulter (eds.), *Youth Mediations and Affective Relations*,
https://doi.org/10.1007/978-3-319-98971-6_13

cultures, questions around resistance seem to plague girlhood and youth scholarship. Jessica Ringrose, a feminist scholar, has noted that "perhaps it is not a grand narrative of 'resistance' that we can lay claim to [but rather] 'traces' or 'residues' of feminist, anti-oppressive discourses, which jar against the regulative rhythm of normative discourses" (2008, p. 54). Such disjunctures, Ringrose notes, open up spaces of criticality and what she calls "small moments of rupture" (2008, p. 54). This chapter interrogates one of these ruptures—an event in the online fan community of popular YA author John Green that sent ripples through his online fanbase and network of fellow writers. The event in question serves as not only as an example of how politics are mediated throughout digital space, but also the ways in which girls attempt to navigate these nuances and continue to find complex ways of articulating their opinions, affect, and identity in a world that demands so much of its girlish subjects.

This chapter argues in favour of expanding definitions of resistance, grounded in a tradition of feminist theory that privileges subversive actions undertaken in everyday moments of conflict as well as traditionally recognizable modes of protest. Unfortunately, a full exploration of the politics and nuances of the event in question is beyond the scope of this particular piece, this chapter instead focuses on how the discourses that emerged in the event's aftermath raise questions about authorial relationships and responsibilities in the context of the collapsed contexts and networked publics of millennial social media. Using theory on the mechanics of networked publics, online virality, and affect theory, this chapter interrogates how the architectures of girls' digital spaces allow for the unprecedented visibility and sharing of their opinions while also leaving room for the continued surveillance and policing of their dissent. I argue for a deeper analysis of the collapsed contexts of online spaces as they relate to adult media creators' proximity to teenaged readers/consumers and what this might mean for the frameworks outlined by girlhood studies scholar Anita Harris, who posits that teen girls' online practices offer a space for them to realize their identities as agentive citizens (2008). What implications does this have for discourses of digital utopianism when the feelings and reputations of male authors continue to take precedence in those digital spaces hailed by girls and girlhood scholars as fertile ground for feminist resistance? How might the design of websites support these continued power imbalances, and how does this particular media event reflect cultural anxieties about virality, support offline gendered hegemonies, and curtail the possibility of teen girls' online citizenship?

Background and Context

Sometime during the evening of June 10 or early morning hours of June 11, 2015, Tumblr user "*virjn*" posted a text post to the popular microblogging site (see Appendix A). This particular text post raised questions about popular author John Green and expressed some discomfort around his relationship to his young, largely female fanbase. Green had been roundly critiqued for his continued use of formulaic, heteronormative romance plots and problematic utterances in fan spaces before. At first glance, the antagonism in *virjn*'s post comes nowhere near the force with which Green had been called out in the past for everything from cultural appropriation to offhand misogynistic comments (Your Fave is Problematic 2013). This specific event was complicated, however, by two resounding factors which raised the visibility of both the original post as well as the subsequent response from Green's readers and fellow authors to an unprecedented and arguably disproportionate degree. The frequency of John Green's interactions with his fans as well as the invocation of broader discourses of gender, sexuality, and victimhood complicate the original post in numerous and significant ways. In the days following the original posts, the rhetoric of the reactionary posts raised numerous, theoretically significant questions about the resistive capabilities of teenagers embedded in online counterpublics and—I argue—serve as proof of a need to reevaluate the ability of girls within online fan spaces to express their critique of white, male creators that remain the most visible content creators, both online and off.

John Green represents a kind of creative personality that appears, at least on the surface, to straddle the divide between online and offline worlds. In 2007, John and his brother Hank began a video blog project called *Brotherhood 2.0*, which ran from January 2007 to December 2007. The two agreed that they would forgo any text-based communication with each other for the duration of the project, communicating instead by exchanging video blogs uploaded to a video channel on YouTube for a wider audience to watch and engage with accordingly (Dean 2018). As of 2018, the Greens continue to upload two videos a week, about "nothing in particular," and continue to interact with a community of viewers who call themselves Nerdfighters. Both brothers have produced a wide variety of educational projects for YouTube in addition to their existing jobs–John as a best-selling young adult author and Hank as a musician and entrepreneur. These side projects have included such initiatives as SciShow and Crash Course, channels dedicated to teaching viewers lessons on science, world history, and literature, and Truth or Fail, a Youtube-based game show (Pot 2012). In this way, John Green has effectively positioned himself as a digitally literate content creator who engages in many of the same online practices and frequents many of the same digital spaces as fans of his books and other ventures.

Likely as a direct result of John Green's familiarity with conventions of online community, his online presence has also resulted in close relationships and constant dialogue with many of his teen readers. In 2011, Green opened an account on popular microblogging platform Tumblr.com and began posting on a regular basis, often engaging directly with fans. Girlhood studies scholars such as McRobbie and Keller have identified girls' blogging practices as potential sites of resistance, and many of these resistive practices take the shape of engaging with and critiquing media objects through activities such as fan writing, fan art, and community building through sharing information and materials online. Green joined this community of fans in 2011 as a way to foster conversations about his books and, for many of his readers, his presence there was welcomed and even celebrated. It quickly became a game to tag his blog in a post about his books or YouTube projects and see how long it would take for Green to comment (Romano 2013). For four years, Green's rapport with his teenaged fans continued in this way, promoting side projects and supporting modes of fan participation that engaged with his various books as well as his other creative ventures. In June of 2015, however, this dynamic shifted abruptly.

Tumblr user *virjn's* post was quickly reblogged, liked, and shared. The post garnered over 15,000 independent "notes" by the time Tumblr user *mattcatashpole* tagged Green's blog in the process of reblogging it.[1] Green responded June 11 by calling the original post "sick and libelous." Green (2015) wrote that he was "tired of seeing the language of social justice [...] misused as a way to dehumanize others and treat them hatefully" and concluded by stating that he would interact less with fans in the future as it was "impossible to continue to use tumblr [sic] in the way [he had] used it since 2011." Within a number of hours, Green had support from other YA authors on Tumblr making similarly defensive posts and decrying *virjn*'s original text post as unfounded libel. One female author called Green an "outstanding friend" and noted that he was undeserving of "spurious accusations of child molestation, threats of violence, and death threats;" another wrote on Twitter that "just because you are creeped out does not make someone a creep" (Johnson 2015; Stiefvater, quoted in Garrett 2015). Somewhere in the midst of all of this, Tumblr user *virjn* deactivated their blog. The post can still be found at the head of many strings of reactionary posts and critiques of the event; however, the original poster's identity and intended meaning is effectively lost forever.

The point of this chapter is not to analyze the ideas contained in *virjn*'s initial text post, nor endorse the reactionary viewpoint. Rather, its focus is to critically analyze Green's response and the ensuing discourse that emerged on Tumblr in the context of complicating author/fan relationships and girls' abilities to express dissent or discomfort with male content creators in digital spaces. Many young fans tend to congregate to engage in what fan scholar Henry Jenkins has described as "participatory culture" (Keller 2012, p. 434). Jenkins' notion of participatory culture "complicates earlier conceptions of the media fan as a passive receptor of culture (and often gendered female)" (Keller 2012, p. 434). This particular media event is fascinating as it exemplifies a number of cultural anxieties around online virality and the legitimacy of ideas expressed in online spaces. Ultimately, this chapter argues that the silencing and public shaming of the original post by Green and his fellow YA authors (many of them women) exemplifies a culture wherein digital spaces are heralded as offering girls and other marginalized youth a place of empowerment and autonomy, but are ultimately controlled by the same modes of patriarchal surveillance and policing that exist offline.

Girls Talking Back on Tumblr

> Tumblr is one of the spaces, even though it is a digital space, where teenagers can exist outside of the behavioral and psychological constraints that adults foist on them. As an adult in this space: you fucking deal with, and respect the hell out of, that. Or you go to Facebook. (aimmyarrowshigh 2015)

The shifting landscape of girls' online resistance is a veritable hallmark of recent feminist literature. According to Jessalynn Keller, the diverse ways that girls use online spaces to participate in feminist activism and media critique reflects their needs as young, millennial subjects within a neoliberal cultural context (2012). Crucially, however, girls' media production and (re)interpretation in the context of fan spaces have also worked to trouble the cultural binary which positions women as passive consumers of male-produced content. In this way, participatory cultures effectively challenge notions of neoliberal consumer citizenship, which posits that young people are best able to "participate in life as citizens through the consumption of consumer goods" (Keller 2012, p. 434). Girlhood studies scholars such as Anita Harris view media production as an increasingly important site where girls enact political agency and "blur the lines" between producing and consuming cultural objects through practices such as blogging (Keller 2012). Other scholars have described third wave networks as being "technologic;" signaling a practice of communicating information digitally and creating "temporary unified political groups made up of unlikely collectivities" (Keller 2012, p. 433). These ideas are also taken up in disciplines beyond girlhood and feminist studies, as subsequent sections of this chapter will demonstrate; however, the centrality of online spaces to theories of millennial feminism and girls' resistance remains a crucial way of grounding the discussion. In the wake of this research, it seems evident that online spaces have become an important site for the troubling of gendered consumption and the staking out of identity.

The Internet and particularly social networks have been key sites of study for feminist scholars because it provides opportunities for feminist solidarity-building not found in many offline spaces. According to blog researchers Lenhardt and Madden, girls tend to gravitate toward producing online media, and particularly blogs, more than boys of a similar demographic (Keller 2012). It is no coincidence that mainstream understandings of fans is deeply gendered, and the activities enjoyed by fan girls (such as fan art or fan fiction) is routinely delegitimized, even by fellow fans.[2] But the digital space of girls' blogs have also been described as "a virtual room of one's own" and understood more widely by feminist scholars as important sites for the development of agency and the sharing of opinions (Keller 2012, p. 434).

Girlhood studies offers two perspectives that become especially important in unpacking *virjn*'s post and the reactionary politics of Green's. The first is Anita Harris's idea that girls' blogging practices often represent the first step towards "viewing oneself as agential citizen and political actor" (Harris 2008, p. 482). Girls' and women's participation in blogging communities, as both bloggers and readers, positions these sites as spaces that offer participants political agency and relative autonomy from the organizing logics of offline society. According to Keller,

> Girls have been active participants of online culture in part because of the unregulated nature of online space that nonetheless remains a *public* way to connect with peer communities and express personal interests outside of adult intervention [...] Girls often occupy a precarious position where they are encouraged to be political in appropriate, adult-approved and supervised ways, while ultimately being excluded. (2012, pp. 434–435)

The publics and counterpublics of Tumblr and other online social networks offer girls and other marginalized youth a unique opportunity to connect and express ideas in spaces that are relatively protected from the norms that regulate offline worlds. The fact that *virjn*'s text post received immediate backlash from Green and his supporters effectively led to the silencing of *virjin*'s voice and the deletion of her blog, is evidence that a culture of surveillance and control still exists in these purportedly freeing online spaces.[3] Digital spaces are not as protected from adult male intervention as Harris and her contemporaries assume; even here, expressing one's opinions has consequences.

The second perspective that is directly relevant to the context and subsequent fallout from *virjn*'s Tumblr post builds off of the reading of digital spaces as a space for girls to engage at a deeper or different level than offline spaces. Girls' participation in blogging "may offer girls more political agency [than] traditional spaces for political activity, such as youth caucuses or other formal organizations, which are often directed and ran by adults" (Keller 2012, p. 434). Blogging and other online modes of engagement also offer girls the opportunity to participate anonymously, with minimal commitment and/or risk. Blogging offers a way to "talk back" to a media culture that often leaves little public space for girls to do so and, not surprisingly, it is the implications of Green's response to the silencing of girls that critics have chosen to focus on in the aftermath of the event. One response from a self-identified feminist states that, regardless of whether or not the blogger agrees with the intent of every person who added to the post or with the idea that John Green is exploitive of his audience, "[she] is going to listen very closely to those girls, [because] too many girls are shut down or gaslighted or made to feel wrong when they express anxiety and discomfort around older men" (teenwitched 2015). Another post echoes the first, noting that the content of the original post is almost irrelevant: "this is about the fact that a young girl should be able to speak out [without] being shut down and lambasted all over a public forum by [individuals who have] positioned themselves as speaking for and on behalf of girls like her" (homodemons 2015). The event in question cannot be separated from the power dynamics at play here, the presence and influence of an adult male author in a fan space saturated with teen girls, and the silencing of many of those same girls.

Tumblr Publics and the Sharing Subject

While girlhood studies provide a rich theoretical basis for understanding girls' online practices and resistance, the field of new media studies and its adaptation of the popular social theory concept of "publics" also offers a number of valuable opportunities for exploring the complexities of the John Green Tumblr debacle. According to Michael Warner, a public is a "self organized [...] space of discourse organized by nothing more other than discourse itself" (2002, p. 50). According to Warner, a public unites strangers through their relationships with texts and their reflexive circulation; it represents an ongoing, socially mediated space of engagement and reproduction (2002, p. 62). danah boyd (2010) introduces the idea of "networked publics" that are restructured by various networked and online technologies. Locating socially understood publics in digital spaces complicates offline ways of understanding context, disrupting the social dynamics of public/private, and collapsing contexts that would otherwise be separate (boyd 2010). Especially, key to a discussion of conflict in digital spaces like Tumblr, however, is the idea that networked publics specifically challenge individuals' sense of control, particularly as it relates to the scalability of online content.

Networked technologies introduce new possibilities for amplifying, documenting, and spreading information and social acts in digital spaces. As boyd (2010) notes in her work, the circulation and eventual reach of content in networked publics is never guaranteed—but publics have never represented guaranteed audiences anyways. Instead, the "scalability" of content in networked publics is always about the ever-present possibility of visibility and what digital scholar Jodi Dean calls "the fantasy of abundance," which presumes all contributions and all sites to be equal, "uncoupled from contexts of action and application [...] the message is simply part of a circulating data stream" (Payne 2013, pp. 551–552). The unpredictable patterns of data sharing and content circulation online promises potential scalability for any user, prompting scholars such as Dean and Robert Payne to argue that the sharing capabilities of Web 2.0

effectively supports the individualistic philosophies of a millennial neoliberal subject in all of her online iterations. This rampant circulation of content online has also prompted new cultural anxieties around media virality, with the realities of media sharing online obscured by the provocative language used to describe such transmissions.

The politics of online virality concern the language used to spread the sharing of online content and also serves to question their social significance and impact. Scholars of participatory fan cultures, such as Jenkins, have been critical of the language of "viral media," arguing that connotations of disease and infection "mystifies how the process [of circulation] works" and positions individuals online as "unknowing carriers of [ideas]" (Payne 2013, p. 548). This type of language effectively constructs those engaging in online sharing as passive or even unknowing transmitters, when in fact digital scholars have long been arguing for more meaningful understandings of online sharing practices. In this way, the spreadability of media is not just circulation of the objects themselves, but a sort of cultural or personal investment of that object with some level of meaning or usefulness. According to Jenkins, so-called viral media objects travel through the web because they are meaningful to those individuals who spread them; "it is precisely because of their meaningfulness to each individual involved in circulation, who is more than simply a 'host' of viral content, that objects spread" (Payne 2013, pp. 548–549). While Payne and other theorists warn against utopian positionings of online subjects as entirely agentive in their role as transmitters of viral media content, the repositioning of individuals involved in the spread of so-called viral content as more than simple consumers or passive participants is an important intervention of recent new media theory and, in many ways, key to understanding the nuances of Tumblr publics.

The ideas of publics and virality are inextricable from the discourse surrounding *virjn*'s Tumblr post and the subsequent fallout and reactionary response on Tumblr. In a post that could be an addendum to Jenkins' theories of viral content, Tumblr user *wayonwayout* cites the fact that some 15,000 independent Tumblr accounts engaged with *virjn*'s original text post in the hours following its creation:

> Posts like this aren't made and reblogged in some kind of absurd vacuum that makes up an entity called Tumblr; they're primarily teenagers and teenage girls trying to find a way to respond to things that feel *wrong* [...] These posts

> don't emerge from a hate-void. [D]ismissing the message just because of the way it's delivered, ESPECIALLY when this stuff is coming from teenagers with few resources [...] is really really [sic] not great. (wayonwayout 2015)

It is especially disheartening to see how such an astute response to the Tumblr debacle compares to those references to virality and online sharing in digital spaces used by John Green's peers and fellow authors in their defenses of him. Author Maggie Stiefvater, in a post to her own Tumblr blog, writes that "the reason why [posts like this] makes a writer like [Green] back away from Tumblr is because it insisted on climbing into his Internet space." Stiefvater's comment clearly appeals to anxieties of online virality and the uncontrollable nature of transmission (Stiefvater 2015). In his own post, Green (2015) notes sadly that studies show that the "complicated dopamine rush that comes with righteous indignation is very powerful," insinuating that the people who reblogged *virjn*'s post did so under the influence of an all-consuming rage rather than consciously or out of some kind of meaningful identification with the message of the original post. Cassandra Clare, another YA author, quotes this section of Green's post in her own response, adding that "this explains so much" (Clare 2015). At different points in the fallout, Green and his defenders dismiss the spread of the original text post using the language of passive consumption and sharing.

It is also worth revisiting here the notion that part of the reason for the immediate and violent backlash against *virjn*'s post has to do with the way in which it was delivered and the types of affect embedded in the original post. Emotion is always also political, both in how it is perceived and how it moves others to action. The turn in feminist scholarship towards affect theory, not to mention the much longer history of women's anger or discomfort being delegitimized in favour of men's careers, logic, and ego, speaks to the power of feelings and patriarchal culture's innate distrust therein. According to scholars Seigworth and Gregg, "[t]here is no single, generalizable theory of affect: not yet, and (thankfully) there never will be" (2010, pp. 3–4). For the purposes of this chapter, it is not necessary to articulate affect theory or draw any clear distinction between affect and emotion. Rather, it is important to consider what these instances *do*—"the effect of [the] affect," to once again quote Seigworth and Gregg (2010, p. 24). In this particular case, affect theory might help us identify the negative gendering and dismissal of one group's emotions (the Tumblr users who reblogged and responded to *virjn*'s post with support) and the legitimation and perceived "realness" of another group's offense (Green and his fellow YA authors) as part of a legacy of denying women's discomfort and distrust of men backed by institutional and societal approval.

While it is undoubtedly important to consciously resist the binaries of active and passive media sharing online, it is evident that the two admittedly heterogeneous groups responding to the online fallout from *virjn*'s post and Green's subsequent response seem to understand the social contexts of content sharing, and the affect embedded in each, in markedly different ways. Rather than taking the time to consider the possibility that *virjn*'s message personally resonated with the over 15,000 Tumblr users who interacted with it before John was tagged and is significant. Green's defenders write off the viral circulation of the post as inflammatory and essentially dismiss the individuals who reblogged it as incendiary and necessarily unimportant. In other words, Clare, Stiefvater, and other authors who came to Green's defense use the rhetoric of passive interaction and virality to reduce the power of *virjn*'s words to the kind of hate-void origin story identified by *wayonwayout* in their sharp critique. Rhetorics of virality and the binary of passive/active online consumption are invoked to preserve the power and affirm the legitimacy of adult creators in digital spaces reacting against a post created by a (presumably) teenaged girl, whose identity is reified and (re)produced as a passive, unknowing consumer and unconscious transmitter of ill-informed ideas whose only explainable origin can be (misplaced) blind rage. Such discourses effectively preserve a paradoxical media culture wherein digital spaces are framed as allowing girls to express an empowered, autonomous selfhood, but remain susceptible to the same strategies of derailment used to silence girls and youth in offline spaces should they engage in unsanctionable discourses—especially those that question the authority of those adults and men with power.

Happiness Politics and Degrees of Silence

A third and final intervention this chapter uses to problematize the impact of *virjn*'s text post on Tumblr publics and the power dynamics already at play is Sara Ahmed's idea of happiness politics and the feminist killjoy. Ahmed's work can be located within the larger body of affect theory that has informed a considerable amount of feminist and queer work. In order to be culturally understood as happy, Ahmed argues that individuals must happen upon "the right things in the right way" (2010, p. 581). If an individual does not have the "right" reaction to texts or objects, or if they act instead to point out the problematic nature of certain discourses or texts, they are reconstituted as affect aliens and reconfigured as what Ahmed describes as "feminist killjoys"—individuals who prevent or actively block the happiness of others by identifying with a critical politics (2010, pp. 582–583). "In the thick sociality everyday spaces, feminists are thus attributed as the origin of bad feelings [...] as the ones who ruin the atmosphere, which is how the atmosphere might be imagined (retrospectively) as shared" (Ahmed 2010, pp. 581–582). We can reimagine this atmosphere in the language of publics and position *virjn* and other Tumblr users who reblogged her original post as killjoys who choose to interact with Green's on-line persona and creative pursuits in "the wrong way."

The feminist killjoy becomes complicated when we take into account the cultural understanding of girlhood. The girl comes to embody hope and future potentialities, frequently positioned as the next generation who can come to be the good, resistant subjects of feminism if they engage in activism in a particular way (Harris and Shields Dobson 2015, p. 146). As Monica Swindle reminds us, *girl* carries an affect all its own, a "pleasurable power [that] is a distinct way of feeling, an orientation toward oneself, objects, and other that creates a collective [...] an affective community" (Swindle 2011). Positive affects "stick" to the figure of the girl feminist due to her discursive positioning as *girl* in ways that the undeniable legacy of the presumably adult feminist killjoy prevents us from seeing (Keller 2012, p. 438). Girls who take up space online in ways that are reminiscent of the killjoy are caught in a kind of double bind; not only do they push against patriarchal expectations of happiness and amicability, they are also acting in direct contradiction to expectations of girlish passivity and positive affect.[4] The impact as Ahmed describes, is that the very act of identifying something as problematic is framed as violence, and the situation is read as being about the unhappiness of feminists rather than about what feminists are actually unhappy about (2010, p. 583). Once again, this rhetoric is reflected in the discourse that emerged on Tumblr in the aftermath of *virjn*'s original post. Author Maggie Stiefvater goes to far as to co-opt popular Tumblr slang in her response:

> You can have your own opinions on Green's books and internet [sic] presence, but the fact remains that he is a very real positive influence on thousands of teens. You're not just making sure you can't have nice things. You're taking away other people's nice things. Get yourself together, internet [sic]. How is it said? Oh, right. *I can't even.*[1] (Steifvater 2015)

The use of Tumblr slang here and the inference to "not having nice things" is no doubt meant to belittle and delegitimize the teen girl voice; however, it also reflects the ideas of happiness and reading texts "the right way". Stiefvater argues explicitly that the girls who reblogged *virjn*'s post were "taking away other people's nice things" and, therefore, did not deserve to be heard.

To return to Ahmed, the intangible nature of online publics and the comparable ease of assigning particular affects to those bodies that inhabit those spaces converge to produce killjoy subjects. "Histories," Ahmed suggests, "are condensed in the very intangibility of an atmosphere, or in the tangibility of bodies that seem to get in the way [...] your proximity gets in the way of other people's enjoyment of the right things" (2010, p. 584). Even discounting the original content of *virjn*'s post and Green's co-option of the teenage girl voice, Green's response and subsequent silencing *virjn*'s and her followers in the hours following its creation is proof that the expansive publics of Tumblr allow for unprecedented visibility alongside unprecedented levels of surveillance and policing of girls' dissent. As Tumblr user *brigidkeely* notes in her response (ironically using the same conventions of Internet slang as Stiefvater, albeit in their correct context), "a group of marginalized people said 'this person makes us feel uncomfortable' and were told they were WRONG and BAD and BULLIES and THIS IS WHY WE CAN'T HAVE NICE THINGS" (delladilly 2015). The feminist killjoy is not undeserving of "nice things" because she points out uncomfortable histories and social patterns wherein adult men hold all the power and teen girls are exploited; to the contrary, "nice things" are withheld when normative systems of power are upheld and unapologetically endorsed. The actions taken to delegitimize the girls who spoke out against Green's presence in digital spaces curated *for* teenaged fan communities is only further evidence that such conversations are, in fact, desperately needed.

Conclusions

According to Keller, the Internet provides girls and young women an opportunity to talk back and "find one's voice" in a culture that frequently refuses to value the voices of girls (Keller 2012, p. 439). I would amend this claim to posit that we survive in a culture that refuses to value the voices of girls *unless* those voices are exploitable, co-opted and used for adult gain. John Green, Maureen Johnson, Maggie Stiefvater, and Cassandra Clare are all internationally renowned YA authors whose successes have been based on understanding and representing the teenaged voice. The fact that these authors converged to use the rhetoric of virality and affect to discredit girls' voices in digital spaces *meant to be their own* is proof of a need to reevaluate the politics of author/reader relationships in the context of networked publics and the collapsed contexts of digital spaces. What does it mean when the teenaged girl voice is valuable when it lands an author like Green on the *New York Times* best sellers list but not valuable when it is expressing discomfort with the same author's online presence? What are the implications of telling young women that their thoughts and feelings are inherently less valuable than an adult man's reputation on Tumblr.com?

If we return to the idea of locating feminist resistance in the everyday, those small moments of rupture that Jessica Ringrose names at the start of this chapter as potentially potent spaces of growth, the critique of Green's post emerges as a space of opportunity. *Virjn*'s post and the subsequent online response reveals the complicated ways in which girlhood can be understood in a context of digital cultures. This chapter suggests that understanding girls' blogging practices as an empowered activity is an inadequate framework as long as authority figures and their allies continue to silence girls' dissent when voiced online, invoking cultural anxieties around virality, digital scalability, and networked publics. The digital footprint or "trace" of such online exchanges, though they fade over time, echo the traces and residues Ringrose (2008) imagines shaping resistive practices and existing to unsettle the regulative rhythms of the mainstream. If we expand our understandings of resistance to include such ruptures, it becomes equally important to feel the aftershocks of such events fully rather than let them fade—a testament to the nuance with which girls continuously and expertly navigate the digital publics that would see their opinions and affect sidelined in favour of "nice(r) things."

Notes

1. For a better explanation of the mechanics of likes and reblogs on Tumblr, see Appendix A.
2. For more context on the gendering of fandom, see Busse (2013).
3. Due to the aforementioned blog deactivation, Tumblr user *virjn*'s identity and gender is not known. However, due to the contents of their post and the demographics of both Tumblr and Green's readership, the pronouns used to describe *virjn* over the course of this piece alternate between they/them and she/her.
4. The fact that Green and his peers have framed *virjn* and their supporters as affectively alien in this way, particularly when the girls in his novels arguably embody this kind of "sticky" positive/ happiness affect described by Harris and Shields Dobson, is an irony deserving of its own paper.

Appendix A: Deactivated Tumblr User's Original Post

The original post that sparked this event was posted by Tumblr user *virjn* at some point on either the evening of June 10 or the early morning hours of June 11, 2015. The exact time of the original post is now impossible to trace because, in the aftermath of the event, Tumblr user *virjn* deactivated their blog. The screenshot below is taken from the exact thread that John Green replied to on June 11, 2015 (see Appendix B for more details), and therefore represents the exact text/implications Green was replying to in the absence of being able to locate the active/authentic blog post.

By the time John Green was tagged in and subsequently responded to this text post, it had already garnered over 15,000 independent "notes." On Tumblr, notes connote one of two actions. Either a Tumblr user can "like" the post, effectively saving it to a list of material to be accessed or reblogged at a later date and presumably demonstrating their agreement with the content therein (although see danah boyd's article for a more nuanced discussion on binaries of affective possibility imposed by digital architecture), or they can reblog the post outright. Reblogging content on Tumblr, posts that content to the user's personal blog and also reproduces it on the Dashboards of those individuals who have chosen to follow the Tumblr user in question. While Tumblr posts can be screened by filtering out certain tags or key words, reblogging effectively widens the circulation of a post (particularly a new post, as in this case) and increases the size of its respective public.

virjn

i bet john green thinks people don't like him because he's a "dork" or a nerd or whatever

when in reality it's because he's a creep who panders to teenage girls so that he can amass some weird cult-like following. and it's always girls who feel misunderstood, you know, and he goes out of his way to make them feel important and desirable. which is fucking? weird?

also he has a social media presence that is equivalent to that dad of a kid in your friend group who always volunteers to "supervise" the pool parties and scoots his lawn chair close to all the girls.

Appendix B: John Green's Reactionary Tumblr Text Post

The text below is taken from a text post created by Tumblr user John Green on June 11, 2015 in response to a text post created by a now-defunct blog (detailed in Appendix A). The post as it appears here has been edited only slightly for some awkward spacing; the text itself remains unchanged.

"You want me to defend myself against the implication that I sexually abuse children?

Okay. I do not sexually abuse children.

Throwing that kind of accusation around is sick and libelous and most importantly damages the discourse around the actual sexual abuse of children. When you use accusations of pedophilia as a way of insulting people whose work you don't like, you trivialize abuse.

I'm tired of seeing the language of social justice – important language doing important work – misused as a way to dehumanize others and treat them hatefully.

So we all seek (and seek to share) the jolt that accompanies outrage and anger. As studies have shown, the complicated dopamine rush that comes with righteous indignation is very powerful, and I'm indulging it simply by responding to the outrageous accusation that my work is somehow evidence of sexual abuse.

But the outrage cycle is exhausting, and while there are wonderful examples of outrage fueling long-term, productive responses to injustice – We Need Diverse Books and the UPLIFT both come to mind – too often the Internet moves from jolt to jolt, from hatred to hatred, ever more convinced of our own righteousness and the world's evil. And getting caught up in that is very painful.

I realize that will seem privileged to many of you (and it is), or like an excuse (maybe it's that too), or lacking in empathy (maybe so), and I'm sure there is plenty here to deconstruct and reveal my various shortcomings (which are legion).

But this stops being a productive place for me to be in conversations if I'm not allowed to be wrong, if my apologies are not acknowledged alongside my misdeeds, and if I'm not treated like a person.

I think at this point it's impossible to continue to use tumblr in the way I've used it since 2011. My life is different (in ways that are both good and bad); this community is different (in ways that are both good and bad); the world is different (in ways that are both good and bad).

So if this blog begins to look more one-way, with more original content and less reblogging/commenting/answering asks/etc., that's why.

I want to emphasize that I am ridiculously lucky to work on stuff I love, from Crash Course to The Art Assignment to writing books. And I trust that many nerdfighter communities – whether vlogbrothers or Dear Hank and John or the Wimbly Womblys or the kiva group – will continue to be open and collaborative and constructive. Also, I'm not angry or anything like that. I just need some distance for my well-being.

Thanks for reading. DFTBA."

References

Ahmed, Sara. 2010. Killing joy: Feminism and the history of happiness. *Signs: Journal of Women in Culture and Society* 35 (3): 571–594.

aimmyarrowshigh. 2015. And then some days I'm like, wow, tumblr [sic] is like.... *Tumblr*, June 16. Web. 12 April 2018. http://www.aimmyarrowshigh.com/post/121677589905.

boyd, danah. 2010. Social network sites as networked publics: Affordances, dynamics, and implications. In *A networked self: Identity, community, and culture on social network sites*, ed. Zizi Papacharissi. New York: Routledge.

brigidkeely. 2015. To me, there was a tonal shift from.... *Tumblr*, June 16. Web. 6 April 2018. http://brigidkeely.tumblr.com/post/121438738441/delladilly-it-is-genuinely-astonishing-to-me.

Busse, Kristina. 2013. Geek hierarchies, boundary policing, and the gendering of the good fan. *Participations: Journal of Audience and Reception Studies* 10 (1): 73–91.

Clare, Cassandra. 2015. As studies have shown, the complicated.... *Tumblr*, June 12. Web. 6 April 2018. http://cassandraclare.tumblr.com/post/121342805219/sarahreesbrennan-fishingboatproceeds.

Dean, Michelle. 2018. A note on nerdfighters. *The New Yorker*, March 13. Web. 12 April 2018. http://www.newyorker.com/culture/culture-desk/a-note-on-nerdfighters.

delladilly. 2015. It is genuinely astonishing to me how many.... *Tumblr*, June 16. Web. 6 April 2018. http://delladilly.tumblr.com/post/121355408458/it-is-genuinely-astonishing-to-me-how-many-female.

Garrett, Camryn. 2015. John Green, YA authors, and rape culture. *The Huffington Post*, July 1. Web. 8 April 2018. http://www.huffingtonpost.com/camryn-garrett/john-green-ya-authors-and-rape-culture_b_7574632.html.

Green, John. 2015. You want me to defend myself against the implication.... *Tumblr*, June 11. Web. 6 April 2018. http://fishingboatproceeds.tumblr.com/post/121316109713/mattcatashpole-astro1995.

Harris, Anita. 2008. Young women, late modern politics, and the participatory possibilities of online cultures. *Journal of Youth Studies* 11 (5): 481–495.

Harris, Anita, and Amy Shields Dobson. 2015. Theorizing agency in post-girl-power times. *Continuum: Journal of Media & Cultural Studies* 29 (2): 145–156.

homodemons. 2015. John green [sic] you are a grown man you should be.... *Tumblr*, June 16. Web. 6 April 2018. http://homodemons.tumblr.com/post/121685038668/catface-mcgee-anandrine-marielubooks.

Johnson, Maureen. 2015. Reblogging for a few reasons, namely.... *Tumblr*, June 12. Web. 6 April 2018. http://maureenjohnsonbooks.tumblr.com/post/121348091233/cassandraclare-sarahreesbrennan.

Keller, Jessalynn. 2012. Virtual feminisms. *Information, Communication & Society* 15 (3): 429–447.

Payne, Robert. 2013. Virality 2.0: Networked promiscuity and the sharing subject pages. *Cultural Studies* 27 (4): 540–560.

Pot, Justin. 2012. Crash course: Entertaining Youtube courses on history and biology. *Make Use Of*, April 7. Web. 12 April 2018. http://www.makeuseof.com/tag/crash-entertaining-youtube-courses-history-biology/.

Ringrose, Jessica. 2008. 'Every time she bends over she pulls up her thong': Teen girls negotiating discourses of competitive, heterosexualized aggression. *Girlhood Studies* 1 (1): 33–59.

Romano, Aja. 2013. How to play Tumblr's John Green game. *The Daily Dot*, June 7. Web. 8 April 2018. http://www.dailydot.com/fandom/is-that-john-green-tumblr-game-meme/.

Seigworth, Gregory, and Melissa Gregg. 2010. *The affect theory reader*. Durham, NC: Duke University Press.

Stiefvater, Maggie. 2015. I watched this blow up before my eyes and.... *Tumblr*, June 11. Web. 6 April 2018. http://maggie-stiefvater.tumblr.com/post/121317287026/fishingboatproceeds-mattcatashpole.

Swindle, Monica. 2011. Feeling girl, girling feeling: An examination of 'girl' as affect. *Rhizomes: Cultural Studies in Emerging Knowledge* 22. Web. 8 April 2018. http://www.rhizomes.net/issue22/swindle.html.

teenwitched. 2015. I can definitely identify and understand the feeling.... *Tumblr*, June 19. Web. 6 April 2018. http://teenwitched.tumblr.com/post/121938662385.

Warner, Michael. 2002. Publics and counterpublics. *Public Culture* 14 (1): 49–90.

wayonwayout. 2015. I'm on my way to Jurassic World so this has to be short.... *Tumblr*, June 11. Web. 6 April 2018. http://wayonwayout.tumblr.com/post/121319047526/maggie-stiefvater-fishingboatproceeds.

Your Fave is Problematic. 2013. John Green. *Tumblr*, April 17. Web. 6 April 2018. http://yourfaveisproblematic.tumblr.com/post/48215439254/john-green.

The manufacturer's authorised representative in the EU is Springer
Nature Customer Service Centre GmbH, Europaplatz 3, 69115 Heidelberg,
Germany. If you have any concerns regarding our products, please
contact ProductSafety@springernature.com

Printed and bound by CPI Group (UK) Ltd, Croydon, CR0 4YY
30/09/2026
02225653-0006